In Search of the Good Society

Compelling reading, this book both reinforces and elevates the role of art in the exploration and analysis of the concepts of democracy, globalization and capitalism. In the book, the author describes a post-human world, a state we have already entered. But how should we think about it, given we have already been co-opted? Can we articulate the future outside the false discipline that the market often dictates, beyond the clutches of a few social media companies, and maintain our rich diversities while holding on to those things that make life possible and worthwhile: love, hope and art?

Running throughout the book is the central theme of uncertainty and divergence. It is uncompromising in asking the question about the need for a new global creation story, which has at its core not the certainties of one defined creation myth but the need to feel comfortable with the uncertainty principle both in physics and the political economy. It is up to artists, scientists and philosophers to articulate this wonder and to help us write a new global creation story based on art (the arts), uncertainty, diversity, risk and wonder – and of course knowledge. This book has the capacity to both clarify and reshape your thinking.

T0320958

This book is an outstanding reflection on the crucial challenges of our time and a path toward a positive future. How can the good life be delivered? The author argues that decisions made through deliberate public policy can enhance and promote health, social care, education, equality and social mobility – all keys to a good society. Yet we must advance public policy with public reasoning. We must win the argument with reason. The author fears that voters today, especially in the UK and the USA, are like turkeys voting for Thanksgiving and Christmas. If you only read one book this year, this should be the one.

Oliver F. Williams, Director, Center for Ethics and Religious Values in Business, Mendoza College of Business, University of Notre Dame, USA

This book is TRULY BRILLIANT. I feel as if I have travelled with the author to far-flung places, back in time and close to death. It conjures up pictures of extraordinarily diverse places, yet subtly reminds us how similar, frail and yet strong we are. It weaves together such different themes so seamlessly. The text cleverly connects major world events and issues, the context of all our lives. With amazing clarity, it is a perfect balance of reflection and positivity, leaving me with a sense of connection to the world and hope.

Carol Adams, Professor of Accountancy, University of Durham, UK

In this illuminating book, *In Search of the Good Society*, Malcolm McIntosh engages in a wide-ranging contemplation of the theory and practice of the good society. With McIntosh's background and experience, he is ideally suited to craft such a quest. Using optics of love, hope and art, he envisions the good life being delivered within a global society and economy. This thoughtful, well-written and insightful essay will be appealing both to optimists and realists. I strongly recommend this book for academics, practitioners and concerned citizens.

Archie B. Carroll, Professor Emeritus, Terry College of Business, University of Georgia, USA

Malcolm McIntosh's latest book is a true gem. It gives all of us pause as we consider the dark realities of the world we face today, then offers hope through glimpses of what creating a good society really means. Read this book. You will be glad you did! It is brilliant. I am blown away and hope the book has great success. The last three chapters in particular are stunning in their scope and impact.

Sandra Waddock, Professor of Management, Galligan School of Management, Boston College, USA

The chapter on health is both refreshing and inspiring. Whilst acknowledging that some diseases are incurable, it takes a very positive approach as to how we can maximize our chances of being around for as long as possible, with some very practical and achievable suggestions. The chapter very clearly highlights the uncertainty over prognosis and, as a medical community, our inability to be accurate in our predictions. It outlines a number of lifestyle steps that as individuals we can all take to improve our chances of defying the odds and being long-term survivors. More than that, it shows the power of positive thinking and of living life to the full.

Mark Beresford, Consultant Oncologist and Clinical Lead for Oncology and Haematology, Royal United Hospital, Bath

Centred on his courageous story of surviving and thriving terminal cancer over six years, Malcolm takes us on an insightful, enlightening, and sometimes painful, experiential journey. It's compelling reading. Don't miss it . . .

Bimal Arora, Chairperson, Centre for Responsible Business, India

About the author

Dr Malcolm McIntosh FRSA (1953–2017) advised UN Secretary-Generals Kofi Annan and Ban Ki-moon as a Special Advisor to the UN Global Compact on business and society, sustainability, human rights and responsible management education; the governments of the UK, Canada and Norway; and numerous supraterritorial corporations and NGOs. He was also heavily involved in many local community initiatives.

After a period teaching English and starting businesses in Sweden, Japan and Australia, he worked for BBC TV as a filmmaker and journalist in current affairs and in the Natural History Unit for ten years.

His subsequent career was as an activist academic for 25 years in the fields of corporate responsibility, sustainability and global governance. He lectured in some 20 countries, notably South Africa, New Zealand, Australia, Canada, Japan, Brazil and the USA, and produced more than 30 books and edited collections.

He had a first degree in education and English from the University of London, a Masters in peace studies, and a PhD in accountability and defence management from the University of Bradford. He was latterly a Senior Fellow in the Centre for Business, Organisations and Society in the School of Management at Bath University. He ran research and teaching centres at Warwick and Coventry Universities in the UK, and was until 2014 Professor of Sustainable Enterprise at Griffith University in Australia.

In Search of the Good Society

An Essay on Love, Hope, Art and Social Progress

Malcolm McIntosh

LONDON AND NEW YORK

First published 2018
by Routledge
2 Park Square, Milton Park, Abingdon, Oxon OX14 4RN

and by Routledge
711 Third Avenue, New York, NY 10017

Routledge is an imprint of the Taylor & Francis Group, an informa business

British Library Cataloguing-in-Publication Data
A catalogue record for this book is available from the British Library.

Library of Congress Cataloging-in-Publication Data
A catalog record for this book has been requested.

ISBN: 978-1-78353-812-6 (hbk)
ISBN: 978-1-78353-742-6 (pbk)
ISBN: 978-1-78353-744-0 (ebk)

Contents

Foreword

Malcolm was a thought leader and a pioneer of the modern corporate responsibility movement. Through his work with the UK Foreign Office in the late 1990s and his involvement with the United Nations Global Compact he played an important role in spreading the idea and practice of responsible business practices and making it a global movement. Always driven to push the boundaries of knowledge about the role of business in society, he inspired and encouraged countless people through his many activities, writings and teaching. His positive outlook on life – even when battling cancer – and his ability to build bridges between ideas and people across many geographies made him a genuine network and community builder of our modern age.

Georg Kell

Founder and former Executive Director
of the United Nations Global Compact

Foreword

Preface

Since the 1970s and the start of global environmental awareness, and more recently the financial crash of 2008/9, there
have been many books and articles on post-capitalism, alterna-
tive-capitalism, new-capitalism, how-to-save-capitalism (and
the world). One of this book's reference points is the esteemed
and much-awarded economist J.K. Galbraith's 1996 book *The
Good Society: The Humane Agenda*, but I could have chosen
any number of other similar-sounding books.[1]

I'm a transdisciplinarian, both as an academic for 25 years
and a serious journalist for many years. I tend not to see the
divisibility between good science, good art, politics and a fantastic cup of coffee. The biggest charge against many of the
theoretical pieces on how we make the good society is that they
miss those things that keep us all going through the best and
worst of days: a sunny day; the driver who takes care while we
cross the road; a joke with a stranger; a safe and secure town
centre; an environment that cherishes artistic endeavour for all;
an ambulance that arrives every time, for everyone; a gun- and

crime-free community – and an immaculate cup of coffee. They often focus on theory with an absence of practical examples. Often it is the little and the hidden things that make your day.

Finally, and not in any way least, the emphasis on libertarianism, individualism and personal change in some models is in many ways radically different from the collective, welfare concerns of what has become the European, Scandinavian and Japanese tradition, and is the guiding motif for many other countries. It is also strange that many classical and political economists fail to incorporate such crucial issues as feminism, environmentalism, racism, collectivism and a good cup of coffee in their theorizing, not to mention a fresh baguette.

This book does four things. First, it tells stories about a number of countries that I have been visiting for the last 40 years to see if they measure up in any way to what might now be regarded as the good society. Second, it examines our desire to find one model that fits all, and to find a unifying theory in science and politics. Third, it includes art and a good cup of coffee as measures of a good society alongside publicly funded universal healthcare and equal opportunities. Fourth, it looks ahead to see if the significant changes that are presaged by the post-human world are compatible with ideas of the good society. This book is a journey using analysis *and* impressionism, insight *and* reportage, data mining *and* humour.

What seems to be most important in seeking a good life for oneself, and a good society for all, is making these two compatible. It is difficult to have one without the other – unless one lacks empathy. For both oneself and society, safety, security and being wanted seem to be fundamental prerequisites whatever may follow in terms of wealth and income. A society founded on love and hope is also founded on a wide variety of ways of expressing itself and its inner thoughts through literature, art, film, dance and music. Also, there is an old Chinese adage that says that a good life is based on having someone to love, having something to do, and having something to look forward to. These I know are sound starting points for a discussion on the good society. And this was as true in the average community of 150 people throughout millennia as it is now when we are connected to millions.[2]

This book looks at the components of a good society. The fundamentals are as concluded in Chapter 4 and given shape throughout the book. Universal health and social care, education and skills, and equal opportunities and social mobility are the keys to a good society. These are fundamental civil rights within a human rights mental framework. All those societies that work for all their members have similar characteristics, whether they be big or small, resource-based, manufacturing or information societies. In order to deliver these fundamental rights, it is necessary for there to be low discrimination in all areas and high social mobility; sound institutions, good governance and low corruption; the rule of law must apply universally; and there must be a separation between the state and the judiciary to provide an oversight of decision-making and provide a place for exposition, debate, and reasoned thinking beyond the necessary political debate. And, at all times, in every way, we must try to establish good, peaceful relations with neighbours near and far in international affairs and trade. Unlike Galbraith, I do not attempt here to make rules for fiscal or financial decision-making: that would be another book.

The greatest threats to world peace are nationalism, tribalism (including religious fundamentalism) and misogyny. This book has been out to review around the world. I have not been kind to some countries and have argued that they do not represent what I have tried to capture as "the good society";

among these are the USA, India and some elements of the UK. I have used both reportage and anecdote, *and* hard data, in my writing. I should not have been surprised by some of the nationalistic feedback that has come my way, but this has been useful in refining my thinking. I note, however, that nationalism is more prevalent in some minds than others and that we still have a long way to go in becoming global citizens while retaining a sense of local identity without resorting to nationalism. Perhaps this is why Galbraith did not venture to apply his theory to practice around the world. This century will sink or swim according to our ability to rise above ethnocentrism and to embrace and manage our connectivity and sense of one shared place.

Acknowledgements

I am very grateful to Clare Brass and Silvio Caputo for lending me their wonderful house in Candelara, Italy, midst the hills, olive groves, snakes and pecorino, which gave me space to think, read and write – and eat cheese and drink the best coffee.

Thank you to all the people at Greenleaf Publishing, particularly Rebecca Marsh, Dean Bargh and Rebecca Macklin, who have believed in me all the while and worked so hard to promote my many books with them over the last quarter of a century.

I have had a relationship with Bath University for some 25 years but lately Andy Crane, head of the Centre for Business, Organisations and Society in the School of Management, has welcomed me back as a Senior Fellow, for which much gratitude.

My close family and friends know who they are. You have put up with me talking about matters economic, cosmic, spiritual, artistic and emotional – sometimes intellectual – and more than anything loved and supported me through six years of cancer thriving. Thank you so much. May the love you make be equal to the love you take.

In my life there have been professional people who helped me immensely but who may not have realized it, because they have helped so many others too, perhaps. This is my opportunity to list some of them. First, Colin Turner, an English teacher at my second-rate independent secondary school, who, as a member of the then revolutionary Royal Court Theatre, staged Joan Littlewood's *Oh, What a Lovely War!* as the school play and presented me with roles that gave immense meaning to what was otherwise a period of little formal learning. I can sing every song even now! Second is Sandy Grant, the teacher who introduced me to E.M. Forster during my "A" Levels at Putney College of Further Education and tutored me while I lay in bed with a drug overdose and pneumonia in the Brompton Hospital when I was in my late teens. Third is Jean Gooding at St Mary's College, Strawberry Hill (now St Mary's University, Twickenham), whose humanity meant she accepted my poetry as part of overall grades for my first degree. Fourth is Paul Rogers at Bradford University's Department of Peace Studies who supervised my MA thesis on post-war Japanese defence policy (still on sale as Malcolm McIntosh, *Japan Rearmed* [Pinter, 1989 and Bloomsbury, 2012]), and encouraged me through my PhD and recommended me for my first job at BBC TV on a series on defence management issues broadcast in 1986 (still on sale as Malcolm McIntosh, *Managing Britain's Defence* [Macmillan, 1979]). Fifth, Georg Kell, Executive Director of the UN Global Compact from 2000–15, was a good friend and a great colleague and appointed me as a Special Advisor to what was then one of UN Secretary-General Kofi Annan's personal initiatives. Sixth, my sometimes co-writer Professor

Sandra Waddock from Boston College has been a wonderful sounding board and enthuser for ideas and writing, as well as a good friend.

In the time that it has taken to write this lengthy essay I have special gratitude for the staff of Britain's National Health Service (NHS). In particular, I would like to acknowledge and thank the wonderful people in the A&E (Accident & Emergency) department at the NHS Royal United Hospital in Bath, the surgeons in the coronary care unit, and most affectionately my oncologists in both Australia's Medicare and the UK's NHS who won't mind me saying that they have been useless at predicting my demise.

It wasn't until the end of this book that I realized that certain companies crop up in every chapter, and in every country: the Hyatt hotel chain, Starbucks coffee, McDonald's fast food restaurants and IKEA. They are not necessarily my preferred ports of call. I prefer the local, the authentic and the delicious. Resisting the extreme blandness, conformity and homogenization of globalization and Americanization were some of the challenges of the twentieth century whether they came from Hollywood, Heinz or Happiness indexes.

Also, we all need reputable editors and portals in an age awash with information, but lacking in veracity. Certain sources seem to recur in my writing, as arbiters of truth and debunkers of fake news: the BBC, the CIA World Factbook, various UN websites, the *New York Times*, the *Guardian* newspaper and others. And praise for Wikipedia as a starting point for some research. These sources are not always accurate, but then that's true of many academic papers I read. All of them make mistakes, *but they all publicly correct themselves and have established reality-check systems*. How unlike some democratically elected politicians (I'm thinking of the USA) and some self-appointed leaders (I'm thinking of China). I have at times been impressionistic in this book, but I have tried not to present any "alternative facts".

Malcolm McIntosh
Bath, England
and
Candelara, Italy
Europe
2017

Introduction:
The reflective observer

We make art elliptically. It comes to you by surprise, out of the corner of your eye, around a corner unexpectedly, sitting across a café smiling at you while you drink coffee. So, art is about the unexpected and the ambiguous. Albert Einstein imagined standing on a railway station and seeing a stream of light and a train passing him at comparable speeds. But what of the lady on the train, he thought? At what speed did the light pass her? It cannot be the same as the stream of light that passed him, or could it be? And relativity was born. This was a creative act not dissimilar to Claude Monet's imperative to paint. Both saw life in a new light.

Small matters matter, or, as Mark Zuckerberg, Facebook CEO and founder, that wise old sage of a man, said after Trump's shock 2016 US presidential election win, "people vote by their lived experience".[3] Ruchir Sharma, chief investment strategist at Morgan Stanley Investment Management, has said that looking at the little things – daily matters – is as important in understanding global trends as looking at global strategic projections by headline economists. So it is that he finds talking to Indians at a local level about the price and availability of potatoes, lentils and onions is just as useful as looking at global patterns and grand narratives.[4] And for Angus Deaton, Nobel prize-winning economist, discussing the correlations between suicide, the use of opioids and votes for Donald Trump has given us a new insight into despair, capitalism and democracy.[5]

We now know that the pollsters were wrong in 2016 in not predicting both the UK's Brexit vote and Trump's victory in the US because they did not listen to the street. Their models did not take into account the price of economic globalization to most people, nor the echo-chamber effect of social media and peer-group pressure. The day after the Brexit vote in the UK, as many of us staggered around in shock, our gardener told me that I didn't understand him and his friends voting to leave the European Union because "you move in different circles". This was tribal as much as anything, and it was visceral. It seems the same was true in the vote for Trump. It didn't matter in both cases that lies were told; what did matter was angry solidarity from a significantly disadvantaged proportion of people in both countries who held hands across the Atlantic to say, "Where's the cake? We want some!"

So, with an ear to the ground, I have included in this book anecdotes and reportage from years of travelling and talking to people around the world, as pointers towards deeper analysis. People's stories are their lifeblood, and narrative is the way we humans understand life and the magic and mystery of living. This is what is known as long-form journalism versus the short, quick, dirty and unchecked scramble for words that's posted instantly on Facebook, Twitter, Whateversup, etc. As a former BBC journalist, I know the value of the first-hand account; and, as an academic, I know the value of the reflective observer.

Emily Brontë said, "I am happiest when I am writing." And so too am I.

If you are looking for misery or despair, don't read this book. If you are looking for how to see life afresh and are seeking some resurgence, then read on. There is misery and desperation, but the book is determinedly positive, even though, as Spock often reported to Captain Kirk from the surface of another place in space: "It's life, but not as we know it." In other words, the future can be different.

The central message is that around the world there are many examples of the good society built on the solid foundations of love, hope, art and social progress. This is not unobtainably utopian; this is reality for millions of people who live in good places with long lives in solid neighbourhoods, with no gun crime, and with fantastic health and social care, shared wealth and many opportunities for greeting, meeting and talking – and expressing themselves in various artistic forms.

This book is a sequel to *Thinking the Twenty-First Century: Ideas for the New Political Economy* (2015) and it picks up on and expands on some of the issues raised by that book. It relates to feedback to that book, in print, on social media and in many public forums. But this book, *In Search of the Good Society,* also introduces new ideas. In the earlier book I asked, "What does it mean to be human in the twenty-first century, now that we know what we know about ourselves and the planet?"[6]

This question has been brought into sharper focus by the events of 2016. Both Britain's vote to exit the European Union and the election of Donald Trump as President of the USA came about through disinformation, lies and playing on fear. And both were led by affluent elitists who used hate and vitriol rather than inclusivity to win the popular vote. But both of them happened in democratic societies; and many people reading this book will be living in more autocratic states. Less than 50% of the world live in so-called democratic states.

In these two democratic events, Brexit and Trump, new social media was used to subvert democratic, open and evidence-based discussion. The question remains, then: what does it mean to be human in a post-factual, post-ideology century, and, some would say, a post-human world? How do we hang on to our essential goodness – "the better angels of our nature", as Abraham Lincoln said in his inaugural speech in 1861. Thomas Paine wrote that human nature is not of itself vicious, so why now are we struggling with the forces of fear and hate?

Martin Luther King said that "the arc of the moral universe is long, but it bends towards justice", but the arc is made up of individuals who form a collective. This is missed by many who fail to see that their individualism is only measured when it is collectivist, as in the 1960s civil rights, feminism and environmental movements. The neoliberal "left" in the US failed to see the beyond-experts masses assembled on the White House lawn because they were so busy comfortably navel-gazing. The same is true of the liberal elite in the UK who failed to measure the resentment against all things smooth and shiny: what people wanted was hard things like jobs, public transport that worked, good healthcare, cheap pizzas and to be able to see their kids progressing in the same way that they had been progressing since 1945.

But these two votes also demonstrate that winning elites are rarely "of the people". Movements may be driven by common cause and collectivism but social drifts are often given momentum by demagogic populists. Such was true in 2016 with Donald Trump in the US who vowed to destroy the "liberal elite" and "drain the (Washington) swamp" and Nigel Farage in the UK, neither of whom had humble origins, and both of whom were part of the 1% pretending to represent the 99%. Trump simply lied and denied his tax return to the US public, while Farage was openly dismissive of those who had worked so hard for his cause. When he stepped down as leader of Ukip (UK Independence Party), he said, "I'm having a great time. I am not having to deal with low-grade people every day. I am not responsible for what a branch secretary in Lower Slaughter posted half-cut on Twitter last night . . . I don't have to spend my life with people I would never have a drink with and who I would never employ." Vilfredo Pareto coined the term "elite" in 1902 as a substitute for aristocracy or ruling class. He divided elite rulers into two groups: foxes and lions. Trump and Farage are cunning, sly foxes; and social progress and liberalism is run by long-term strategic lions.

One of the overall themes in this book – drawing on *Thinking the Twenty-First Century* – is that the future is, and ought to be, feminine, by which I mean negotiated, collaborative and cooperative. The 1980s masculinity of aggressive neoliberal economics was a counter to the birth and growth of movements that gained momentum in the 1960s and '80s: feminism, environmentalism, civil rights and democratization. In 2016 we have seen human progress step backwards and the dangerous, daring, winner-takes-all man reassert himself as if in a last gasp before becoming something else: a rounded human being. The world cannot be inherited by gun-toting, chest-beating, misogynistic, homophobic xenophobes like Donald Trump and Vladimir Putin or we are all the losers.

After a lifetime travelling the world, I have included in this book reflections on the differences and divergences that still exist in different political economies – places I have been remembering for over 40 years. The countries chosen are China, India, Italy, Japan, the USA, South Africa, the UK, Australia, Sweden and Greece. Research on comparative international political economy is principally concerned with divergent capitalisms and it often highlights local-community resistance to the race to the bottom and the subsequent increase in inequality; the tide of global neoliberal economics; and defiance of the absurdity of "the end of history" hypothesis. In this book the measurement of difference is through the lens of personal reflection, reportage, alongside globally recognized indicators ranging from, among others, wealth inequality, infant mortality, obesity, happiness, and defence spending.

Often attempts at writing things down are concerned with talking to oneself *and* to the world (but perhaps not when it's a shopping list). The written iterative process is reflective and refining in a way that often conversation is not. In writing about the drift of the twenty-first century I have tried very hard to dismiss, to judge again, and to absolve myself of the burden of my liberal rights agenda: human rights, civil rights, feminism, democracy, markets, equality, and the fourth estate. But, try as I might, I can't. My mental fudge is as glued as adherence to any religion can be, so maybe my liberal humanism is as great an impediment to my thinking as any other rock and a hard place. And yet, in my secular state with my postmodern hat on, I'm open to anything – well, almost – but in my heart I will not accept unthinking tribalism, bellicose nationalism or misogyny.

I feel as the author Julian Barnes does: that what was once centrist politics is now deemed left-wing to the extreme; and yet the principles are central to the twentieth-century social compact, sanctified in the UN Charter and in numerous internationally ratified agreements.

Barnes lists his ethical relativism this way, like a liturgy: There is such a thing as society; how society looks after its weakest members is a sign of its moral worth; the rich should pay progressive taxes to support the poor; freedom of expression, information and assembly are vital to a state's operation; the free market requires firm regulation; church and state should be separate and faith schools should be banned; the state should run essential public utilities such as health, transport and education which should have no profit motive; wars are generally wrong and stupid; and that all this should be based on a fundamental belief in the rational principles of the Enlightenment.[7] I would add that the death penalty is always wrong, and that equality before the law is paramount – but maybe Barnes has taken these things for granted.

An anthropological view would say that the world is to be studied in and for its diversity, and that cultures should be studied free of one's own values and norms. In other words, in terms of anthropological study, one culture is neither better nor worse than another. But in order to see another culture one has to work very hard to clear the mind of any preconceptions or mental filtering that will cloud the view and impede learning and understanding.

As much of this book is impressionistic and written on the hoof, while travelling around the world, I am guilty of this very sin: of seeing things through my own rose-tinted glasses. We are most uncomfortable when we are away from our safe space, and it tends to be to our tribal and national instincts that we turn in an unthinking way. Is that what happens to me when I'm observing driving habits in Sweden, India, Japan or Italy?

Putting to one side for a moment the values that I might hold dear – for instance, that the death penalty is both morally wrong and evidentially ineffective – it is clear that a society in which everyone feels safe and secure while also understanding our increasing interdependence and the complexity of life is one in which uncertainty, diversity, creativity, enterprise, inclusivity and knowledge creation are taken as everyday norms. That that's just how it is. But how do many of us feel safe and secure? Hence the fuelling of anger, fear, frustration and suspicion that demagogic leaders are so good at manipulating.

The social democratic state is one in which there is a balance between the jealous market and the public good; in which there is art that sells and art that illuminates; and in which there is science that leads to useful technology and science that simply illuminates. The liberal world view is open and closed at the same time: it holds to uncertainty and diversity while also holding firm to human rights, kindness and fairness. And beyond that it says that integral to civilization, per se, is an acceptance and an ability to talk about love, hope and art as part and parcel of everyday life, and that is true in communities, nation-states and all organizations. Just as we don't talk enough of death, so we also don't talk enough of the joy of living and how much we yearn to love and be loved.

And, when it comes to viewing the world outside our cosmos, it is often our expectations that get in the way of an open mind. The international peace negotiator, activist and scholar Adam Curle sometimes used to surprise all sides in peace negotiations by simply listening, and saying nothing. He said he was listening with a completely open mind in order to learn, and not for extraction. He also added that he was no good as an observer "unless I know who I am". Being well centred is important when receiving disparate and often ambiguous information. So too is being incredulous a good state of mind, as long as one is a reflective observer. One could call this the slow thought movement. An ancient Buddhist proverb that appealed to Curle is "the ox is slow, but the earth is patient".[8] In an age of distraction it is often difficult to follow the earth.

Zygmunt Bauman noted in his 1993 book *Postmodern Ethics*[9] – on the merits of secularism – that the postmodernist, having examined all the ethical possibilities, is more aware and therefore more moral than the adopter of faith. Similarly, Nelson Mandela observed in *Conversations with Myself*, published in 2010, "In real life we deal, not with gods, but with ordinary humans like ourselves: men and women who are full of contradictions, who are stable and fickle, strong and weak, famous and infamous."[10] The philosopher John Gray asks, "How could all of humankind not want to be as we imagine ourselves to be? To suggest that large numbers hate and despise values such as tolerance and personal autonomy is, for many people nowadays, an intolerable slur on the species."[11] Surely everyone, really, at heart, is in favour of human and civil rights, feminism, taking care of the planet, democracy and regulated markets?

I've tried to be an ethical relativist, but can only contort myself so far – as a theoretical exercise, but not as a way of life. If I start with "do unto others as you would have done unto yourself", is this an emotional statement lacking in any moral sentiment or a clear statement that accepts that humanity, and myself, flourishes when it loves itself and each other and so supports the statement often attributed to Mahatma Gandhi: "be the change you wish to see"?[12] In the observations that follow in this book I am guilty of sometimes being very clear about some issues and being confused by others.

If, as Herodotus said, and some anthropologists do today, morality is a social construct with its own lines of historical

development, or that morality is the result of emotional attachment – as Hume, Hare and others have said – then there is no
such thing as right and wrong. I am sure, and I have admitted,
that I am the product of everything that has happened to me,
but I have also looked at the evidence for humanity's success,
and its failures; and, while I am often found to be of a postmodernist frame of mind, I argue that there are some fundamental truths that also find me hopping between determinism
or positivism when it comes to what is right and wrong. In this
post-Enlightenment era where the idea of objectivity is ques-
tioned, I stand guilty of confusion. On the one hand, I want
to argue that we must be careful not to think there is a unifying truth in physics or political economy; and on the other
hand I am saying that there are some norms that are inviolable
if we are to continue towards the good society. Do I end up
with a picture of the world with a defined set of values, norms
and behaviours? Yes, to a certain extent, but with the caveat
that within these boundaries there is, as observed in this book,
plenty of room for uncertainty and diversity. In listening and
watching as a reflective observer in slow thinking mode, I can
agree with Nietzsche the need for some sense of perspective.

But – and here is the test for us all – would it be progress
to accept child slavery, or female genital mutilation, or bear
baiting, or gender discrimination, or racism? I think not, and I
think the vast majority of readers of this book would agree. So,
in a similar vein, would it be progress for Europeans to rein-
troduce the death penalty and abandon gun control, or for the
British police to be armed, or smoking to be permitted again in
bars and restaurants in Ireland or China, or to adopt Brazil's
model of capitalism? My answer to all these questions is, of
course, "no": but there will be some readers who will decry
this narrow-mindedness . . .

Much learning is best experienced by chance, over the shoulder, by happenstance, out of context. One morning in 1989 while working at the BBC in the Natural History Unit, I arrived at work to find a note on my desk from my Editor, Peter Salmon, saying "go to the USSR and interview Gorbachev on the environment". Forty-eight hours later, passport and visa in hand, I was on my way to Moscow to see if I could get access to President Mikhail Gorbachev who was in the process of introducing *glasnost* (openness) and *perestroika* (restructuring away from central planning) to the USSR. Given that the state of the environment was, and still is, one of their biggest challenges, we supposed it might be possible to interview the man himself. I didn't manage to interview Gorbachev but we did manage to interview various other high-level people and to make a documentary on the oil and gas industry in northeast Siberia on the Yamal Peninsula. The oil and gas industry had for many years financed Russia's development, and in particular its space exploration and militarization. Gorbachev had flown over some of the oil fields and asked why the gas was flared off rather than being captured and used productively. In doing so he had pointed to what was at the time the largest single cause of global warming, and is now a source of enormous exported wealth to Europe from Russia. In this period of *perestroika*, the strategic aim was to capture the gas, and increase the productivity of the oil fields, by building what would have been the world's largest petrochemical plant. This was to be financed by the Mitsubishi Bank of Japan, the technology was to have come from GE in the USA, and the project was to have been managed by the Finnish petrochemical company Neste. Today, many EU countries are reliant on Russian gas supplies.

Gorbachev fell the following year, but before he left I visited the crumbling USSR several times, soon to become Russia

again, and when we finally got to make the film the story was
about the appalling damage that had been done to the delicate
permafrost tundra on the Yamal Peninsula by the most care-
less oil industry to be found anywhere, and the disruption that
had been caused to the nomadic reindeer-herding Nentsy (or
Nenets) people, and the difficulties that the potential international partners were having in a country without proper
laws and rife with corruption, with an almost complete lack
of enforced environmental regulation, all the while with a
Klondike look to be observed in the eyes of those international
partners.

One day we found ourselves filming the sophisticated Finnish suits in Copenhagen at Neste, the next day interviewing corrupt and incompetent officials in the south-east Siberian town
of Salekhard, and then the third day talking to the supremely
kind-hearted and literally down-to-earth nomadic Nentsy people on the tundra. The Nentsy lived then as they had for hundreds of years moving with their reindeer along the snow line
as it increased and receded, living off the reindeer, the fish in
the rivers and the wild berries that abounded underfoot. They
dressed in reindeer skins and made their *chum* – conical tents
– from the skins. Everything came from the local environment.
They enjoyed both disadvantages and advantages of Stalin's
communism, which had given them access to medicine but also
substantially corralled them into fixed settlements such that
only 10,000 at that time were living nomadically. They could
call a helicopter if they were sick or if one of the women was
having a baby, and they would be whisked away, although the
Russian helicopter crew we were with made it clear that they
saw these nomadic people as savages and barely human.

What an irony that the Nentsy left barely a footprint as they
softly walked across the permafrost and yet the oil industry

had left damage and old equipment that would take thousands of years for nature to take back.[13] During the many months that I spent in Russia, Gorbachev united all the Polar people from the USSR, Scandinavia and the USA with a conference and party in the Kremlin to which I was invited. This meant that peoples with a shared Mongolian past met for the first time. The Inuit met the Eskimos and the Nentsy met the Sami, and it was a glorious exchange of music, language and culture all with the same roots – and the same ability to live in almost perpetual cold and snow.

This anecdote is about the search for fossil fuels; about the clash of civilizations, between centrally controlled, bureaucratic communism and egalitarian, cooperative, agrarian nomads; about geopolitics and the fall of the Soviet Union; and about the tentacles of capitalism reaching for rich pickings in the remote corners of Siberia.

An illusion central to the human condition is that we can understand everything: we can't. We can live in awe, but often we live in fear. This book, and the last, *Thinking the Twenty-First Century*, are about those things that really matter: love, hope, art and social progress. The idea of a single model of the good society is a deliberate delusion: looking for a unifying theory in physics and global economics will not change the need to manage uncertainty and complexity. Uncertainty is at the heart of the scientific enquiry and in diverse political economies. It is a principle of quantum physics and of market economics. Uncertainty means risk and probability, not certainty, dogma or end-game.

This book does not answer all these questions, but by asking them asks the larger question: why can't we have the good society? Where is Utopia now? This seems even more pertinent now that the world is in turmoil and social progress is on hold . . .

This book is interested in what works in society, and where and why and how. Often the answers are not at all obvious, and, as in physics, can only be observed and not fully understood.

Constant themes are uncertainty, divergence and difference – and the power of wondering and wandering. Managing these issues is to celebrate complexity and to revel in ambiguity, paradox and contradiction. Do we need to construct a new global creation story that has at its core not the certainties of one defined creation myth but feeling comfortable with uncertainty both in physics *and* political economy? Physics and political economy are inextricably linked, although few politicians would know or admit as much. It is up to artists, scientists and philosophers to articulate this wonder and to help us write a new global creation myth based on art (the arts), uncertainty, diversity, risk and wonder – and knowledge.

Marxist theorist Terry Eagleton wrote in *After Theory* at the beginning of the twenty-first century that the left had run out of theory, and that the right held the centre ground. In a world of oversupply it is difficult to mount a campaign for cheap food, or universal health services, or free buses, but it is possible to trade on populist disgruntlement and "if them why not me" resentment. This seems to be the mood across much of Europe and the USA as I write. People worldwide have forgotten how we got where we've got today, partly because they're so distracted by their distractions.

The final chapter looks at the post-human world, a state we have perhaps already entered. But how should we think about it, given we have already been co-opted? Can we articulate the future outside the false discipline that the market often dictates, beyond the clutches of a few social media companies, and maintain our rich diversities while holding on to those things that make life possible and worthwhile: love, hope and art?

Three steps forward, two steps back is the history of humanity. Sometimes it feels like three back, two forward – and there are many periods in human history when this has been so, the First and Second World Wars, for instance, and 2016. War is always failure, however justified it may seem at the time.

There are three meta-themes to this book, all of which we are genetically predisposed to, and all of which need nourishing to be fully realized. *Love* binds us all together in varying communities and relationships. *Hope* springs eternal through the passage of time and effort. And *art* is the expression of love and hope. As the book unfolds, each of these themes will become apparent through the use of impressionism, anecdote, reportage and analysis. We are living midst a change to a post-human world where our survival as a species relies on our age-old ability to learn and adapt and where we accept that to survive we must become a form that we have not been, a form in which our multifaceted selves are part of our evolutionary past *and* part of an evolutionary future founded on intelligent adaptation. At all times we must remember the anthropic principle. As the astrophysicist Steven Hawking puts it: "We see the universe the way it is because if it were different we would not be here to observe it."[14]

At any time, we are here, in *Dhuwa* – as Australia's Karingbal people say: to be alive, very much so, ears, eyes and soul attuned to the Earth and the cosmos and to the past and the future. It's all around us forever and they've known this forever – whatever physics may now be telling us is the truth. Or, as *The Tibetan Book of the Dead* poses the paradox, "live everyday as if this is all there is *and* as if you will live forever".

As the book develops, reference will be made to various art forms, a number of countries and the enduring themes of love, hope and art. References to the sculptor Barbara Hepworth ride through the book and the diversity of political economy cultures permeate each chapter. If you travel you cannot but be amazed and delighted at the commonalities *and* the differences, at what it means to be human *and* what it means to live in a local community, whether that be a nation, a town or a forest.

A single form or a theory of everything is only possible to understand laterally, in another dimension, and it is most apparent or easily made aware of in an art form: hence the starting point in Chapter 1 of Barbara Hepworth's work for the UN. It can never be evaluated in a cold, calculated way. A theory of everything would combine what we know about the universe on a macro scale with what we know about quantum physics: two very different sets of ways of being. At the heart of the human condition is a similar conundrum: combining the laws of daily existence with the mystery of unknowing. At the heart of both conundrums is the complexity of the process of trying to arrive at an answer. It's not possible to know all the variables at any one time, and to hold them still in the now for now, for when the now has gone the conditions have changed and so the answers have moved on, infinitely.

But we have created life on Earth, by which I do not mean that we are god (although our gods are our creation), but that we have developed, adapted, grown, dispatched, maimed, given birth to a way of being on Earth. In this organic mass there is more in common than in division, but still there is great diversity in how we manage the human conundrum, the human condition. Living in the Swedish north is to daily manage many of the same functions of life as living in a South African township, but the politics of daily life and weather are wildly different. There's the rub: how we are so similar, and so different in our lives.

1

This century's new creation myth

"World organization is still a new
adventure in human history"

Dag Hammarskjöld[15]

Barbara Hepworth's "Single Form" stands resolute outside the
UN headquarters in New York. It conveys a number of mes-
sages. Any observer is struck by the contrast of this standing
stone with its rounded resonance of indigenous wisdom from
ancient England against the stark conformity and regularity of
the surrounding buildings. As a standing stone it is a flag flying free in the metropolis of New York's constant churn. It is
a signpost back across time to a moment when humanity was
at one with wind and waves and not striving hard to complete
some mission to succeed at all costs. Barbara Hepworth said
as a sculptor, "I am the landscape" – and aren't we all? The

repository of imprinted memories and experiences threading back to our most formative time, our own childhood and the birth of human beings.

If the surrounding skyscrapers are erect phalluses to human frailty writ large as certainty, then "Single Form" is a blade of grass bending in the wind, holding firm to the certainty that the wind blows through us, dust to dust, ashes to ashes.

The "Single Form" represents all of humanity across the ages and for all time; it is both one and many in its strength. It stands erect and sure, not proud but surely sure of itself. The whole is made one by the hole which invites the eye to look through and past the immediate and gives the viewer an insight: that it is an illusion that all that can be seen cannot be seen. Look beyond, it says, through my eyes. Like meerkats on the African plain we have stood and watched out and then darted underground when danger approaches. New York and all its copies stand as masculine testimony to certainty: we can conquer and we can stand forever against the elements. Not so Hepworth's "Single Form" which holds both strength and infirmity as the wind blows through it. One imagines that it will still stand when the city of New York is flattened and is no more – not because it needs to stand but because of what it represents: timelessness and the human endeavour. To be, to watch, to witness, to see, and to count one's blessings. As Hepworth said: "I think that the very nature of art is affirmative, and in being so reflects the laws, and the evolution of the universe."[16] In this, "Single Form" embodies the themes of this book: love, hope, art and progress.

"Single Form" was commissioned in memory of the person who many consider the most enlightened UN leader in the organization's history: Dag Hammarskjöld. When he died in a plane crash in 1961 in Africa, Jacob Blaustein, a former US delegate to the UN, commissioned the piece from Barbara Hepworth who had been a friend of UN Secretary-General Hammarskjöld. The piece was installed in 1964.

Blaustein had been invited by US President Roosevelt to provide expertise on human rights, and it is possible that Blaustein ensured that human rights are at the heart of the UN's Charter and ongoing work.

Hammarskjöld, the UN's second Secretary-General, said in 1959 that it was important for everyone, "the worker, the artist, the scientist and the politician", to experiment in life in order not to be subordinated at a time when the need for "tolerance is as great as ever in the very interests of progress and in the interests of peace". He declared: "What I ask for is absurd: that life shall have a meaning. What I strive for is impossible: that my life shall acquire a meaning."[17] But through Hepworth's "Single Form" life can have meaning in its most lyrical, poetic and transcendent manifestation, beyond the realms of the obvious and the scientific – and, in this century, beyond the algorithmic.

Hammarskjöld famously said that in decades to come the UN would still be dealing with the same issues as he had grappled with during his tenure as UN Secretary-General from 1953–61, because "world organization is still a new adventure in human history". He was thought by many to have been the most visionary leader the UN has ever had and, despite being unanimously appointed, and reappointed for a second term, by the Security Council, stood up to the five permanent members in a robust and honest manner. There are some who think he was murdered because of his efforts to find peace in what is now the Democratic Republic of Congo. In 2016 UN Secretary-General Ban Ki-moon reopened the investigation into his death which may implicate the US and British governments.[18]

Jacob Blaustein and his father Louis were the founders of the US oil giant Amoco, now part of BP, and inventors of the drive-through petrol station and the metered petrol pump. The Blausteins put most of their money into human rights work and Jacob was a member of the US delegation to the 1945 United Nations founding conference where, as business person, he ensured that civil rights became part of the founding principles of the UN along with peace-making.

Hepworth recognized that, imperfect though it is, the UN represents one of our greatest hopes for a good life for all on this planet. As she said:

> The United Nations is our conscience, if it succeeds it is our success. If it fails it is our failure. Throughout my work on the *Single Form* I have kept in mind Dag Hammarskjöld's ideas of human and aesthetic ideology and I have tried to perfect a symbol that would reflect the nobility of his life, and at the same time give us a motive and symbol of both continuity and solidarity for the future . . .[19]

On another day, some months later, I am looking at a painting by Giovanni Battista Tiepolo from the eighteenth century in Venice and I realize how secular Hepworth's "Single Form" is, for it crosses all divides, and lifts all religions beyond the casualness of their creation stories – even though it is so human-centric. Religion is important both as illusion and as narrative, and, of course, illusion and narrative are important in the discovery of knowledge and the creation of art. But being religious need not mean being fixed in one's faith, for it can mean being open to possibility. Religion – as illusion and narrative – is part of what it means to be human, just as atheism – as part of scepticism and agnosticism – is also part of possibility. It is possible to be a believer in the Christian story but not believe in God, so it is also possible to believe in other religious stories without becoming fixed in their faith.

Also outside the United Nations headquarters lies, rather than stands, Henry Moore's "Reclining Figure". Moore and Hepworth, Yorkshire-born contemporaries and friends, studied at Leeds School of Art, joining in 1919 and 1920, later also living near each other in Hampstead, London, in the 1930s and becoming members of the Royal College of Art in London's Exhibition Road. Despite Moore, five years older than Hepworth, being slightly disparaging of Hepworth's postmodern figurative work, "Single Form" and "Reclining Figure" both seem so human – both are of and from the landscape and both speak to the heart, the mind and the spirit. Hepworth said her work was organic "because I'm organic myself". The landscape is Yorkshire where both were born and brought up, but in a sense these two sculptures are also redolent of the industrial age – as a firm reminder of where we come from. And, as we move into the machine-, bio- and artificial-intelligence post-human age we forget our evolutionary past at our peril. We have always had less control than we thought, but now, as we make "intelligent" images of ourselves that can mimic much of what we do but not who we are, we must be sure to retain a sense of wonder and witness to the world. Art in all its forms is the way to preserve this sanity – and try to make sense of our beginning, our middle and our end.

Hepworth is important not just for her art but for what she represents: as a woman who had to confront a world of male artists; as an artist; and as someone with hope for the future. She is the feminist and the feminized future, building monuments to a negotiated, collaborative future.

But, if Hepworth spoke with sculpture, how should we think and write about this century? It is so important to think complexity, to make connections. On complexity, as Klaus Schwab, founder of the World Economic Forum, says, "we are living in the most interdependent era in history: no leader can afford to think in 'silo' terms, but must be much more holistic and adaptive in order to 'connect the dots'".[20]

To be or not to be . . . that is the question

The science of economics has done so much damage by disconnecting economics from daily life, both as it is experienced by individuals and communities, and as it is taught in economics departments and business and management schools around the world. As Cambridge economist Partha Dasgupta said, in writing *Economics: A Very Short Introduction*:

> Even though the analytical and empirical core of economics has grown from strength to strength over the decades, I haven't been at ease with the selection of topics that textbooks offer for discussion (rural life in poor regions – this is the life of some 2.5 billion people – doesn't get mentioned at all), nor with the subjects that are emphasized in leading economics journals (nature rarely appears there as an active player).[21]

The outgoing US President Barack Obama said that one of his continual messages as President was explaining how the world was one, connected in all ways, an interdependent entity.

And as Paul Polman, CEO of Unilever, one of the world's largest companies, observed to an audience at Bath University in 2016, academics are the least progressive people, unable to work outside their narrow boundaries, and incapable of forming partnerships with those outside their rarefied fields.

Self-serving stories are not helpful, but stories that illuminate, elevate and distract in their language and style from the everyday are very important in making some sense of the essential lightness of being. All creation myths begin with a story, so it is that the Bible begins with "In the beginning was the word" and the Japanese creation myth begins with cosmic chaos out of which were formed sexless deities who created gendered gods who formed the islands of Japan. Many Australian creation myths, and there are many different Aboriginal peoples' stories, start with the dreamtime but, as they become more elaborate, they often seem to have some understanding of the science that we now know about the creation of the Earth and the history of its evolution. In South Africa, Cape Town's table mountain, *Umlindi Weningizimu*, is the greatest giant of them all, a dead giant watching over us to keep the other giants peaceful. According to this creation myth, there is one giant at each corner of the world, created by Djobela, the Earth goddess, who had made love with the Sun god Tixo to create Qamata, who needed protection so a number of other giant gods were created around the world which now stand as the world's greatest mountains. And so we can tell creation myths from around the world.

Understanding and telling stories seem to be part of what it means to be human. And this book is but a story. We like to think that we grow out of fairy tales and simple stories and graduate to hard science, truths and patterned ways of seeing the world, but in reality these supposedly more advanced ways

23

of seeing the world are but simple tales. For our age, since the Enlightenment, the way is to catch the drift of the narrative while keeping our feet on the ground, of listening to the music while hearing the whole piece, and of admiring the sculpture while seeing its context and place. Wherever one hears Shakespeare it is transporting, but to see it in the round as it would have been when it was written can be to contextualize it and give it life. So too Hepworth's "Single Form" outside the UN headquarters in New York gives it meaning, and wouldn't Antony Gormley's "Another Place", with its 100 iron figures staring out to sea on Crosby beach outside the port of Liverpool, be radically reduced in meaning if placed elsewhere? Hepworth and Gormley point out that place gives meaning to their art, just as Einstein said that where you are and what you're doing gives time and space relativism.

As an example of difference, diversity and interpretation the Royal Shakespeare Company, on the 400th anniversary of his birth in 2016, tested and teased the limits of *that* scene in Hamlet:

Papa Essiedu, then playing Hamlet for the RSC at Stratford upon Avon:

"... to *be* or *not* to be ..."

Tim Minchin – Australian musician:

"... to be *or* not to be ..."

Benedict Cumberbatch – "Sherlock Holmes" – who had just played Hamlet in London:

"... to be or *not* to be ..."

Harriet Walter, RSC actor:

> ". . . to be or not to *be* . . ."

Rory Kinnear, RSC actor:

> ". . . to be or not to be: that *is* the question . . ."

David Tennant – *Dr Who*, *Broadchurch*, *Hamlet*:

> ". . . to be or not to be: *that* is the question . . ."

Sir Ian McKellen, RSC member – *Hamlet et al.*:

> ". . . to be or not to be: that is *the* question . . ."

Dame Judi Dench, RSC actor and former "M" in James Bond films:

> ". . . to be or not *to* be . . ."

Prince Charles, elitist hereditary bloke and heir to the British throne:

> ". . . to be or not to be: that is the *question* . . ."[22]

Interpretation is everything; humour and stress can be found everywhere; and nobody is right but we all have a role in telling the human story. In being we are struggling. The sculptor Antony Gormley expresses the human condition: "Our need is to leave a trace: a trace of our living and dying on the face of an indifferent universe."[23] For, as theoretical physicist Stephen Hawking says, our view of the universe is always an anthropic view, otherwise we wouldn't see what we see and the universe would be different, but it would be just as indifferent.

Fellow scientist Brian Cox, a particle physicist at Manchester University, agrees: "It has always been self-evident to me that there is meaning in the universe, because the universe means something to me . . . the question is whether that meaning is local and temporary to the Milky Way."[24] But, while there is uncertainty on two levels – because we're observing the phenomena and because our knowledge always moves on – Cox is a model-maker, as was Einstein. In other words, we can use the evidence to continually test our models. Some people start with the evidence, some start with the mathematics, and some start with their intuitive perceptions of possible worlds. The art of knowledge, and the beauty of the human brain – to synthesize Hawking, Cox, Einstein, Shakespeare and Hepworth – is in the roaming, in the dreaming of possibilities and alternatives to knowledge *and* to the way society works. In both cases we're looking for patterns because patterns are what we know best. The extraordinary paradox is that, while some of the most influential thinkers today are collectors of evidence – think Thomas Piketty and Steven Pinker – politics in many countries is dominated by what are termed "post-truth" politicians who trade on lies and disinformation and for whom experts are history.

Art transcends. In a study of Shakespeare worldwide,[25] Andrew Dickson said that more than 1 billion people were acquainted with the world's greatest playwright, and many of the interpretations stretched the plays to their absolute limits. Good art transcends the petty particulars of individuals, politicians, nation-state squabbles and day-to-day bigotry and raises the spirit and sets us free: hence the need for art to be the third part of my triumvirate for the good society, for a successful political economy. Words written during one of England's flowerings of art in the sixteenth and early seventeenth centuries still resonate today and ensure the continuing mellifluousness of the English language, even if the transactional basis of modern "Globlish" is less rich a tongue.

It is notable that Shakespeare appeals to freedom fighters and dictators, to humanists and human rights abusers alike. The Robben Island bible – the complete works of Shakespeare – went from prisoner to prisoner clad in pictures of Hindu deities to disguise its penetration – Shakespeare being seen as subversive by South Africa's White administration, but Hinduism not. Each inmate noted in the margin their favourite lines. Nelson Mandela's were from *Julius Caesar*: "Cowards die many times before their deaths; / The valiant never taste death but once."

Not many people know that Adolf Hitler also had a German translation of Shakespeare and his Minister of Propaganda Joseph Goebbels had a PhD in drama and thought Shakespeare a "huge genius … more modern than the moderns"; his favourite play was also *Julius Caesar*.

Shakespeare's genius is as a wordsmith, most of his plays being derivative, and he became the representative of the magical burst of language and art in sixteenth-century England.

Another derivative writer and poet is Bob Dylan, who often references Shakespeare in his songs, and is the representative of the flowering of alternative thinking, reflection and art in the 1960s and '70s in the Anglo-American world. Bob took his name from the Welsh poet Dylan Thomas and both owed much to a man who should have won the Nobel Prize for literature, James Joyce. Being dead, like Shakespeare, doesn't count, of course.[26]

Much of this book treats war as the apotheosis of civilization and the good society. That war is always a failure may be a truism, but it seems fitting to quote Shakespeare:[27]

... O war! thou son of hell
Whom angry heavens do make their minister
Throw in the frozen bosoms of our part
Hot coals of vengeance! Let no soldier fly.
He that is truly dedicate to war
Hath no self-love, nor he that loves himself
Hath not essentially but by circumstance
The name of valour.

William Shakespeare,
Henry IV Act V, Scene 2, line 33

Bob Dylan did not want to be the spokesperson for his generation because he said he was a chronicler, a storyteller, and so too Shakespeare, who still, across 400 years, speaks for generations.

War, and the use of force, and the denial of peace, has been one of the stories of humankind – and it continues. Since 1945 the world has lived through the most peaceful period in human history, partly because of standoff, and partly because we have learnt to talk, to collaborate and to negotiate – to be tolerant of each other and hope for a better future – but mostly because of the recognition of MAD – mutually assured destruction – should anyone start a nuclear conflagration. War, or not war, constantly raises its ugly head when examining how we love, hope and make art – it's a recurring theme in this book.

On time, nothing and God

Aristotle was concerned about the idea of creation because it postulated a beginning, and Kant argued that time could have started any time (no joke intended), and Hawking said that thinking about consciousness (as in the two previous statements) was to be avoided as too difficult. We live in a world where everything is apparently explicable, not least so that we can manage or control it. This masculine attribute is a false economy and leads to a lack of time for awe and wonder, for allowing the heart to wander and the soul to rest. At the heart of the century is uncertainty, both in physics and politics. The void for most people will be filled by *apparent* certainty: a religious mythology, a life lived in a box, or the shutting-out of reason. In the whirl of instant comment and social media it has been said that we live in a post-factual world, a world where the expert is no longer recognized. This accords with the uncertainty principle which is at the heart of quantum physics, but could lead humanity away from staying in balance with knowledge and awe.

That most people do not understand advancements in physics is well known, so it is a supreme surprise when a leading politician calmly answers a question on physics. In April 2016 the Prime Minister of Canada, Justine Trudeau, was asked if he could explain quantum computing. He said:

> Very simply, normal computers work, either there's power going through a wire, or not. It's a 1, or a 0, they're a binary system. What quantum states allow is for much more complex information to be encoded into a single bit.[28]

The audience at Canada's Perimeter Institute for Theoretical Physics in Ontario gave him a standing ovation so surprised were they he understood that life may not be this or that, but this, that and whatever.

Given that all that we do, including the development of government policy, is governed by both classical physics and quantum mechanics, it does not seem unreasonable for us all to ask our politicians if they understand the issues related to a grand unifying theory. Their answers will tell us a great deal about how they approach issues of uncertainty, flexibility and consultation – and, of course, the funding of open-ended research in physics and other areas of knowledge development.

Many globally recognized physicists have also been progressive social reformers. Einstein campaigned for nuclear disarmament (after the end of World War II, during which he had advocated that the USA gain nuclear weapons to counter the Germans); Martin Rees, the UK's Astronomer Royal, has said that, unless we urgently reform global climate change policy, we only have a 50/50 chance of surviving the twenty-first century; and Stephen Hawking has said that we have as great a certainty of blowing ourselves up (through nuclear war) as destroying life on Earth through climate change.

From the International Space Station it is possible to understand the relationship between physics, awe and experience. An astronaut looking out will have had to trust classical physics and gravity to hold the ISS in orbit and not spin off into dark space. All astronauts have talked of the awe of looking both at space and back at planethome. And, as the ISS flies around Earth, observations can be made of cosmic, planetary, celestial and human activity in the moment, in one shot. There is lightning and newly observed lightning sprites, along with other weather patterns that affect life on Earth: cyclones, empty skies and grey days. And beneath all these are the lights of cities and urban sprawl as the Earth's resources are released into the atmosphere. The great conurbations of frenetic human activity show our success at colonizing time and space in one 24-hour economy, never sleeping, but rarely awakening to the real awe of the universe. And we know that the individuals that make up these cities are as complex and inexplicable as the smallest of things understood in quantum physics.

But the quest to understand or marry classical physics and the uncertainty principle (as made apparent by quantum physics) may be beyond our ken: it may not be possible to bring together two sets of ideas that each exist on different planes. In a similar way, it may not be possible to understand the love of a forest with the fear of getting lost in the same forest. Experience tells us that we may gaze in wonder forever but never find the answer, and yet the modern world is determined to find answers to everything. For all questions there is an answer, and for all problems there is a solution, and for all joy there is a reason. But – and this may be a non sequitur – why should we seek solutions for all the perceived problems that we have invented in our affluent world?

Today, 12 February 2016, as I sit waiting for a plane at Tokyo's Narita airport, one of Albert Einstein's propositions has fallen into place: gravitational ripples have been detected for the first time, as he predicted 100 years previously, according to a paper in the *Physical Review Letters* signed by more than 1,000 scientists.[29] This is fundamental to the idea that matter and energy are indivisible. Gravitational fields are created when matter collapses into black holes creating massive amounts of energy and stopping time – because nothing can escape. One scientist said:

> up until now we have only seen warped space-time when it's calm. It's as though we had only seen the ocean's surface on a calm day but had never seen it roiled in a storm, with crashing waves in which the flow of time speeded up, then slowed, then speeded up. A storm with space bending this way, then that.[30]

With language like this, it is possible to sympathize with Wittgenstein in thinking that all that is left to do is linguistic analysis!

I like the idea that this latest discovery was recognized through the hearing of sound rather than the seeing of light – there being no light in dark matter – hence the reference to black holes. One scientist described the sound as being a chirp. This I can understand: I can hear it. Now we know the sound of one hand clapping (paradox: we are desperate to "understand"): the evidence of the gravitational wave that was "heard" by the Laser Interferometer Gravitational-Wave Observatory (LIGO) team in the USA is not dissimilar to dropping a pebble into a bucket of water. If you do this you can hear the sound of colliding black holes a billion light years away. The distant is here, now. You are in the still, small place if you want to be now – being able to hear discovery, rather than read about it, or see it in numbers; on this occasion we can hear its music. Einstein said he thought in terms of music, and would have become a musician if he had not become a physicist. Between thinking, he played the violin apparently to a very high standard. Nietzsche said that "without music, life would be a mistake" and I would add that without love, hope and artistic interpretation life would be meaningless. Despite his mental roaming, Einstein was reputed to find it difficult to accept that his theories might need refinement and rethinking. This is also true of Charles Darwin, who is said to have become inflexible towards the end of his life. But don't we all?

It strikes me that the interior of a black hole – where lies infinity, nothing and no time, only potential energy – is the still point of the turning universe. This I can reach if I meditate or muse for long enough and get myself in "the right state of mind". This lack of mind is the real mindfulness so beloved of this generation's chatter. In other words, I say to myself that I can reach into the idea – for it is only an idea – of a black hole anytime I wish, simply by thinking.

So many statements, so many ideas, so much fun is to be had by blowing your mind. In *A Universe from Nothing* Lawrence M. Krauss says, "if you looked far enough in any direction, you would see the back of your head" and "the further you look the younger and hotter the universe" and "nothing is everything".[31] For us in the material world, in our mostly urban sprawls, "nothing is everything" is a mental construct. What should we make of the Higgs boson – the "god particle" – or that light is everything? Are we really stardust? Is it just avarice, competition and masculinity that have kept us slow and stopped us moving forward, or have they been the secret of our success as a species? Are they not the anchors of temporality that keep our feet on the ground and run the course of each day?

"Nothing" is such a misguided word, a concept that means the opposite . . . Before the Big Bang there was everything and nothing which is the stillness, the now. And dark matter is everywhere all the time – passing through us. In an infinite universe, an infinite nothing, anywhere is the middle. This thought inevitably puts me at the centre of the universe: am I God and all creation flows from me, as Descartes suggested? The most recent theory is that the Big Bang was created by two black holes hitting each other. This can never be known: it is just a mathematical idea – but how should or could I get my mind around it?! Socrates said that he knew nothing except the fact of his own ignorance.

Do I have nightmares? About this? Or do I feel elevated to affirm our undivided past as humans and be humbled by the magnificence of what I don't, and can never, know. I may wake in the night with an idea for a book, with a horror that a misogynist, xenophobic teenager will be elected President of the USA, a worry about my children, a terror about a near car crash, a fear of dying, but I never wake in the night worrying about the beginning of time or the end of the universe or the third law of thermodynamics. But, as Krauss has said, "one person's dream is another person's nightmare".[32]

There will be those who, through their belief in Christ, Jehovah, Allah or whatever, find deeply offensive the two symbiotic, but seemingly contradictory, ideas that we can know but not know everything: but when has religion ever been humble? Greek philosophers could not cope with the idea of creation (human) because humans had always existed (even if the world's oldest religious texts which predate the Greek empire, the Vedas, say that God came after creation). And here's a conundrum: if God created time, and time stood still, would God still exist? In other words, time must be the creation of humans, like God, who also, presumably, created the universe in which time exists. Did God know what (he) was doing when he created the universe? If he didn't, then he's not God. Similarly, present-day creationists believe, with no empirical evidence, that dinosaurs walked the Earth alongside humans.

Walking Charles Darwin's walk along the sandy path in his garden at Down House in Kent is to think the same thoughts as Claude Monet working in his garden at Giverny in Normandy. Darwin never said that it was the fittest (i.e. the strongest or most intelligent) of the species that survive: it is the ones most responsive to change. Monet's house is full of prints by Hiroshige and Hokusai and his garden is inspired by their art. He said he had "the deepest admiration for Japanese art and a real appreciation for the Japanese"[33] and it was he who introduced

Japanese art to Europe. With an open heart and mind, both Darwin and Monet thought the unthinkable.

A good story which makes us smile (and why shouldn't we smile while contemplating the universe?) is told of Albert Einstein who became impatient with the many people who wanted to talk to him. He reluctantly agreed to meet a young woman who had travelled from Bombay to Princeton University, greeting her with the line "I suppose I have to go and play God again." He also said that time runs very fast when you're sitting next to a pretty girl, but very slowly when you're waiting for a bus. Everything's relative.

Relativity, Fauré and human fallibility

We are easily fooled. As Winston Churchill said, "it has been said that democracy is the worst form of government except for all those other forms that have been tried from time to time".[34] And often mistakenly attributed to him is the assertion that "the best argument against democracy is a five-minute conversation with the average voter". Here we might think of those fooled by Adolf Hitler in the 1930s in Germany and those misled in the UK by the "Vote Leave" campaign on the EU in 2016, and lied to in Donald Trump's 2016 US presidential campaign. One UK government minister, Michael Gove, then the UK's Minister for *Justice*, said during the campaign "we've had enough of experts".[35] The same is true of Donald Trump's 2016 presidential campaign. Similarly, Mao Tse Tung encouraged millions to turn against their fellow Chinese because they were teachers, doctors and lawyers. How gullible are we in the face of determined misadventure and evil?

In what is being called the "post-truth" world, we must call on people's ability to sort bullshit from fact, to question everything they hear, to be discerning. Politicians, like second-hand car salesmen, have always lied, or at least hyperboled, in their search for power, and we know that in the vast majority of cases to want to be a political or business leader involves a significant dose of sociopathology – to be inured to attacks, to play on opponents' weaknesses, and to focus solely on personal reward.

Over breakfast with a scientist, the discussion moved to the relationship between quantum theory and biodiversity. The well-published and internationally recognized expert on slime moulds and biodiversity was demonstrating his love of life on Earth by waving his hands excitedly in the air as he talked about the sex lives and predatory nature of these enigmatic living beings. What, I asked him, is the relationship between your work on biodiversity and quantum theory? Knowing the café manager had a sense of humour – and the ridiculous – as she stacked the shelves with organic tomatoes and purple flowering broccoli, we asked what she thought of the space-time continuum? Her reply: "I don't have time to think about that: I've got a job to do!" Well, that told us!

And what do we know about physics and the universe, and why does it matter? Are we easily fooled? Yes, we are. In the conjunction of conventional physics, which describes large-scale gravitational matters, and quantum mechanics, which describes non-gravitational subatomic physics, is what is described as unified theory. This is the final solution, the end-game, the meaning of everything. But be very careful, because we cannot know everything, however much we attempt to do so. Stephen Hawking said, "I think there is a good chance that the study of the early universe . . . will lead us to a complete unified theory within the lifetime of some of us who are around today" (always assuming we don't blow ourselves up first). "Only time (whatever that may be) will tell."[36] He, like Einstein, has a sense of humour.

We have a hundred billion neurons in our brains, the same as there are stars in the universe. Which came first? A space cannot be both a space and a conjunction or a theory of everything: I'm just playing with ideas – and your mind. Empty your mind and you will understand the universe. Just as we created God, so too we created time as a concomitant of an understanding of the beginnings of time. And we will not last long; just as we created God(s) and time, they too will fall by the wayside. And so I cast some of you into a hell of your own making, which, as St Augustine said, is what God created, after (he) created time and heaven – in response to people who asked the question "What did God do before (he) created the universe?" Do not ask! Ignorance is bliss. Ah, the problem of knowing and consciousness.

In his bestselling *Seven Brief Lessons on Physics* Carlo Rovelli compares Einstein's 1915 article on "The General Theory of Relativity", which he says is "very moving and beautiful and awe inspiring", to Mozart's *Requiem,* Homer's *Odyssey,* Michelangelo's painting on the ceiling of the Sistine Chapel, and Shakespeare's *King Lear.*[37] Each of these examples has a completeness in its attempt to construct a view that reaches beyond the conventional and transport us to another realm beyond the obvious and everyday. In a later interview, when he had become an international bestseller translated into 41 languages, he said that it was the connecting of beauty, emotions and science that had struck a chord: "I don't think those things should ever be separated from science."[38] Referring to his mild use of drugs as a young man he said that stepping back, and seeing things outside our established perceptions, "helps in losing the idea that what we see is reality". That great attender to scientific detail, Charles Darwin, said in his autobiography that "If I had to live my life again I would have made a rule to read some poetry and listen to some music at least once every week."[39]

Looking down from the International Space Station, astronauts can see phenomenal beauty and the everyday burning of fossil fuels in cities *as well as* natural phenomena that will presumably still exist after humans have burned themselves out. And so the conjunction of physics, awe and experience. In a grain of sand. I have chosen Barbara Hepworth's sculptures as my transcendent art, but playing Fauré's *Requiem* or looking at Rothko's paintings would be just as good, and doing all three would surely blow your mind. As sculptor Antony Gormley says, "I believe in the ability of sculpture as a first-hand experience to move us and to shift our goal-orientated consciousness somewhere deeper and wider."[40] It is one of the main themes of this book to weave a story between the values-driven goals of political economy, whatever side they come from, and the wider appreciation that art gives us. The former gives us hope and drive while the latter gives us hope, contemplation, context and understanding. Without art we are lost.

And yet we are not so far from C.P. Snow's 1950s two cultures:

> A good many times I have been present at gatherings of people who, by the standards of the traditional culture, are thought highly educated and who have with considerable gusto been expressing their incredulity at the illiteracy of scientists. Once or twice I have been provoked and have asked the company how many of them could describe the

Second Law of Thermodynamics. The response
was cold: it was also negative. Yet I was asking
something which is about the scientific equivalent
of: *Have you read a work of Shakespeare's?*[41]

But perhaps culture, or discussions about it, have become a
melange of ideas: not so much a clash between science and art
as Snow discussed, but between diversity and completeness. In
a sense there are three forces at work. One: the desire to find a
unifying theory of everything in physics (which is an illusion as
it will lead to uncertainty); two: the "end of history" hypothesis (which is mostly delusional myopic US thinking); and three:
a feeling that, now that two-thirds of the world use Facebook
or some such platform, and know that Lennon is more famous
than Lenin or Jesus, and expect potatoes to be ubiquitous, culture may be harmonized and homogeneous (which is all true,
but misses the point about community cohesion).

As commentators like Terry Eagleton have pointed out,
cultural politics is both trivial and momentous. It can mean
a glossy brochure or a photo of an emaciated child, *and*
it can be worth dying for, as in Northern Ireland or South
Africa.[42] In other words, culture can be equated with political economy, with the very ways and means of production,
consumption and decision-making. This is important because
it moves the discussion away from the idea of economics as
deus ex machina, as much of modern (neoliberal) economics
is discussed, and into the realms of systems, controls, norms,
agreements, history – and, love, hope and art as the basis for
political economy.

Is culture the same as, or synonymous with, political
economy? The lives of two prominent cultural theorists, Stuart Hall and James Baldwin, overlapped; and both have been

enormously influential in cultural *and* postcolonial studies. On Hall's death in 2014, the *Guardian* obituary said that his work "lay in an insistence on taking popular, low-status cultural forms seriously and tracing the interweaving threads of culture, power and politics".[43] This interdisciplinary perspective is all-encompassing. The view is the one taken here in placing love, art and progress as that heart of political economy.

The cultural theorist James Baldwin said that artists kept "the human race alive" as "incorrigible disturber[s] of the peace" because our "visible reality hides a deeper one". This action "make[s] the world a more human dwelling place". In support of the artist, that is all of us as interpreters of existence, a "nation is healthiest which has the least necessity to distrust or ostracize these people – whom, as I say, honor, once they are gone, because somewhere in our hearts we know that we cannot live without them".[44]

John Berger was a disturber of the peace, and is still controversial today. How many men see that the world is made in their image? Berger was an art critic and writer who made an important BBC television series in the 1970s called *Ways of Seeing* in which he said "the 'ideal' spectator is always designed to be male and the image of the woman is designed to flatter him ... if you doubt this (as a man) transform the woman into a man ... then notice the violence this transformation does ...". He argued that this was part of the construct of capitalism, which "survives by forcing the majority, whom it exploits, to define their interests as narrowly as possible ... it is achieved by imposing a false standard of what is and what is not desirable".[45] And so we need to build the sort of society where Baldwin, Hall, Einstein and Berger can thrive and are welcome, and where their work is not burned as were books in 1930s Germany, and Beatles records in 1966 in the Southern

States. The civilized society is tolerant and welcomes the artist, and mystics like Einstein.

And so to beauty and science. Einstein drew a distinction between mysticism and religiosity, the former being a natural result of looking hard at the joy of scientific discovery and the latter being where people go when they want certainty leading to mental starch. He said:

> ... everyone who is seriously involved in the pursuit of science becomes convinced that a spirit is manifest in the laws of the Universe – a spirit vastly superior to that of man, and one in the face of which we with our modest powers must feel humble. In this way the pursuit of science leads to a religious feeling of a special sort, which is indeed quite different from the religiosity of someone more naive.

For the ancient Greeks beauty was moral goodness, and ugliness sin. Herbert Read, writing in *The Meaning of Art* in 1931 said, "Art is so much more significant than economics or philosophy. It is the direct measure of man's spiritual vision."[46] I see knowledge as art – and its denial the antithesis of the love and hope that keeps us going, just as art is knowledge.

The theory of nothing is important here on Earth, among us mortals who play with time and each other's lives because so much of what we believe is based on nothing more than trust. Prick the bubble and we're lost. In the end: "Life's but a walking shadow, a poor player / That struts and frets his hour upon the stage / And then is heard no more."[47] So it is that Ai Weiwei's and Banksy's art is transitory, both political in their way, but both saying "first I am an artist; if it's political, then OK" – and, of course, it is. Bob Dylan, Nobel Prize winner for literature, said the same, declaiming the idea that he was the spokesperson for a generation, just an artist, a storyteller. Author Colm Tóibín said he is "a soft liberal during the day and a socialist at night ... [but] I have never won a political argument. I am a novelist. I see every side."[48]

Some of Banksy's street art still exists where it originally appeared when local authorities realized that graffiti could be art rather than despoliation. Go see some of his few remaining original works around the docks in Bristol, England, where he was born in 1974.

That people all over the world flock to art galleries and live events is either testimony to a desire for the real, to see the original, to hear the wobbles and see the smears, to be in touch with the authentic, *or* to have their culture packaged, for culture to be organized: "We go to the gallery." So much is digitized, distant, virtual and delivered to an electronic platform that the authentic has a very real appeal. The actor Colin Firth spoke to this when he said that he had chosen a particularly expensive watch, but he made the point well: "We live in such a digitized, fossil-fuel and electrical age, so to see a piece of engineering that isn't dependent on any of those things, and what's more, to see it crafted by human hands, resulting in an object that is both exquisite and precise is miraculous."[49] We wear art on our wrists; and in using this quote am I guilty of falling for that trick – aligning capitalism with art with nature with sensibility?

Such is the appeal of the 1,000 or so music, arts and literature festivals in Britain every year. With one paradox: so much of life is random, unmanaged, badly produced, and so much verbiage is posted online without a moment of intelligent thought that there is also a desire for things that are curated, produced and crafted. This is the appeal of the BBC, CNN and good newspapers which have audiences and people willing to

42

pay for someone to edit the world and show them a product, and fact-check. My time as a journalist at the BBC was mostly a lesson in deliberation and reflection: Have we got this right? Do we need to fact-check? Is there a second source for this idea? And how can we craft this narrative so that it's most effective – and watchable? And attendance at art galleries and museums is up, even though some find them aseptic and distant.

The good society not only promotes art and cultural development that challenges the establishment and the status quo but also provides free access to it when possible. While doing some research on Charles Darwin, I was standing at the information desk of London's Natural History Museum and the man in front of me, an overweight middle-aged American male, asked where he paid to get in. The woman said, "It's free." "No," he said, "where do I buy a ticket?" "You don't need a ticket" she replied carrying on with her other tasks. He turned to me and said, "I don't understand. You mean all these people haven't paid? How do you do it?" I started to explain about access, a public good, a national asset, a free society, open to all ... He said, "That's crazy. It must cost a fortune!" It does, but it's worth it. Just like universal health and social care, access to art and cultural artifacts is fundamental to a good society.

I am passing through an airport somewhere and the camera takes the data necessary to recognize my face: the shape of my nose, the angle of my eyes, the space between my lips and my ears. But it doesn't feel my heart beat, or know that I need to be hugged or have a coffee. Soon it will, and the machine in your pocket will know precisely these things and tell you before you were aware of them, what you might have experienced if you'd had the experience, and on and on.

Algorithms are pattern recognition forms and we, as humans not machines, are also programmed to recognize patterns. The difference is that our recognition takes in many complex factors and balances them in a way that mechanical algorithmic software does not, even if originally programmed by humans. Google is homogeniz(s)ing my language so that even though this computer is set to default to UK English, not American, I still have to manually correct "homogenize" to "homogenise". There will be no more Dylans (both of them), Shakespeares, Brechts, Okris or Murakamis. Everything will be homogenized, standardized and commoditized – and then fed back to me as a financial service within a market economy. Even my need for a hug. What's the algorithm for a hug?

Somewhere in the mountains by the sea there is a community that knows all of this and nothing too. Is it Lake Wobegon, Candelara or Stratford-upon-Avon?

I am more convinced that evolution has given us complex brains and that that Darwinian complexity is at the heart of our condition to be lost and only found in the single simplicity of a story or the simplicity of meditative transcendence where we seemingly go beyond beyond. To really search for the truth is to always lead on and be frustrated. But settle back and enjoy patterns that satisfy: art, music and nature. We can find endeavour in work and striving sometimes but we can only find peace in the flow.

My complex brain is an extraordinary thing – half machine, half open system, half living organism – but it can never be beaten, assumed or understood.

I find real solace in Shakespeare, speaking across the years, 400 years after his death, and not just in relation to the previous reference to C.P. Snow. There is comfort in the thought that there is nothing new, but that there are those who through art and literature spell it out with beauty. I am reminded of the contention that perhaps we have not bettered the English language since this brief Elizabethan flowering of literature, art and music amid the devastation of the plagues that scoured Europe in the sixteenth century.

Trees

There are Siberian Actinobacteria that have been alive for about 500,000 years, and are thought to be the oldest known forms of life on Earth. And just outside Perth in Western Australia it is possible to gaze in wonder at 2,000–3,000-year-old stromatolites growing in ponds by the side of the road. Their origins date back some 3.5 billion[50] years and are linked to the beginnings of life on Earth. Older, but less accessible, are some protected Mallee eucalyptus trees in New South Wales, Australia, which are about 13,000 years old. Almost 10,000 years old is the Fulufjället Spruce Gran Picea in Sweden, known as Old Tjikko, and in the Kruger National Park in South Africa the 2,000-year-old Pafuri Baobab can be hugged and listened to while on safari. I have stood next to this tree in South Africa, and the stromatolites in Australia, along with a 600-year-old tree just near where I live in Bath which marks an ancient parish boundary and a walking right of way. Every traveller who meets this remarkable tree muses, "If only this tree could talk, what stories would it tell?"

I was reminded of the centrality of trees in our history by a guide at Shakespeare's birthplace in Stratford-upon-Avon, who made two, now very obvious, points that all fuel for warmth and light 400 years ago came from collected surface carbon in the form of wood, and that, because of bandits, it was a necessity for most people to be inside after dark – hence the very large number of inns and resting houses. Wood was central to everyone's lives.

In *Meetings with Remarkable Trees* and *Remarkable Trees of the World* Thomas Pakenham spoke of seeking out old trees in the same way one might seek out a previously unsighted whale or goanna, and of the personal bereavement at the end of a tree's life. He found a pagoda tree planted by Thomas Milton in 1833 blocking the sidewalk in Martha's Vineyard in the USA, baobabs in South Africa that are thousands of years old, and the cedar at Kirishima that has become a Shinto shrine in Japan.[51]

Recently books such as *H is for Hawk* by Helen Macdonald[52] have reconnected us with nature and its power to anchor us to our spiritual and physical home. As she says, learning the names and origins of species is transformative: they transport you to another place where lineage and history become enthralling – "you have to learn how to read them against the messiness of reality".[53]

There is an old adage that "The best time to plant a tree was 20 years ago. The second best time is now." I would add that the very best time is several hundred years ago, depending on the tree. Remember that the world sailed and was built on trees, and that in Europe until the Industrial Revolution trees were a premium crop. In the case of oak, it had to be planted as a long-term investment for your grandchildren or their children. Many churches and houses in Britain were accompanied by an oak grove. Just outside Oxford, there is a seventeenth-century church whose roof timbers had to be repaired after 400 years. Conveniently, when the church was built foresight prevailed and the oak was procured from the nearby forest – which belonged to the church as it had been planted for just this purpose. A number of Oxford and Cambridge colleges dating back to the same period can tell similar stories of propitious planting. Recently in the UK the National Trust needed to re-lay the roof of Dyrham Park, a historic stately home built by a significant beneficiary of the slave trade and British colonialism, William Blathwayt. *Remains of the Day* was filmed there. After 300 years, most of the roof timbers were still in good repair which meant that in the twenty-first century this building still stands with timbers some 500–700 years old.

These examples of long-term investment hold obvious lessons for us today in a world of short-termism and instant, microsecond decision-making. Bettys and Taylors, a family-run Yorkshire-based tea and tearoom company, was founded by a Swiss confectioner in the early twentieth century. This company's commitment to sustainability, as the *FT* put it, "would put many corporations to shame".[54] The grand-nephew of the founder, another example of long-term investment (!), retired in 2011 and he and his wife established the United Bank of Carbon in an attempt to trade in carbon rather than felled trees.

The divide between economy and ecology has become so deep that we forget our evolutionary past and our reliance on our host, Earth. In 1854 Henry Thoreau's *Walden, or Life in the Woods* became a bestseller as it described his reconnection with nature. His writing is lyrical and beautiful and he has remained a reference point in nature writing (even though he scarcely lived a subsistence or sustainable life in his woods, enjoying frequent visitors and trips home to a very nearby village most weekends to get his washing done). He said that "he has never met a man who is quite awake" and that he "went to the woods because I wished to live deliberately, to front only the essential facts of life, and see if I could not learn what it had to teach, and not, when I came to die, discover what I had not lived".[55]

Almost a century earlier in 1789, the Reverend Gilbert White's *The Natural History and Antiquities of Selborne* was published in which he chronicled the state of changing nature in his Hampshire village. It has become a classic of observational details and careful analysis, full of wonder, surprise and delight. While Thomas Pakenham may have travelled the world looking for trees, Gilbert White, a trained naturalist first and an ecclesiastical practitioner second, stayed at home minutely recording the details of flora and fauna in one location. Part of the captivation of Thoreau, Pakenham and White for the reader is not just their insights but also their lyricism in writing. Here is White:

> On September the 21st, 1741, being then on a visit, and intent on field-diversions, I rose before daybreak: when I came into the enclosures, I found the stubbles and clover-grounds matted all over with a thick coat of cobweb, in the meshes of which a copious and heavy dew hung so plentifully that the whole face of the country seemed, as it were, covered with two or three setting-nets one over another.[56]

Barbara Hepworth worked in various materials – brass, wood, plaster and marble – and she describes the same feeling and reverie of being so connected with the real, the here and now, the Earth: "The strokes of the hammer on the chisel should be in time with your heartbeat. You breathe easily. The whole of your body is involved. You move around the sculpture, and the whole of you, from the toes up, is concentrated in your left hand, which dictates the creation".[57]

It is love, hope and art that define human existence, and understanding of science is bound up with all three. Love is our social dimension: it's what binds us together, makes us complex interactive individuals who have survived by being in groups, by working together, and who have died by being too tribal and fearful of other tribes. Hope is what makes us get out of bed every morning, what makes us believe that our next best idea, our creativity, our enterprise will see us through the day. Our best hope is that working with others, through love, we will find collective solutions. Finally, art expresses hope. Hope is best expressed in collectivism and art. Collectivism because we know we cannot survive alone, and art because it is our way of talking to the past, the present and the future. Art is how we connect through all its forms to explain whatever it is we might be in another universe, a different form, another way of seeing the world – and there are many "others".

A love of others and of the Earth is what anchors us and our institutions, and provides the diversity and divergences in political economies around the world. Barbara Hepworth's life work moved from naturalism to abstraction. As she said in the 1940s, "Working realistically replenishes one's *love* for life, humanity and the earth."[58] Such is the connection and resurgence and vitality of art in our lives, as it has been in ages of humanity across ten of thousands of years. Art gives hope and meaning to life. Art is part of culture as much as economy and ecology.

In the late 1960s we all potentially became bohemians and art was allowed and blossomed across all social classes, in all areas of life, and in all forms – as it also did during Shakespeare's period. Art became classless and stopped being the preserve of the few; there was an attempt to make art everywhere for everyone. There is still a sense sometimes of a distinction between fine art and popular culture. Nietzsche believed that slavery was a good idea because it allowed the "master race" to be creative, and Flaubert similarly thought that the mob could never be cultured.

But art is part of what it means to be human – for all of us, and not something separate from us. It is given to some to be artists, and others not. It is given through education, skill, aptitude and hard work for some to be more able artists than others, but it is for everyone: it is not elitist. And, most importantly, it is a language that speaks across languages and breaks barriers and surmounts boundaries. Barbara Hepworth said that it was "the only language which nations speak together and they don't quarrel. And yet in times of stress and war, the tiny grant which the state provides to maintain visual arts is the first to go."[59]

So, here, by art I mean art that is of everyone and for everyone, even if it's not always appreciated, understood or liked. Sometimes it elevates, sometimes it coarsens, but that's its role: it gives life to love, hope and human existence and is as old as language, exchange and procreation. We could have a debate about what sort of art "Like a Rolling Stone" or "Yesterday" are, but it is facile and pointless: art is what illuminates, lights up, challenges, confronts, comforts and is other-worldly. Andy Warhol said that "an artist is someone who produces things that people don't need to have but that he – for some reason – thinks it would be a good idea to give them".[60] And Barbara Hepworth said that "the very nature of art is affirmative, and in being so it reflects the laws and the evolution of the universe".[61]

Tolerance and Utopia

But wait: perhaps love is too high an aspiration for the world. Notably, US politicians often talk about love, hope, faith and aspiration amid a deeply divided country brimming with weapons of personal and global mass destruction. Martin Luther King famously embodied the spirit of a new-found country – for White European migrants and Black slaves – when he preached: "I have a dream . . ." America is all about dreaming and faith politics, even if the faith is nowadays in wealth and guns. But he made a very important distinction between love and politics, which, as we proceed with a book subtitled "love, hope and art" is well worth remembering. "Morality", he said, "cannot be legislated, but behaviour can be regulated. The law cannot make a man love me, but it can stop him lynching me, and that is quite important".[62]

UK and other European politicians do not talk of love: that is reserved for individuals. Japanese politicians use memory, nationhood and creation as symbols of their ability to take the country forward.

But perhaps the lesson of Nelson Mandela is the most recent practical example of showing love by acting out a personal commitment to compromise, to collaboration and to listening. The obvious, and most immediate, act was putting on the symbol of the White South African community – the team rugby shirt – when South Africa won the World Cup in 1995.

If King and Mandela were major influences during my growing-up, so too in my late teens was the novelist, pacifist, broadcaster and social activist E.M. Forster who lived from 1879 to 1970. His novels are now well known, partly because of the films and television series that have been made of *A*

Passage to India, Where Angels Fear to Tread and *A Room with a View*. Throughout World War II Forster broadcast on the BBC and was heard around the world. In 1934 he was asked to become president of the newly formed National Council on Civil Liberties, now Liberty. I was influenced by an intelligent man who talked of nuance, complexity and subtlety in art and human relations. His talks and essays united the themes that I am presenting in this book: of love, hope and art as one idea in humans. As indivisible. Of one unifying theory in search of a way of being for individuals and societies.

In one of his talks in 1941, near the beginning of World War II, he said that at the end of the war the world would have to learn to live with those who were currently the enemy. In a sense, he was propounding the vision and values that were to lay foundation for what is now the European Union. Having lived through World War I, and been affected by the Crimean (1853–1856) and the Boer War (1899–1902), and now experiencing World War II, he acknowledged that force was often the way humanity tended, but that in between all this brutality was space for creativity and for cultural blooming. At the heart of culture and art was the bohemian: someone who maybe looked outlandish and would think the unthinkable, articulating ideas with no presumption of a direct political act, but nonetheless ultimately conducting politics by subversion or ellipsis. Forster claimed that we needed politicians who could think beyond the necessity of winning the war to the future beyond. These people should not talk of love nor raise the stakes too high, for we would fail, but should talk of tolerance. Tolerance, like prudence, kindness and fairness, is not a spirit-raising word, but these are the stuff of civilization as he saw it, which embrace the fundamentals of democracy: "So two cheers for Democracy:

one because it admits variety and two because it permits criticism."

As he said in a broadcast in 1941:

> Love is a great force in private affairs: it is indeed the greatest of things: but love in public affairs does not work ... The idea that nations should love each other, or that business concerns should love one another ... it is absurd, unreal, dangerous ... In public affairs, in the rebuilding of civilisation, something much less dramatic and emotional is needed, namely tolerance. Tolerance is a very dull virtue.

The world is full of people, many of whom you don't like because they listen to the wrong jazz, smell differently, or wear the wrong clothes. One solution is the "Nazi solution. If you don't like people, kill them, banish them, segregate them." The other way, tolerance, is the only "foundation for the post-war world". "On the basis of tolerance a civilised future may be built."[63]

I quote Forster at length here because it seems that the same message is true now in a moment of great personal, national, community and global change. So I do not renege on my commitment to love, hope and art but temper them with some sense of realism in building the good society, and a socially just political economy. In the same vein, Barbara Hepworth said of Dag Hammarskjöld: "[He] had a pure and exact perception of aesthetic principles, as exact as it was over ethical and moral principles. I believe they were, to him, one and the same thing."[64] But Hammarskjöld was a realist: "The United Nations was not created to bring us to heaven," he told an audience in 1954, "but to save us from hell."[65]

The UN, which came into being in June 1945, was established "to save succeeding generations from the scourge of war, which twice in our lifetime has brought untold sorrow to mankind" so that the peoples of the world "practice tolerance and live together in peace with one another as good neighbours".[66] We live in the shadow of the world wars, and with a hope invested in the succeeding charter, conventions and institutions that arose in the immediate years thereafter: not just because of the development and use of weapons of mass destruction – the ultimate "final solution" – but also because of the millions of people from all parts of the world who had lost their lives in the pursuit of war as a means of solving disputes. Lest we forget. Remember, remember, remember.

The world's new creation myth is based on the principles enshrined in the UN Charter alongside the development of knowledge and the use of technology. As a unifying principle – a single form – the UN Charter is a good starting point, and much complemented by further international agreements and developments. How this relates to our quest for a unifying theory in the search for knowledge can only be surmised through art, through investigations and interpretations which enhance our love for each other and hope for the future.

A note on hope, aside from the links to art. There will be some who will equate this book's focus on love, hope and art as utopian. This is to miss the point. As John Carey says in his wonderful compendium,[67] "Utopia" means *nowhere*. *Searching for the Good Society* says that the three elements of love, hope and art, singly or in conjunction, can be found in many societies around the world, and this book samples some of them. Much of what I would think of as Utopia already exists, and has existed through history. This could be mainfested in the first time you heard the hope in "Nkosi Sikelel' iAfrika",

54

or the birth of your first child, or sitting drinking coffee in an Italian piazza on a warm sunny morning, or voting for the first time, or travelling on the Shinkansen, or feeling safe when seeing your GP for free, or feeling ecstatic when you get the Olympic vibe, or knowing that your rights are no lesser or greater than the leader of your country. Or watching the sun rise over the mountain knowing you have a good day ahead of you.

Oscar Wilde said that "a map of the world that does not include Utopia is not worth glancing at, for it leaves out the one country at which humanity is always landing. And when humanity lands there, it looks out, and seeing a better country, sets sail. Progress is the realization of Utopias".[68] This is what Charlotte Brontë means in *Shirley*: "I approve nothing utopian: look life in its brassy face – stare Reality out of its brassy countenance."[69] Dream big and progressive.

2

Good capitalism: love, hope, art and progress

> ". . . the virtue of prudence,
> of all the virtues that which is
> most useful to the individual . . .
> Humanity, justice, generosity,
> and public spirit, are the qualities
> most useful to others."

Adam Smith[70]

The fertile twentieth century

We all live surrounded by prudence, humanity, justice, generosity and public spirit. That is our daily experience. This is possible because of institutional arrangements made 250 years after Adam Smith wrote of the limits of the market that allow me to feel safe, loved, trusting, and in companionship with those around me – hopeful of a good day, and a good life, and hopeful that I will find joy and transcendence in artistic expression, from a child's drawing to street music to a Rodin and a Hepworth in the town square.

This isn't some pious sentimentality on my part but the realities of life everywhere. In the informal township of Kayamandi in Stellenbosch, South Africa to Penn Station in New York, USA to Shenzhen in China I have found social relations that uplift the soul and acknowledge our common humanity. I have also found divisions, tribalism and misogyny in these places which require healing. War is the greater destroyer of love, hope and humanity. War is always the manifestation of failure. Today Aleppo is being destroyed but yesterday it was Beirut, Warsaw or Carthage. And people's lives. Out of the ashes we rebuild, we rebuild, we rebuild and only fools, warmongers or sociopaths forget.

It's the second decade of the twenty-first century and the world is in a mess, partly because we don't seem to understand how we got here. Historians on both the left and right such as Eric Hobsbawm and Niall Ferguson agree. Hobsbawm has said that we are living in a "permanent present",[71] with little connection of events now to events past. Niall Ferguson agrees we are not getting "the big picture".[72]

We have been riding a wave of change since the last decade of the last century, a wave of change that has been almost universally accepted and embraced wherever humans have been touched by its enveloping enrapturement. I'm not referring to the economic project that is the current wave of globalization, but the technology that has accompanied this wave. The information–communications revolution has touched us all, and, despite having benefits and disbenefits, it has been accepted on all sides. It isn't an issue of left or right, green or brown. We have had to swallow it hook, line and sinker as to sneer at it or reject its frenzied demands is to appear so antediluvian and Thoreauish. And yet Marshall McLuhan was so right when he talked in 1964 of the global village and that "the medium is the message" – or the massage. We hadn't become so cynical about mass media then – or perhaps McLuhan had. Anthropologist Margaret Mead said that, in the mid-1960s, "thanks to television, for the first time the young are seeing history made, before it is censored by their elders" in reference to the Vietnam War appearing horrifically on television screens nightly.

As Eric Hobsbawm exclaimed in summing up a historian's life in *Age of Extremes: The Short Twentieth Century*,

> perhaps the most striking characteristic of the end of the twentieth century is the tension between [the] accelerating process of globalization and the inability of both public institutions and the collective behaviour of human beings to come to terms with it. Curiously enough, private human behaviour has had less trouble in adjusting to the world of satellite television, E-mail, holidays in the Seychelles and trans-oceanic commuting.[73]

Nearly 30 years on from Hobsbawm's comment it is still true, but writ larger: the ferment around the globalization process has been made apparent by the internet and the availability of limitless information. But this limitless information has failed to lead the general population to greater wisdom, for they cannot see beyond the next nanosecond of digitized, algorithmic activity, let alone back to their parents' day.

The Communist Manifesto of 1888 said that, in the struggle of dialectical materialism, "the proletarians have nothing to lose but their chains"[74] and, 60 years later, George Orwell's satire *Nineteen Eighty-Four* was published, in which he wrote that

> so long as they [the Proles] continued to work and breed, their other activities were without importance. Left to themselves . . . they had reverted to a style of life that appeared to be natural to them, a sort of ancestral pattern . . . heavy physical work, the care of home and children, petty quarrels with neighbours, films, football, beer and above all, gambling filled up the horizon of their minds. To keep them in control was not difficult.[75]

And now social media fulfils this role.

It's some years since the cultural commentator and philosopher Terry Eagleton was able to write, in 2003, that "traditionally it has been the political left which thought in universal terms, and the conservative right which preferred to be modestly piecemeal. Now, these roles have been reversed with a vengeance".[76] If the early twentieth century was the battle of big ideas – between communism and fascism aided by several capitalist meltdowns – then the early twenty-first century is the clash of civilizations between planetary and human care and the dictates of neoliberal economics with the market as god. But the left has yet to fully embrace environmentalism, sustainability or the new economic agenda because it is still fighting many of the battles left over from the twentieth century and the vestiges of communism – and in some cases Marxism. (Marx himself displayed his wit, or simply saw himself as an analyst not a politician, when he said, "If anything is certain it is that I myself am not a Marxist".)

The two-thirds of the world that is connected to the internet and uses social media is in distraction mode, constantly updating their narcissistic profiles or checking in on the issues that Orwell talks about. They do not understand our global interdependence and co-determination except that they know and feel the growing global inequality even if they have no idea about the extraordinary levels of wealth and health increases for most people since the end of World War II in 1945. And although many of the two-thirds may be wealthier and healthier than previous generations, they still have to pedal hard on the treadmill to keep up and not fall into the poverty trap and out of the consumer flood.

The stupefying fact that 85 individuals have the same wealth as 50% of the world's population is reinforced for many by zero-hour contracts in the UK and food banks for the poor, 50% youth unemployment in Spain, stagnant or falling wages in the USA, and the rush from the country to the city to work in factories in China. Many of us are richer, but the rich are richer still.

Social media lets us know, and lets us know what we don't have and how dangerous the world is. It does not remind us of the road we have travelled, the wealth that cannot be measured or that, despite the dreadful images, the world is more peaceful now than it's ever been. And this is not to praise the rise since the 1980s of a model of global capitalism that has supported the accumulation of wealth for a few and the enslavement of the many on the treadmill or the denial of basic rights and security for some 2.7 billion people.

Different political economies

The debate about capitalism is often sterile because of its binary nature. A thinking political economy is better. Politics is personal, and the personal involves love, hope and creativity, expression, enterprise, discovery – and art.

There are vast divergences globally, and yet we are all being measured and quantified – as nations, communities and individuals – by metrics largely devised in the USA which take no account of the love, hope and art that exists locally. It is not that enterprise hasn't been the driver of increased wealth and well-being globally, particularly since the end of World War II, but that the model and matrices are unhelpful and sometimes destructive. After all, as Nobel Prize-winning economist Amartya Sen has said, enterprise and exchange are as much part of being human as conversation, procreation and eating. He does point out that some conversations are of course foul, and that some food is unhealthy, and that some sex is unwelcome, but the point is made.[77] But it is true that the hegemony of a model of capitalism and economics that dictates that all economies must comply with one set of rules is destroying local cultures and dismantling whole economies.

Artist Tim Etchells provoked discussion at Tate Modern in London in 2016 by talking about all the different forms of exchange we engage in every day: between generations, cultures, people, the past and the present, between women, inside the family, with the unknown, in ideas, and in economics.[78]

But it is only in the last few hundred years, since the rise of mercantilism in Europe and the Middle East in the twelfth century and the Industrial Revolution led by the UK in the seventeenth century, that exchange or bartering between (essentially) equals led to capitalism per se. Until this point, over the previous 15,000 years of humanity's history, business people – mostly men – were seen as the lowest of the caste and class systems, whereas farmers, who provided food, were just below the aristocracy or power holders in any society, whether this be in China, Britain or Japan. But capital-holding power holders only emerged when foraging stopped, because foraging, hunting wild animals and gathering wild plants requires equality of effort and equal distribution of what meagre wealth can be gathered.

Farming, emerging about 11,000 years ago, produced sedentariness, wealth, rulers and a population surge. But most people still lived subsistence lifestyles on between $1.50 and $2.20 a day by today's prices, according to historian Ian Morris. Here we begin to see the beginnings of popular uprisings and revolution – of populism itself. Foraging societies had Gini coefficients of about 0.25, the Roman Empire 0.43, seventeenth-century England about 0.47; but on the eve of the French Revolution the measure of inequality was 0.59, and the accumulated wealth disparity in France was 0.80. This is similar to today's global wealth inequality; we should wonder at how little we learn from the long view.[79] Morris points out that, just as farming swept away foraging, and farming capitulated to industrialization as the dominant economic driver, so we are now in the middle of another humanity-shifting point where we have enough personal energy, where we can create energy from new technology, and where mind, machine and space are interchangeable.[80]

Capitalism, rather than exchange, barter or entrepreneurship, is a problem – and a virtue. A problem in that it attracts the avaricious, the greedy and the unscrupulous, and a virtue in that, when it works well, it creates wealth and distributes it equitably. For an economy to be seen as capitalist, economic transactions have to be based on markets, and the spoils owned by the risk-taking investor in the form of property or other accumulation. Central to this process is the profit motive. How capitalism is managed is what makes a sound political economy and leads to the good society or leads to the rip-off economy and the divided society. But all sound political economies rely on non-market institutions which provide support for the risk-taking, the profit-making, and the wealth accumulation. These can include education and healthcare systems, justice and peace-making apparatus, and public pensions and transport logistics.

Capitalism has had a bad press over the years, from Plato, Aristotle, Jesus, St Paul, Thomas Aquinas, Charles Dickens and Keynes. It could even be argued that Adam Smith was only interested in prudent capitalism, understanding that capitalism worked naturally in conjunction with "humanity, justice, generosity, and public spirit". At no point does Smith say that unfettered capitalism, or free markets, could provide the moral basis for the good society.[81]

Smith wrote about the relationship of the individual to the community, and it is this area that makes, or destroys, the good society. And it is this issue that is the most important, now that inequality is so extreme across societies worldwide, from India to China, from the USA to the UK. But, even though it is not as much an issue in countries such as Finland, Australia and

Canada, it still raises its ugly head even in these exemplars of the better society.

It is this mix of institutions that make the good society, as we shall see. As I write, the pendulum has swung towards the profit-takers and away from the non-market institutional builders with the belief that the market is god, even when it comes to healthcare and the provision of basic rights, such as water. As John Kay has said, "the premise of the new right is austere. Private property is the most important social institution; self-interest the central human motive; insecurity the engine of progress".[82] Don't let the peasants get too comfortable! And then in 2016 they did – and voted for populism, the post-truth agenda, and demagogic politicians. Does economic efficiency go hand in hand with selfishness? And which should rule? And didn't the votes for Brexit and Trump, engineered by rich elites, play into the hands of right-wing economic thinkers rather than providing the momentum for a good society?

Many industrialized countries today face a situation similar to Europe in the 1930s. Then unemployment was over 25% in most countries and led to significant state intervention in the form of relief and infrastructure projects – and the rise of communism, central planning and fascism. Tribalism, rather than internationalism, became the dominant force and culminated in World War II and xenophobic, homophobic, misogynist populist leaders. Today, these conditions, coupled with social media and the role of propaganda and misinformation, as in the 1930s, are even more alarming for two reasons. First, humanity must ensure that planethome is habitable, and it may not be in many more decades if we don't take every care to change our trajectory; and, second, since 1945 we have the technological capacity to destroy ourselves. It only takes one madman, one irrational person, one peeved individual. So the issues to be very urgently addressed concern the threat of nuclear war, inequality, information and lies, responsible leadership, governance at all levels, and climate change.

Good societies

And so how should we measure the world and its difference, diversity and distinctiveness? Beyond the grossly simplistic gross national product or average income figures lies a wealth of data to be mined that can be compiled depending on the result desired, or the attitude needed. How should we measure the subtitle of this book: love, hope, art and progress? Here are some ways and means of looking at the world afresh, and perhaps some combination of them would give us an answer, as they all contain the seeds of a world that constantly has the good society in mind.

But first, which country would you like to live in, given a choice?

- Which country has the lowest crime rates and the most effective gun control?
    - *Japan, the European countries and New Zealand*

- Which country has the lowest obesity rates?
    - *Japan*

- And the most cost-efficient healthcare system?
    - *Overall, UK*

- And which countries have the best publicly accessible sports facilities?
    - *Australia and Costa Rica*

- Which countries have the most literate and numerate people?
  - *Among others, Cuba and Costa Rica*

- Which countries have the lowest carbon emissions rate *and* are some of the happiest?
  - *Costa Rica, Jamaica and Vietnam*

- Which country has had the longest continuous economic growth in the last 100 years?
  - *Australia*

- Which country has the longest record of giving women the vote?
  - *New Zealand*

- Which countries incarcerate the largest percentage of their own citizens?
  - *USA, China and Turkey*

- Which countries have the highest education ratings?
  - *Among others, Singapore and Finland*

- Which city is the most pleasant to live in?
  - *Copenhagen*

- Which country has the highest personal tax rate?
  - *Denmark*

- Which country has the highest corporate tax rate?
  - *USA*

- Which is the safest densely populated country to drive in?
  - *UK*

- Which is the only OECD country still to have hereditary parliamentarians?
  - *UK*

- Which advanced industrial democracy has one of the lowest numbers of billionaires?
  - *Japan*

- The highest?
  - *China – but that's not a democracy and it's ten times the population!*

- Which is the best country to be born in, according to the Economist?
  - *Switzerland, followed by Australia, Norway, Sweden and Denmark*

- Which country has the highest individual gun ownership?
  - *USA*

- Which is the only OECD country that does not have a universal publicly funded health and social care system?
  - *USA*

- Which countries have the highest educational attainment ratings?
  - *Singapore, Japan, Estonia, Chinese Taipei, Finland*

- Which countries have the lowest gender gap?
  - *Iceland, Finland, Norway, Sweden, Rwanda*

Lessons from this chapter:

- It is not poverty or affluence that create the good society; it is the cultural content of political economy.

- It is not poverty or affluence that create good health and educational outcomes; it is public policy decisions and a focus on equality.

- Equal opportunities are as important as equal outcomes, and it is finding the balance that makes for a vibrant democracy.

- Markets are always supported by public infrastructure.

- If the winner always takes all, society is the long-term loser.

- Collectivism is as important as individual effort.

- Removing violence from everyday life is one of the greatest universal liberators.

- Providing universal publicly funded education, health and social care are the greatest markers of a civilized society.

- Upholding the rule of law and ridding society of social, economic and nepotistic corruption are keys to opportunity and social mobility.

For this chapter I trawled a vast number of databases, and, as with travelling, it broadens the mind. Where there had been prejudice came enlightenment, and, where I was sure, I had to unlearn and learn again. Where I had a suspicion, sometimes the results were worse than expected. Given that I started with countries that I have been visiting and writing about for 40 years, I was surprised how liberating it was to be confronted with the hard data. Most prominent in my fishing were the CIA's World Factbook, the Human Development Index, the World Economic Forum, the New Economics Foundation, the *Economist*'s "Where to be Born Index", the Global Peace Index, World Bank GINI, the World Happiness Report, Oxfam, SIPRI. And many others.

But most of all, or alongside this, there was visiting and standing and staring and wondering, and then asking friends and colleagues "How do you do that?" or "Why do you do that?" How else would I have noticed that Swedish drivers slow ten metres from a pedestrian crossing, Australian drivers always stop but only after intimidating pedestrians, Italians never stop unless challenged to do so, and when crossing the road in India one prays first. And how would I have observed the minutiae of Italian, American and Japanese eating habits unless I'd been there and formed impressions? None of this is included in any of the big data. In other words, even in a homogenizing world there is no substitute for travelling and being there. But I still don't know why the British litter so much and why Australians are so clean, and how Italians still make the best coffee in the world, and why New York still gives me a buzz, and why I feel so safe and free in Stockholm and Tokyo. And how have some countries – Japan, Italy and France among them – resisted the Americanization of eating, when others haven't (UK, Mexico and South Africa). And the answer is most certainly not just economics. And why is it magic to stand at Cape Point looking out at the Atlantic in one direction and the Pacific in the other with the Antarctic just over the horizon? And why has Fauré's *Requiem* been my soundtrack while writing this book?

Between 1967 and 1973 Geert Hofstede, a Dutch social psychologist, former IBM employee and organizational anthropologist, was commissioned by IBM to look at cross-cultural issues in countries around the world. He settled on six dimensions: power distance, individualism, uncertainty avoidance, masculinity, long-term orientation, and indulgence versus restraint. Recently, Hofstede's work (he was born in 1920) has been continued by his son who has updated the initial findings.[83]

Hofstede's findings were an important step towards under-standing comparative economies. They showed then, and via updates continue to show today, that, while capitalism may operate successfully in different countries, different political cultures tell us that capitalism needs culture to work, and that love, hope and art are part and parcel of capitalism's successful operation. For instance, Hofstede's research showed that Japan is a masculine culture that avoids uncertainty, has a long-term orientation and low indulgence towards its children. In the first three of these categories it mirrors France, which is fascinating because both countries have been accused of not changing fast enough with the current conditions of globalization: they are both stuck in the past. As you will see from other parts of this book, I profoundly disagree: to hold on to what works and to resist change for change's sake is a virtue, and should not be thought of as failure.

Other stand-out findings show that China and Japan have low individualism scores whereas the UK, Australia and the USA ranked very high. It is worth interrogating Hofstede's defi-nition of masculinity and individuality as he indicates, as an anthropologist, that the future is negotiated, shared and col-laborative (a feminized future, as I have previously written) rather than assertive, competitive, aggressive and masculine. Could it be that Brexit, Trump and Putin are throwbacks, tem-porary aberrations, or a sign that humanity cannot cope with a feminized future?

Given the ferment that exists today around post-truth and populism, the other striking result from Hofstede's findings is on power distance, which is relatively high in Japan, India and China and relatively low in the UK and Australia. Does this mean that these latter countries are more dynamic and respon-sive to change? Or that this is a measure of turbulence and an inability to stand up to the savage winds of market-based capitalism?

By way of a caveat, many of these findings raise more questions than they answer, not least on Hofstede's definitions, but also because, in my experience, they confound evidence on the ground. They are an interesting take on ways of seeing the world and provide fascinating insights into the 70 or so countries examined, but they also shed light on the way the researchers see the world.

Charles Hampden-Turner and Fons Trompenaars tried, as others had done before and have since, to understand the different cultures of capitalism. Their 1993 book *The Seven Cultures of Capitalism* looked at wealth creation, but not distribution, in the USA, Britain, Japan, Germany, France, Sweden and the Netherlands – but not India, China, Brazil, Russia or Indonesia, the rising economies.[84] They concluded that, although there were a number of outstanding capitalist and free trade economies, the way in which they each operated was radically different. They found, and it may sound obvious in the context of this book, that "wealth or values creation is in essence a moral act" and they concurred with Tawney's 1922 book *Religion and the Rise of Capitalism* that there is a direct link between successful capitalism and puritanism and a belief in making life work on Earth now, for *this* generation.[85] Hampden-Turner and Trompenaars said that the USA was the champion of capitalism and "no other nation has so tirelessly defended capitalism with arms and words throughout the world".[86] It is as true now as it was in the late twentieth century that "despite numerous claims of growing convergence and the 'globalization' of managerial structures and strategies the ways in which economic activities are organized and controlled (around the world) differ considerably from those in the USA and the

UK".[87] Hampden-Turner and Trompenaars were interested in what makes a good capitalist economy, not in what necessarily makes a good society, although all the political economies they chose to examine would be regarded by many as great places to live then and now, more than 20 years later. This is despite the fact that, then and now, the differences between living in Japan and the USA, and Britain and Sweden, are considerable. The cultures that all these countries embody has not changed radically over the last few decades. The authors were good enough to recognize their own myopia and personal preferences having been trained in the US model of capitalism: "Our dream is of a world culture in which all paths lead to a shareable integrity. The vision is American because it would constitute a new kind of world order created by cross-cultural communication." Perhaps they could not foresee the downsides of globalization or the rise of India and China and the muscling of Russia. Just a few years after the liberalization of financial services led by the UK and the USA they were unable to foresee that banking would spiral out of control on a wave of irresponsibility, greed and ineptitude. And they could only have begun to see that, largely because of globalization and the financial services, industry wealth would accumulate so dramatically in the 1% with an enormous divide from the 99%.

It is worth mentioning Michael Porter's work here, although he was principally interested in competitive advantage by countries and companies rather than economic well-being, wealth distribution or the good society. His basic lesson is that companies, and countries, can create wealth through price or differentiation – by being cheap or by being different and novel. The former condition is a necessary concomitant of a country's wealth creation but not if by so doing it reduces the quality of life of its inhabitants, which is one of India's largest problems.

He went on to delineate five forces that understood how a company, or a country, could compete: bargaining power of suppliers, threat of new entrants, threat of substitutes, the bargaining power of buyers, and the position of rivals.[88]

Capitalism has developed over millennia from personal or group bartering and exchange to a situation where global financial deregulation today is beyond the purview of most mortal beings. In the last few hundred years, the cultures of greed and acquisition have grown and have led to increased discussion about morality, increased regulation and calls for greater transparency and tighter reporting of all institutions: commercial, governmental and non-governmental. We have recognized that with more capitalism comes more risk, more booms and busts, and a greater need for state intervention to manage the vicissitudes and inexactitudes that markets inevitably bring. They do self-regulate but not to humanity's advantage. The current wave of globalization, and the cries of crisis, are not new – in the last century one wave led to World War I and the second to World War II. We must learn, but we don't. In each case, the collapse of capitalism has led to war. In other words, democracy, capitalism and peace do not march hand in hand. In the twenty-first century it is not just that this model of capitalism is failing but that the institutions that might moderate its excesses are also in need of rejuvenation, and this includes models of democracy. How is it that Americans could elect a man who defies civilized norms, is ignorant of international standards, and who decries the democratic process unless it works in his favour? And how is it that the British were so easily fooled by lies told about the EU and their future? What does this say about democracy, education and the fourth estate – the "free" media?

We are interested in answering the question: which model of political economy delivers wealth and equality and a range of other indicators to produce what might be described as the good society in the twenty-first century? There is a wealth of literature on inclusive growth, the inclusive economy, wealth creation and wealth distribution, and growth or no-growth economics. What we are interested in is the sort of research carried out by William Judge, Stav Fainshmidt and Lee Brown, which uses four dimensions to look at the links between wealth creation and wealth distribution: trust, power relations, education, and regulation, in 48 developed and developing political economies.[89] Their research suggested that the most effective economies at delivering *both* wealth creation *and* wealth distribution has high trust in society and low corruption, low power relations between people and decision-makers (in other words, those in power were sensitive and well connected to the people affected by their decisions), there was a high level of universal education and high-quality ongoing training within society, and there was a high level of regulation quality (the regulations were good, effective, implemented and respected). They accepted the premises of capitalism: private ownership, labour markets and market price signals. Not surprisingly, most Scandinavian countries came out well in this research, and countries such as Chile, Mexico and South Africa floundered at the bottom, with most European countries coming somewhere in the middle and the UK and USA scoring significant wealth inequality ratings over the last few decades. Australia, New Zealand and Canada scored well on all four matrices with less wealth inequality than most European countries, and, as we have noted elsewhere, with continued social mobility, unlike the UK and the USA where social mobility has stopped for the bottom 20% and reversed for the lowest 10%. Globally, the shift between the top richest 1% and the remaining 99% has increased dramatically since the introduction of aggressive neoliberalism and financial deregulation in the late 1980s; but in the UK and the USA this has become particularly marked. Countries such as India, Russia and China also show astonishing wealth inequality, but as these countries are in transition they cannot be lumped into one package. China is working to move wealth across society as a whole, and the survival of the Chinese Communist Party depends on this; whereas in India, South Africa, Mexico and Brazil this extreme wealth inequality is entrenched in their models of political economy. It will take a revolution for that to change in those countries.

Globalization, like capitalism and collectivism (or that "there is no such thing as society"), is part of life and to argue for its removal is as ridiculous as arguing against sex, eating and conversation. The biggest political challenge has always been how to mix sex, eating, conversation *and* globalization, capitalism and collectivism – and produce a civilized society that is fair for all.

Detailed research highlights the need to understand the links between all institutional arrangements in any given society and between institutions at an international level, market and non-market. Within an economy, wealth distribution can take place through state intervention or the regulation of private organizations such that equitability occurs and it is the subtle relationship between these sets of entities that can determine the effectiveness of distribution. Similarly, wealth can be spread via equity or credit-based mechanisms each of which might give individuals a stake in society and provide for shared wealth, inclusiveness and social cohesion. Sweden, Denmark, Australia, Norway and Switzerland form a cluster at the apex of the two indices: wealth creation and wealth distribution, because they score highest on the four dimensions measured. Switzerland's and Norway's personal incomes are in a range of their own, but it is worth noting that the highest scores in this research are from small countries where voters have direct contact with their leaders and where, even in the boardroom, representation is mandatory for all parts of society. It is worth remembering that most commentators note that the wave of anti-expert and populist sentiment around the democratic world is based on low trust for democratic institutions and expertism, declining wealth distribution, and the perceived mass disruption of badly managed migration. In regard to failed institutions, poor regulatory management and elite corruption, these are the definitions of failed states, according to Daron Acemoglu and James Robinson in *Why Nations Fail*.[90]

Finland, and some of its near neighbours, comes out on top using Judge *et al.*'s indices. This country "appears to represent the highly developed and relatively equitable social democratic form of capitalism". Numerous lessons arise from their research, but two seem paramount: first, that too much research has been focused on company or business competitive advantage and not enough on the good society in a capitalist economy; and, second, that public policy, especially when it involves radical economic change as happened in the UK under Prime Minister Thatcher in the late 1970s, must not (cannot) ignore whole systems involving the history and culture of society. A country's loves, hopes and arts are as important as its productivity, efficiency and economic performance. The Dalai Lama, commenting on the dryness of economics over political economy, said that humanity "can live without religion and meditation, but we cannot live without human affection".

On this basis I want to expand Judge *et al.*'s four dimensions to look at what creates a good society in the twenty-first century, beyond simply wealth creation and wealth distribution. For instance, wealth creation is too broad a heading: for how was the wealth created? Did that wealth creation impede the distribution of wealth in another country? But, also, some breakdown and expansion of issues of power, regulation and education are necessary if we are to better understand how the good society operates in small pockets around the world. And work it does, as I have seen in many places where love, hope and art are the overriding virtues that make the wider political economy tick. It may be the tens of thousands of migrants who have been treated generally with great kindness by the Germans after making their way perilously from North Africa; or the way the Japanese always help a lost foreigner and are eternally polite; or the way Indians manage to rub along despite ethnic and religious differences and vast wealth disparity; or the way every cup of coffee in Italy is good, everywhere. It is an art and served with love for quality. It's as important as saying good morning to your neighbour every day.

The four indices are fundamental, and form an inner circle:

1. High trust

2. Low power distance

3. High regulatory quality

4. High training and education

An outer circle, not part of Judge *et al.*'s diagnosis, should contain the following important facets of a developed good society:

1. Social mobility with a recognition that diversity, including wealth, ethnicity, gender, disability and sexuality, should not be determinants of movement

2. High logistical mobility and a good public non-car-based transport system, with high environmental

standards, a sustainability strategy and a low carbon footprint at its core

3. Incentives, and enabling legislation and frameworks that promote sustainable outcomes

4. Universal healthcare free at the point of delivery

5. A peaceful and peace-making internationalist outlook

6. Low-conflict and peacefulness community social relations, including full gun control, no death penalty, low crime and reintegration not incarceration at the heart of the justice system

7. Easy, flexible models of business incorporation including profit, not-for-profit models and a range of other models that encourage cooperation

8. Easy entrepreneurship and emphasis on enterprise and creativity

9. Recognition and funding of the arts

10. Recognition and protection of public places and spaces

11. Transparency, reporting and open management of information on all media to promote discussion, democracy and information flow, but to limit hate speech, vitriol, defamation and inaccuracy

12. Wealth creation that recognizes and accounts for all the above

Utopian? No. All of these points are covered in some degree or more in many countries around the world. All of them can be researched and analysed for best practice, implementation and drawbacks. What are the problems? Culture, history and external and internal threats can make the journey difficult!

However, much progress has been made in evaluating different aspects of these 16 points by different organizations looking at various indices. But few of the models start from Judge *et al.*'s premise that wealth creation should be attached to wealth distribution and with the intervening issues in their four determinants of wealth distribution and my further 12 points of detail.

Following the 2008/9 financial debacle and the lurch towards nihilism, xenophobia and protectionism in 2016, there is much talk of a "post-capitalist society" and the like, and there is even more talk of robotization taking over many jobs and livelihoods, and artificial intelligence being the new human. Whatever the "post-capitalist society" comes to look like, this century Brexit and Trump are the logical outcomes of reordering the world around a race to the bottom, too-free markets and corporate manipulation of prices, labour and taxes. This is time to pause, if we can see beyond the hiatus that has been created. It is a chance to look again at how we might see the world afresh, because it's not that we haven't been trying for a while. Gross domestic product measures everything but not a lot that matters to most people, while the Human Development Index has been a wonderfully enlightened leap into a more progressive future but it fails to take into account our ecological footprint or, indeed, whether we are happy or not. The World Happiness Report, among other methodology, does just this and these factors combined make up the Happy Planet Index (HPI) produced by the New Economics Foundation. Elsewhere I cite Cuba as an extraordinary example of the delivery of universal healthcare and longevity in a poor country, and the HPI consistently places Costa Rica at the top of its rankings. The HPI combines well-being, life expectancy, inequality of outcomes, and ecological footprint and arrives at a measure that points us in the direction of living long, happy lives within the Earth's limits. Do all of these rankings have serious criticisms? Yes, but they all contain the germs of something new: a way of looking at the world based on only one planet and human contentedness. In a sense, they are based on mindfulness, but we have a way to go collectively even if some individuals have found a way to live with the vicissitudes of the current neoliberal globalization project.

So much of what makes life worthwhile is handed down from generation to generation. It may be a recipe for apple pie, a motif on a pillowcase, a place of worship, or the streets we cycle down every day that are full of laughter and tears from centuries gone by. George W. Bush famously wrote Europe off by saying that it was a museum (when most European countries, apart from the UK, would not support the Iraq War in 2003), which is strange considering Americans eat pizza by the ton and Walt Disney made a fortune adapting European fairy tales. The peaceful European vision is based on the baguette, the pizza, pumpernickel, medieval towns, soaring renaissance music and a searing memory of two world wars – and Christianity. These cultural assets may be immeasurable, but a better measure of what's worthwhile than simple GDP.

We could continue, but the point is that there are vast divergences globally, and yet we are all being measured and quantified – as nations, communities and individuals – by metrics that often take no account of the love, hope and art that exists locally. It is not that enterprise hasn't been the driver of increased wealth and well-being globally, particularly since the end of World War II, but that the model and matrices are unhelpful and sometimes destructive. But the hegemony of a model of capitalism and economics that dictates that all economies must comply with one set of rules is destroying local cultures and dismantling whole economies.

In an article entitled "Adam Smith's market never stood alone", the Nobel Prize-winning economist Amartya Sen said that, since 1945, "all the affluent countries in the world have depended for some time on transactions that occur largely outside markets, such as unemployment benefit, public pensions and other features of social security, and the public provision of school education and healthcare"; however, "a reliance on markets for economic transactions is a necessary qualification for an economy to be seen as capitalist".[91]

This point is illuminated by the annual statistics from the World Economic Forum (WEF) which complement the myriad useful statistics from various UN agencies and other ratings organizations listed elsewhere, albeit that the WEF tables include income, wealth and competitive performance – and draw on the UN's work. Many of the indices discussed in this book, from the role of art to the quality of a cup of coffee to the need for places for peaceful, sociable meetings, are now of paramount importance as the world steps back from the precipice of ignorance, fear and isolationism. That way leads to fascism, war, declining wealth distribution and deteriorating environmental resource management.

WEF's Inclusive Growth and Development Growth reports and annual Risks Perception variously include measures that make the simplicity of GDP figures look just that: over-simplistic. Societies and risks are integrated and managing public policy is a hard juggling task, however much politicians may want to over-simplify and sloganize on the stump. WEF's seven pillars of inclusive growth and development are: education that builds human potential and opportunity; the provision of basic services such as transport and digital infrastructure;

sound institutions, including low corruption and sound business and political ethics; the allocation of financial resources; good jobs, wages and livelihoods; equitable taxation and social protection; and asset building and entrepreneurship. Based on these indices, the top ten countries, with the highest "inclusive advanced economies" in the world, are Norway, Luxembourg, Switzerland, Iceland, Denmark, Sweden, Netherlands, Australia, New Zealand and Austria.[92] It is worth matching the earlier quote from Amartya Sen and WEF's citation for Norway because they go a long way in describing that which makes for the good society in the twenty-first century, and acknowledging that, far from being utopian, this is reality for many people. "Norway tops the IDI [Inclusive Development Index], with high and rising living standards, effective social protection and low inequality. There is a high degree of social mobility, low unemployment and a large share of women participate in the work force, helped by sound parental leave policies and affordable childcare."

However, one caveat. All these countries either have small homogenous populations and abundant natural resources (topped by Norway and Australia) or highly attractive financial sectors that attract the secretive (topped by Switzerland and Luxembourg). But, having made that point, they can all point to maintaining a balance between private and public policy for the benefit of all citizens *and* entrepreneurship. They have all resisted the worst ravages of globalization.

Slightly adjusted weights are given to different indices in WEF's Global Competiveness Index which includes Singapore, USA, Germany, UK, Japan, Hong Kong and Finland.

Sewage and social progress

Emily Brontë's *Wuthering Heights* regularly features among the most important novels published in the English language; she and her two sisters wrote novels that have stood the test of time, and have also been made into numerous films. I am in the Brontë's home of Haworth in England, where, in the 1850s, while the sisters wrote and the father preached, the villagers died of disease and poverty. I am struck now, as I was in India last year, by the juxtaposition of religion and politics – in mid-nineteenth-century England and India today. Haworth church, where the Reverend Patrick Brontë preached, is grand, and a testimony to wealth in pocket and spirit, and yet the wealthy refused to contribute to improved sewerage in Haworth in the 1850s. One of Patrick Brontë's sponsors at Oxford was William Wilberforce who led the parliamentary reforms against slavery, and we know that *The Tenant of Wildfell Hall*, written by Anne Brontë, is concerned with women's rights. But, while the sisters wrote brilliantly about the human condition, none of them wrote specifically about social conditions – or sewage.

For those who haven't visited the haunting Brontë parsonage, it looks out over the cemetery where lie buried the villagers, most of whom had died of poverty, bad sanitation and disease. The Babbage Report of April 1850 concluded that people had been burying their diseased dead at the top of the hill and this had contaminated the water supply that ran down the hill into the village. So it was a cycle of contamination and death as the bodies' disease and dis-ease drained into the rivers and streams.

The local history society is to the point:

> Over 40% of children died before attaining the
> age of six years, and the school records from this
> time are testament to the poor health of local chil-
> dren with smallpox, measles, whooping cough and
> scarlet fever frequently mentioned as the cause
> of death. The average age of death in the village
> was 25.8 [years], which was about the same as in
> Whitechapel, St. George-in-the-East, and St. Luke,
> three of the unhealthiest of the London districts.[93]

The Brontë sisters all died in their thirties, but Reverend Patrick Brontë lived until he was 84.

The main high street, now a bucolic if steep walk through
history for the millions of annual tourists, was a sewer in the
mid-nineteeth century. Twenty-five families lived in cellars,
below street level, and everyone must have prayed for the frequent rain to wash away the filth.

India has lowered infant mortality in most states to about
30 per 1,000 live births but this compares badly with the UK at
3.6 per 1,000 live births. Some will argue that this is an unfair
comparison, but I make it because of the fabulous wealth that
India now has due to the dramatic expansion of its economy.
The situation is similar to Brazil, Mexico and South Africa.
The good society provides not just a health and social safety
net but is judged by how it treats its poorest and most vulnerable people. This is a test for all societies and at the heart of
love, hope and art being central to political economy. What
was true in Haworth is true around the world now. For comparison, infant mortality in Shakespeare's time was such that
about one-third of all children died before the age of one.

Fast-forward to 1945. The end of World War II brought
about changes that are still with us today, albeit some rather
shaky and many misunderstood or unrecognized. In the UK

Churchill and the Conservative Party were very surprised to be thrown out of power and succeeded by the Deputy Prime Minister Clement Attlee, leader of the Labour Party. Just as Patrick Brontë had to fight hard to have the water contamination issue recognized and dealt with in Haworth in the mid-nineteenth century, so too must elites be engaged and confronted in order for those beneath them to be to allowed to have what they have. This book attests to the role that markets and trade have played in the twentieth century, but most would also reference the role of non-market ideas and movements. Until the mid-nineteenth century, most people around the world experienced virtually zero wealth increase for thousands of years, and nothing during their lives. The advent of the Industrial Revolution coupled with increased world trade meant that most people in the West then saw their standard of living rise year on year. But in the UK, with the advent of World War I, tests carried out on conscripts showed that the average male was seriously malnourished and suffering from a range of diseases. The reintroduction of conscription just before World War II reignited the debate about wealth inequality and the lack of social and health safety nets in Britain. A united coalition government during the period 1939–45 asked the question again: "What are we fighting for? A country with rich and poor, or a country where everyone benefits from the nation's wealth?"

Europe dreaming

The European dream is falling apart as I write these words. A project that was supposed to unite has disillusioned people and set them against each other. But this was because the European dream failed to do what the American constitutional pioneers did – which was to work hard and fast enough to use the horrors of World Wars I and II and so make one political currency, to not only see a dam but to realize the promised land on the other side. Most people I speak to around the world, outside Europe, do not understand Europe. I sing a hymn of praise for its vision and values, even though it has stumbled on governance and policy. Americans, Australians, Japanese, Chinese listen but do not understand.

Travelling across Europe, this vast continent with some 400 million people, I am reminded so often of how hard it was to come together, to make peace, and how easy it is now at this time of existential crisis for it to fall apart. Non-Europeans ask me how can so many people with such a violent past with so many languages hang together, have one vision. And yet this has mostly been the reality since 1945.

On the quay in this little place in Switzerland sit two young Muslim people, the woman wearing a hijab. They speak to me in German, then in English – hers is quite good. They look out of place here in this little German-speaking Swiss lakeside town with its three hotels. We do not understand each other, and only afterwards do I realize she was scared of me and was saying, "I have a ticket on the ship. I'm going back." I believe they felt they shouldn't be here, in this little place. I wanted to help them; they looked so fragile looking for a room at the inn. And the German-speaking lot here growl in their looks: no nods, no comments, they look suspiciously – at me. And yet when they open, they are open. And I am reminded of European history again, and again. How can one forget the first savage half of the last century and the heroic struggle to make peace. Remember, remember, remember. And now the streets are clean; order prevails.

Across Europe the coffee is always good and strong; this is not a small issue but the very stuff of life, which would be unrecognizable to most Americans and Brits who seem not to understand quality and consistency issues. This is why Starbucks hasn't taken off in Italy and Australia where it lowered, not raised, standards. I am reminded of sociologist Anthony Giddens's example of coffee in his introduction to sociology. There are a myriad complex connections if one can adopt a "sociological imagination" and see the links to globalization, legal drug use, colonialism, development, sociability, and life-time rituals. Swedish IKEA members worldwide are offered free coffee, but IKEA Italy had to offer the real thing served by trained baristas, not some weak slop from a stand-alone machine, such is the significance of good coffee in daily life there. IKEA Shanghai has had to limit free coffee to those who can show they also shopped, for in China their shops were being used as free day-long meeting places for older citizens. For the Italians the quality of the coffee is matched by their sociability, and for the Chinese it was the meeting space and place that mattered. Italy IKEA also has smoking rooms for up to 25 people, a practice that is not allowed in any other IKEA store around the world, such is the intransigence of Italians to observe international scientifically based health practice. If Indians and Irish and New Yorkers can give up smoking, why not Italians?

And in Italy there are patisseries everywhere, but hardly an obese person to be seen! It's down to portion sizes, which are 25% of UK and US portion sizes – and self-control: no pigging. This is not, as some would say, about poverty: where I'm writing this book, in Italy, there is no vast wealth and life is cheap, but peaceful, and there is little sign of obesity despite the love of pasta and pizza. This is about the unshakeability of local customs and communities. The non-obese countries of the world refute the link that is often made between poverty and obesity, or that poverty causes obesity. No, it is about culture, contentment, self-control and normalization. As Robert and Edward Skidelsky say, "Pre-enlightenment economic thought is often dismissed as a hotch-potch of bigotry and ignorance. But the failure of the modern age to make good its utopian promise casts it in a friendlier light. Capitalism ... has no spontaneous tendency to evolve into something nobler."[94]

Red, red geraniums – and poppies

I am driving across northern France in a thick fog. And the shuttered houses have red, red geraniums, like the blood the soil has washed away. Remember, remember. Across these fields millions of men died and a vivid dream rose to make Europe peaceful once and for all time. And the denouement was not here: it was in Hiroshima. In Europe high technology was used in the gas chambers, and companies like BASF and IBM aided, abetted and profited from the slaughter of millions of Romas, disabled, gays, street sleepers and Jews. In Japan the terror fell from the sky one bright blue morning delivered from the belly of a Boeing B-29 called *Enola Gay*, named after the pilot's mother.

And those who are dead worked so hard for this peace, so easily blown asunder by populism led by despots who have no sense of longer time and place. They are everywhere these shrill and greedy voices, pursued by guns and poppies. And this is why the peace is difficult.

I order coffee in a European square. It's good, the cup is clean and the taste pronounced. And I know where it's from. I pay and know the waiter can live, and when he calls an ambulance for his sick mother with a heart condition it'll transport her quickly to as-good-as-it-gets medically in the world. And, despite outrages across Europe, I drink my coffee without fear of a bomb, a theft, a gun or being poisoned. And tonight I will sleep in a dry, warm and secure room in my guesthouse knowing there'll be no knock at the door or bomb through the roof to disturb my gentle sleep. For this is a peaceful, largely gun-free society. It's not without work to be done, and it's ongoing in its deliberations, argumentation and it has agreed divisions, but it's purposeful in its equality before the law, its desire (if not always in its practice) to be kind and non-violent, and its space for dissent. This is France, a country underpinned by the motto of the late-eighteenth-century revolution: *liberté, égalité, fraternité*, fermented by the British civil rights writer and activist Thomas Paine who found fame in France and the USA but not in his homeland. Since 2000 the EU has had a charter of fundamental rights and Europe also has a "social democratic economic model" that is trying to defy, in the words of the *Financial Times*'s Wolfgang Münchau, "transactional, finance-based US-style capitalism".[95]

So this is what peace looks like. Sergeant Martin Hauser of the British Army wrote these words, near Trieste, France, in early May 1945 at the end of World War II:

> I hold a glass of beer in my hand, look into the transparent yellow liquid, and my thoughts wander. So this is the end. Is this what peace looks like? Here we sit, a group of men ... happy to have got through these years full of danger and horror sound of limb and mind. But where is the joy, the

enthusiasm that can be expected of us? ... Time
passes with an exchange of memories – memories
of past times, serious struggles, friends who have
fallen. The past weighs heavily on everyone.[96]

The German playwright Berthold Brecht was in New York
when World War II ended. He wrote a haiku:

nazi germany surrenders unconditionally
six in the morning on the radio the president
    delivers a speech
listening i look at the blossoming californian
    garden[97]

The worms have left casts, and the moles have tunnelled
under all and there are men tending the graves of young men,
mostly in their early twenties, long dead and buried, all named,
all remembered for having short lives. And the French, German, British and European Union flags fly here.

I stood, tears rolling down my face, in homage to the 589
men in this graveyard. Mostly British, but from all over the
world. One grave, of A. Parkin 14624865, catches my eye, for
its inscription echoes and amplifies the four flags flying here:
"peace perfect peace". The end of life, and the end of war: the
European dream.

And I stop at the nearest roadside restaurant for *un café*
and *une baguette avec confiture* in front of a roaring fire and a
bar dating back from before the last war, and probably the war
before that, "the war to end all wars".

If you want the best example of how companies and
capitalism fail because of the lack of intelligence and political will, those companies that survive war are testimony. So
next I'm standing next to a Krupp anti-tank gun on the beach

at Arromanches in Normandy. And I don't forget IBM's and BASF's involvement in the gas chambers. And what about Boeing and Hiroshima? Neutral. Allowed to be. Better strategically than government.

The things we can do when we put our minds to it. I've thought this when arriving by train into Hiroshima expecting there to be no trees but struck by the extent of the regeneration. And I've thought it too going down coalmines and contemplating the physical endurance of mineworkers. And here I am again at Omaha Beach in Normandy. We can do great things when we organize. Some business leaders know this and make Kit Kats, Dyson vacuum cleaners, Boeings and Hondas.

It's a bright November day, just above freezing, but the sun is shining. I can hear the guns and see the ghosts; or is it the films playing in my head? Omaha Beach looks deserted, but there is one other man there. I can see he's talking on the phone standing next to the memorial on the bluff that took the Americans all day to capture from the Germans on the first day of the D-Day Normandy landings in 1945. Thousands landed that first day; only hundreds survived. So I climb higher and wait for him to end his call. It's very cold and after a while I walk down the memorial to read the inscriptions to the dead from across America who came "to liberate the world". He is polite and greets me with "Bonjour". His phone conversation punctuates the silence and the waves and the sea birds, so I walk towards the beach to get some quiet and peace. We are the only two people for a hundred kilometres but he follows me. I stop and turn and say, "We are the only people here and it's very peaceful but full of ghosts – and you are on the phone. Why?" He smiles, raises his shoulders in that Gallic way and says, to elicit sympathy, "I'm sorry, it's work." The words tumble from my mouth: "This is a place of peace and remembrance, and you are on the phone! There is just you and me and you have followed me on the phone from up there to down here on the beach. Please have some respect." And more words, unspoken, tumble into my head: "That these many, many men died so that you could be on the phone for work!" The clash of the twentieth century with the twenty-first. The apparent "end of history". We're all on the phone facing *FOMO* – fear of missing out.

The British and the American war graves are immaculate. We can keep our war graves just so, but in Britain we can't keep our streets clean and our potholes filled. The American war graves, and there are thousands, are sentinelled, marble white against time and weather. It is clean and tidy and well organized. It is such a contrast to flying into JFK or LA airports which always feels like arriving into a scruffy, hastily erected transit camp. It shows a country's priorities.

In the early twenty-first century, France, the country of haute cuisine, is McDonald's' most profitable European country. You order from machines dotted around the restaurant. There are nine language choices – English, Russian, Japanese, Chinese, Spanish, Italian, Dutch, German and of course French. I wonder how often these language choices are used in Lèves, France. It certainly caters for a global audience, and for migration from around Europe. My "french fries" are tired and not so crisp, and my burger is very average. And it costs me €7.40 including a "biodynamic" apple juice.

And yet there is enormous diversity within Europe – and the rest of the world. It seems extraordinary that what has been banned and become largely socially unacceptable in all public places and restaurants in Dublin and London – and in New York, Delhi, Beijing and Sydney – is still so prevalent in Paris, Geneva, Bologna and Tokyo. In these still-smoking countries their people and places smell of smoke, even if some people do not smoke; it reminds me of how it was growing up in Britain. And can you believe it used to be possible to smoke on aircraft? To strike a light, to have naked flames on planes! Lung cancer has a long tail and those who are dying now started many decades ago. It will take a generation or two for the public policy in this area to flow through, so at the moment the UK and Australia have death rates related to lung cancer similar to Italy and France. But it is interesting to note how the science and public policy have converged in some countries but not in others. Just as I felt violated in some places in the USA by the obvious presence of guns, so I felt polluted by smoke while dining in many places in Italy, such is my piousness and sensitivity. But I think I'm on the side of the angels – or they're on my side. Surely it's best for people not to carry guns and not to smoke, or have I got something very wrong? Is peace not just the absence of war but the presence of good public policy?

And yet the twentieth-century European holocausts on the battlefield and in gas chambers took place only a hundred years after Europe had ceased to benefit from the transatlantic slave trade. The African slave trade, of which the transatlantic component was only one part, has estimates of between 15 and 37 million victims and ran for ten centuries. World War I from 1914–18 caused at least 17 million deaths and World War II from 1939–45 caused at least 120 million deaths. Both wars started in Europe. Genocide was a feature of the slave trade and both world wars.

The two world wars led to enormous dislocation of people and the rearrangement of borders, and as I write both are still in flux. State territorial borders are challenged by social media and the internet, and social media, globalization, climate change and war have encouraged, and in many cases forced, millions of people to uproot themselves and seek a new life elsewhere. Whether they be refugees, asylum seekers or economic migrants, the desire to leave behind what is most sacred and head for the unknown and some other world is not what most of us would choose. They travel in desperation, with the hope of a better life where normal human relations can be restored and a better life gained. They often move with loved ones, carrying children and supporting older folk.

Seventy years of peace in Europe was shattered in Yugoslavia. Christiane Amanpour, a war reporter and now a CNN anchor, was asked about confronting those who caused this dislocation. As an example of confronting the horror and facing the truth, she cited an interview with the psychopath Slobodan Milosevic – a Serbian politician who was known as "the butcher of the Balkans" – during the war in former Yugoslavia in the 1990s: "I asked Slobodan Milosevic how he would sleep at night. You have the facts and you have been there on the ground and seen the carnage and the destruction – and they just deny it!"[98] Donald Trump is not a psychopath, even if he is a serial abuser, misogynist and xenophobe, but this propensity for denial seems to be a trait of demagogic leaders who are not held in check by constitutions and the separation of the judiciary, the state and government – and the fourth estate, the media.

We had hoped that war in Europe belonged to the twentieth century, but the current confusion and rise of right-wing xenophobia does not augur well. The philosopher Isaiah Berlin said of the last century: "I have lived through most of the twentieth century, without, I must add, suffering personal hardship. I remember it only as the most terrible century in Western history."[99] This was echoed by the violinist Yehudi Menuhin: "If I had to sum up the twentieth century, I would say that it raised the greatest hopes ever conceived of humanity, and destroyed all illusions and ideals."[100]

The Greek legacy

While writing this book, a moment to cherish took place at London's Heathrow Terminal 3. It confirmed the melange that is the world today and the delight that I find in surprise, ambiguity and being open all hours.

Richard Curtis's 2003 film *Love Actually* begins and ends with people meeting at an airport. The meetings, greetings, waitings and partings are full of expectation, love, grief, hope, tears and smiles. And so it has always been at crossroads, rail stations and mundane bus stops. *Love Actually* unravels a complex interaction of lives that mirrors us all in its fiction. Romeo says to Juliet that parting is "such sweet sorrow" until we meet again, and Robert Johnson's 1936 blues number *Cross Road Blues,* made popular by Eric Clapton and Cream in the 1960s, speaks of decisions and junctions on the road travelled – and also dubious deals with the devil. The internet was supposed to herald the end of movement, or at least a diminution, but in reality the churn has increased. Today, Ryanair, Europe's largest airline, founded only in 1984, aims to carry 180 million passengers a year by the end of the 2020s.

While waiting for a friend in the arrivals area, because his plane was delayed, I had coffee in a branch of Carluccio's, an Italian restaurant chain. One of the issues in thinking about political economy and the good society is making links between values and value, between wealth, health and well-being. Research into longevity in communities with long life expectancies and low levels of many of the illnesses and frailties of affluent societies often leads us to the all-male Mount Athos religious community in Greece where many men live well into their hundreds. This community hardly suffers cancers, Alzheimer or cardiovascular problems: people die of old age. As a cancer survivor myself, I'm intensely interested in lifestyles that last.

I'm sitting there, minding my own business, when I am suddenly surrounded by tall men in black robes speaking Greek (this is Terminal 3 at Heathrow Airport). I asked a younger member of the group, not in robes, who they were and he said they were Mount Athos priests changing flights . . . there is nothing like the mountain coming to you rather than you having to travel to it. The Mount Athos life has much to recommend it, and many praise its austerity and its meditative aspects; and the monks claim that freedom from relationships with women, because they are celibate, leads to a stress-free life! But at the heart of their lives is the Mediterranean diet, now well understood to be the healthiest in the world, so long as you consume its constituent litre of olive oil every month. The monks' regime also includes eight hours of prayer over four sessions a day, regular exercise looking after vegetables, fruit and goats, and – this is very important – feeling useful within the community. This group had been invited to the USA to share their experience and are en route back home to Greece via London. Airports are the melting pots of the global community. What they made of Carluccio's Italian food I don't know. I do know that many of them had a beer.

The sun rises across the shimmering Mediterranean. Pick a country that is experiencing the worst of the global debt crisis, that has a long and influential history, a highly literate people with some of the longest lives in the world, which attracts millions of visitors every year for sun, sea and inspiration – and you have Greece. Greece is a good example of an economy and people that have suffered at the hand of credit liberalization. At the launch of the euro in 1999, Greece had almost zero debt, and by the time of the global debt crash in 2008 it was in need of bailing out, so high was its debt at 175% of GDP. Most Greek people's lifestyles had not changed, apart from playing host to both the European football championships and the Olympic Games. But at this point they have been forced to dramatically change their lifestyles to repay the debt, and the beneficiaries of the repayments have mostly been German and French banks.

In 2003 when I last visited the small port of Epidavros, famous for its ancient Greek pre-Christian open-air amphi-theatre, a silver truck would pull up every morning and park as close as it could to the fishing boats as they docked. Sneak-ing a look, you saw big fat tuna being loaded direct from the sea into a semi-refrigerated container. Within a few hours they were being loaded onto a flight to Japan. And yet there was no tuna on the menu locally. More than a decade later there are few large tuna left to be caught in the Med and the old men return from short fishing trips with a few fish if they're lucky. The young men have mostly left for the city and there is little fish on the menu now, and what you can find is expensive.

Marx and Engels said that all societies have their hierar-chies, but what distinguishes industrial and feudal society is the distinction between the bourgeoisie and the proletariat, between those who own the means of production and those who simply labour. Today the Greeks profoundly believe that they are all proles, even the petite bourgeoisie, now working their souls off for international capital. You don't have to be a

Marxist, or a communist, to know that this situation is unsustainable and will inevitably lead to disruption if not revolution.

As one US commentator pointed out, with full European political union Greece's 11 million people would be like the US state of Mississippi which receives federal support every year as part of the union with no vicious debt negotiations. The same is true of a federation like Australia where the annual discussions over redistribution to poorer states are vigourous but not punitive. And yet this country, Greece, has helped keep the value of the euro low and enabled countries like Germany to export expansively by remaining largely what is referred to as a "backward" and peasant economy. The Greeks have exported feta cheese, yoghurt, democracy (in its fledgling form), drama, and, until the 1980s, ships.

The Christina Hotel in Epidavros looks out across the blue Mediterranean. This hotel is a lesson in the whirlwind of instant capitalism. The hotel has been run by the Paraskevopoulos family since they returned from Toronto in 1978 to build the dream – a hotel named after the mother. Most of the fixtures and fittings are today as they were then, but not in need of repair as they are loved every day and kept fully functioning. This is by no means a run-down hotel, and everything works perfectly: it has not succumbed to the mad consumerism of the market to replace everything every day with more junk. Here there has been an investment in quality from day one; here the staff are the bedrock of society and enterprise capitalism. This hotel, from top to bottom, is family-run – the costs and the risks are shared, the work is shared, and the burden is enjoyed. That was until 2015 when Greece's debtors decreed that sales tax should be 23% and corporate tax 30%, and to be paid in advance. On top of this, for the first time property taxes must be on ownership, not just on conveyancing or transfers, which topples one of the pillars of stability and continuity. Greece is a case study of the derivative-made financial system let loose on the world in the late 1970s.

If there is a model of how to grind a population down and foment revolution through resentment, stress and discontent, this is it. But this myopic system measures not these human frailties. Its internal logic, its algorithm of life, is as cancer is to the human body; and until we find a cure to both it will destroy us. Perhaps one could wish that those working on cancer cures could work in close cooperation with those working on remodelling capitalism for the many not the few. Greece's austerity measures, while necessary in one sense, for obviously there is no logic to paying interest on insurmountable debt, reward the rich, punish the poor – and do nothing about climate change. And, as I learnt first-hand here in Epidavros, current austerity measures are punishing what used to be thought of as the very foundation of capitalism: the family firm, those hard-working people so courted and seduced by the political parties of the elite. As another local, a resolutely positive and successful restaurateur, says, "We can stand this for maybe two or three years, but not for any longer!"

The village of Epidavros is a cohesive, largely crime-free, low-impact village on the Peloponnese. Its main attraction, apart from the blue of the shimmering Mediterranean and in the past the fishing, is the largest open-air amphitheatre in the world, built more than 2,500 years ago. It is also the birthplace of modern medicine: Asclepius was the Greek god of healing and had two daughters, Hygieia and Panacea.

From here – from the amphitheatre – you can hear everything, so good are the acoustics. Every visitor claps her hands, does a turn, tears a sheet of paper or whoops to see if she can be heard in the amphitheatre and across the universe. And she can. It continues to reward, still vital after all these years, still an extraordinary feat of engineering wrought from the rock of the universe. Presumably the amphitheatre could be used to collect sounds from the universe and 14,000 people could listen to the Big Bang just as the gods were listening 2,500 years ago. And if you listen carefully you can hear the comedy and tragedy of all time down through the ages. Has anything changed?

Twentieth-century civilization was built upwards with giant phalluses careering skyward as signs of dominance and prosperity. Twenty-five thousand years ago the Greeks built temples, but they also built into the hillside to make public venues for expression, for art, for music, for healing of mind and body. It is known that at Epidavros the theatre was part of the healing of Asclepius. Open to the sky and within hearing of the gods, the plays were attended by all – a democratic space in a fledgling democracy. Only elite men had real power but everyone could learn, and laugh and cry. I've been to Olympic stadiums, to London's Royal Albert Hall and the Hollywood Bowl, but nothing beats the resonance of the ancient amphitheatre at Epidavros. I've sat in seats previously occupied by men in robes; I've looked across the same hills that our forebears gazed at during losses of attention (for they happen to us all!); and I've felt my backside nestle into the curves of these comfortable seats where history sits, come rain or shine, come night or day. For we are a passing thought, settled in our regular ways yet discomfited by our mortality, both individually and as a species. Tonight I shall scream at the stars while also sleeping peacefully under the blanket of blindness that is our daily bread. Forgive us for we have not sinned, we just fell awake on this beautiful planet with these gods and stars looking down benignly. And now to sleep I go, at peace, at home, at rest, for I have heard so many voices at Epidavros from around the world. And they all clap and whoop the same.

Christina is 80. In 1956 she and her husband emigrated from the village they were born in, Epidavros to live in Montreal, Canada, returning to Greece in 1978 with enough money to build their own hotel in their home village, on the Greek Peloponnese. "With these two hands, we built our lives. Now even though we have for 60 years run a good business we have nothing – they have stolen everything!" "They", in her eyes, are the global financial community. From these formerly apolitical people a lesson can be learnt: how to politicize a whole nation. This is what the bailout package from the troika means to Christina and her family-run business. The eldest son, Georgios, cannot afford to run a car as the road tax in 2015 is €600, and he refuses to drive without tax and insurance. Sales tax is now 23%, and this year he must pay this year's corporate tax *and* next year's in advance. This good, honest, family-run business is being bled dry to feed the voracious lenders to the Greek economy, when, ironically, this family have never borrowed anything.

There is a rising tide across Europe that knows that they are allowed to think of an alternative. The problem is: that alternative may be captured by right-wing populist demagogues who find traction in blaming not sophisticated elites and bankers but some "other": migrants, the country next door, or an internal element in society. In Greece this has already begun, with charitable groups helping the thousands of boat people who have arrived on the Adriatic islands and Golden Dawn saying they will only give food to Greeks.

There are solutions to be found in societies around the world, but those solutions are to be found in rethinking the problem. In Greece's case, the only number that mattered was the debt-to-GDP ratio – 175% or so. They were not interested in the other wealth that keeps a country wealthy: love, hope and art. They were not interested in the Paraskevopoulos family. So it is that I have measured the countries I am interested in against a range of rankings that lead us to a different future: what matters. Christina may not be destitute or living a subsistence life but she has come to be part of the global community rather savagely. Any model of economics has to take on board her issues: her love of the Greek tragedies played out every summer in the amphitheatre; her love of her four grandchildren; her stuffed peppers and tomatoes that are a Greek speciality; and her beloved customers who return again and again to drink their organic orange juice and olive oil, to smell the herbs, and swim in the warm sea – and to wonder at operations carried out 2,500 years ago without anaesthetic!

Flatpack Sweden

Is sex dying out? Or is childbirth? In Japan there is a growing aversion to sex among some young people and in Sweden the government has launched an enquiry into the low birth rate and the declining interest in sex. The average age for a woman's first birth is now 29 across Sweden and 38 in Stockholm, the capital. The government will pay to have any fertile woman's eggs frozen, which is one of a number of features that make Sweden stand out in Europe, and in the world.

On almost all human security rankings – those measures that are considered marks of a civilized society, the height of human achievement – Sweden comes near the top. But of course we have to be careful, because this implies that other societies are not civilized, or some are more civilized than others. It is a question of the social contract between the state, the people and business. One of the characteristics of Britain and Australia, for example, is that voters in those two countries expect good public services and low taxes: an unfixable problem and always a compromise for politicians. Swedes, by comparison, along with their near neighbours in Scandinavia, fully support high taxes because they recognize that they get good value for money: they like the state supporting society. Swedes pay an average of 48.2% of GDP in taxes, whereas the average in the UK is 36.6%. But then in Sweden most people receive direct benefits from the state either because they are employed by it or because they are in receipt of state benefits. As in Japan, Swedes believe they are all in it together and that the state is a beneficial parent who will look after them. There is no delusion, as there is, for instance, in the US, that small government would be a good idea because they understand that the state not only pays benefits but also maintains the roads, pays for the police, sends an ambulance and invests in the arts.

Probably the most extraordinary indicator of how different Sweden is from most other countries, even those that think of themselves as child-friendly and civilized, is the 480 days' paid parental leave. And most people receive about 70% of their income when they retire. These figures are the highest in the world. Most interesting is that, despite changes of government and an increase in diversity with migration over the last few decades, this social contract continues. And this is not a country without an enterprise culture: indeed, it ranks very favourably, albeit not as favourably as a few decades ago, against most other counties in the OECD. The capital city, Stockholm, with less than one million inhabitants, has delivered IKEA to the world and such inspirations as Spotify – the app that killed the CD and maybe the music download.

The Swedish village of Leksand, population 6,000 (16,000 for the local administrative area), has an excellent library, as has every small community in this country, like Australia and Costa Rica. This contrasts with the world's fifth richest economy in the world, the UK, where the redistribution of wealth under the so-called austerity programme has left most small communities without such facilities unless they can be paid for and staffed by volunteers. Most alarmingly – at first – in Sweden, cars slow down sometimes 10 metres from a pedestrian crossing, and there is no intimidation – unlike in Australia, Italy and France where cars sometimes stop at crossings but drivers intimidate pedestrians by racing up to them. Sweden is such an unaggressive society, and yet it is not unenterprising or lacking in get-up-and-go.

Here is a story that epitomizes Sweden's good-natured and fair society. There is no ticket office or machine at Leksand railway station due to efficiency cuts. I am told by an ever-so-friendly waiting passenger that I can buy a ticket on the train. I am travelling from Leksand to Stockholm further south, and I have to change trains in Borlänge, which I duly do, all trains being on time. On the train from Borlänge, I discover, belatedly, there are no on-board ticket sales – and I face a possible fine equivalent to four times the original ticket price. At first, the train conductor is severe but soon searches for a solution. She phones through to the ticket office in Stockholm for me to buy an online ticket but all my credit cards are refused for security reasons – because we're on the phone! So she comes up with another ingenious and intelligent solution. I have to spend the equivalent ticket price in the train bistro using a credit card, which is OK. By so doing I get ten bars of chocolate (organic, of course!) and a free ticket! There is much laughter and I am not arrested. I tell the conductor she is a genius, but that this is madness. She says, "But of course. This is Sweden. We have found a solution – and", she says proudly, "the train company is the largest employer in Sweden!"

An intelligent country with traditions but also with a strong tradition of problem-solving has solved another problem, seemingly insurmountable in some other countries, particularly the USA where there is a debate about whether transgender people should use male or female toilets. At Stockholm station, as at all public venues, they have unisex toilet cubicles so there is no issue. It is an obvious solution to a number of problems but it is still unnerving as a newcomer as I queue sandwiched between two women for the loo: am I in the wrong place? Will I get arrested for going into the ladies' toilet? Then another man joins the queue. All is well.

And another first, which is coming to all countries: the street coffee shop does not take cash, only cards – "because it's cheaper for us!" In Italy in the market, and in France on the seafront at Cannes, I am told they don't take cards – "it's too expensive for us!" In the UK only about 50% of all transactions are now made with cash across the whole economy and the same is true of most advanced economies.

And the global ubiquity of IKEA, exporting a flatpack sanitized version of Sweden – to China, Italy, Australia, the UK and everywhere. If it's a cold wet grey day in Bristol, or blisteringly hot in Brisbane, or noisy in Beijing, IKEA is always Swedish: well designed, cheap, and comforting inside. But where am I? Nowhere man in nowhere land. In the lift the poster says "Leksand in Dalarna", where I used to live, in the heart of Sweden. And every home I visit around the world has some part of IKEA at its heart. Proclaiming its global citizenship values,

IKEA shouts, gently, "There is one world of fish, labour and wood". Responsible sourcing, good management, efficient value supply chains, some elements of the circular economy, a dose of clean lines like the Google login page: am I being taken for a ride?

From Stockholm to Saigon to Saskatchewan I am in heaven, a heaven made in Sweden. This is the country that gave us the Dalarna Hest (the red horse), the bastu (the Finnish sauna), neutrality during World War II, and the Volvo (now Chinese-owned, where most IKEA furniture is made). In Bristol, IKEA is packed to the rafters: cheap products, good food, clean, bright, safe, multicultural, tolerant, organic. Apparently, IKEA's brilliance is not just because of the Swedish design principles: it's because their design staff spent time in customers' "most intimate spaces . . . observing their bathroom habits". To observe is to understand, a principle for Sweden's IKEA just as it was when Japan's Honda started out.

From Google in China to McDonald's in India, companies are learning to be relativistic in their trading practices, integrating with local political cultures and often abandoning their espousement of universality and global human rights. Cowhides are on sale in IKEA Italy, but not in UK. Is this because of UK animal rights or because the British wouldn't buy them?

I was in Moscow the day the first McDonald's opened in 1978 and there was a queue round the block, not just for the American fast-food way of life, but also for the unheard-of quick service! And McDonald's brought better hygiene conditions and reduced instances of food poisoning. According to one now slightly tarnished theory, American overseas fast-food countries, particularly those with McDonald's, don't attack each other. Peace is a fatty, salty burger in a sugary bun brought to the world from Germany via the USA.

There is something about building well for the future, rather than, as in England now, building for today's profit. Swedish housing is designed to withstand the long savage winters, down to minus 30°C and below, and to be energy-efficient and literally long-standing. Japanese housing is efficient and profitable, but collapsible too – for earthquakes and for development. Most twentieth-century British housing seems to be built without much reference to how it might be used or the exigencies of the prevalent weather, particularly cold, damp and wind. And traditional Swedish design is so simple, so well proportioned, and so beautiful.

A United Kingdom?

The UK, Britain or the British Isles (as it is variously known around the world, even if these are in reality different political and geographical entities) is an anomaly among advanced industrial states. As the world's fifth largest economy, it precariously balances between the values and norms of neoliberalism in the US and those of the welfare economies of Europe and Australasia. But it also stands out as exceptional in still having a hereditary contingent in its upper house in Parliament, *and* having the lowest social mobility among OECD countries (apart from Portugal) due to its archaic and elitist independent school sector which caters for just 7% of the population but takes most of the prizes at the top of society, 71% in the case of high-court judges. Overall, its educational scores are not in the top ten.

UK wealth inequality is similar to the US, as is obesity, but it still has the most cost-effective publicly funded healthcare system in the world. Wealth inequality, having narrowed during the 1960s and '70s, is now roughly the same as it was during World War I, 100 years ago. On gender issues it is middle-ranking, on human development it is nowhere near the top ten, and its global happiness and "where to be born" rankings languish in the 20s. But it is a safe and relatively crime-free country where, even after the Brexit vote, 66 million people rub along together relatively harmoniously by global comparison, and whose capital city, London, is one of the most ethnically diverse and exciting cities in the world (it voted 80% to remain in the EU). It also has the most respected broadcaster in the world, the BBC, which is publicly funded by a universal licence fee which means that all of its 30 or so radio stations and four main television channels run without commercial advertising.

There is a truism of the UK, which is that the people want to pay low taxes but expect the best public services. This doesn't add up, and is the abiding post World War II political problem for those coming to power. It is neither a global power, nor a sophisticated sharing Scandinavian economy. And yet it hosts the third largest number of individuals worth more than $50 million after the US and Japan. Only the US, Luxembourg and Austria have a larger share of the 1% than the UK, whose wealthy are drawn to London by its globally dominant financial services sector, and, ironically, given the profile of the 1% (who dislike paying taxes and often engage in nefarious business activities), its stable democracy, application of the rule of law and safe environment.

On 5 December 1962, US Secretary of State Dean Acheson said of the UK, "Great Britain has lost an Empire and has not yet found a role." As the UK leaves the European Union, this is perhaps more true in the twenty-first century than it was then.

It may also be true of the USA that it is losing an empire, now, in the twenty-first century. It could be said, to adapt Acheson's line, that in 1945 Europe lost a war and hasn't quite found a way of being, even if it has found peace for the last 70 years. In 1973 the UK belatedly joined the European Community and the direction of travel became clearer as a senior member of the world's largest trading bloc. Most importantly, the Community became a Union following the Maastricht Treaty in 1992, with a commitment by all members to four freedoms of movement: goods, workers, services and finance. In subsequent years, millions of people moved around Europe with about 1.5 million British people moving to work and retire, particularly in France and Spain; London became the second largest French community in Europe; and some 2 million workers from former Eastern Europe came to work in the UK.

To travel in Europe is to meet the world, some of whom have travelled from another part of the EU, some of whom have travelled from further afield. It has added to the cosmopolitan and vibrant feel of cities like London, Paris, Rome, Madrid and Berlin. This feeling is not as obvious in smaller cities outside the main hubs, and this is where the bulk of the fear and xenophobia lies, partly because these small towns and rural areas can argue that they have been left behind both by European integration and globalization.

In Fano, Italy, I am welcomed by Sudanese umbrella sellers; near Mont Blanc in Switzerland at the top of a mountain I am served by Portuguese; in England, in Stratford-upon-Avon, Shakespeare's birth, marriage and death place, many restaurants are waited on by Poles; and in Beaune, France, my beautiful coffee is served by a Colombian. In several places as I travel we have a joke about which language to use, and, of course, we settle on the lingua franca, English.

The vote in the UK, on 23 June 2016, to leave the EU demonstrated the enormous cultural variety across this disunited kingdom. Cities such as London, Cambridge, Edinburgh and Belfast voted more than 70% to remain in the EU, while cities like Yarmouth, Blackpool and Burnley voted more than 70% to leave. Although 81.5% of British people live in cities, there is a divide between the large and the small, the south and north, and between the cosmopolitan and the parochial. In other words, those places that have benefited most from the union, and globalization, and have higher levels of education and less poverty, voted to remain – life is essentially good to them. This feeling is reflected across the EU and in North America: we have been told that the world is richer and we have seen some people getting very rich but we don't all feel the effect; and what are now described as echo chambers have increased the reassuring chat between those who think like we do.

Today, Londoners have more in common with sophisticated cosmopolitan urbanites in Berlin, Edinburgh, New York and Sydney than they do with people who live in Penzance, Bingley, Great Yarmouth, Dallas and Dijon. We all belong now more to global social tribes than nations. Increasingly, we trust Facebook and Twitter rather than external experts – in other words, "people like me". The narcissism of the Facebook generation is also the generation that says "I think" and "I believe" when confronted with a truth that doesn't fit with their prejudices. Accordingly, during the UK's EU referendum debate, the "leave" campaign's consistent line that, if the UK left the EU the country could spend £350 million a week more on the National Health Service – despite being challenged by all intelligent bodies and informed people – was still believed on polling day by nearly 50% of the electorate. What are those organizations to do that have relied on people finding them reliable and accurate sources of information? Mark Thompson, former Director-General of the BBC and since 2015 CEO of the *New York Times*, says that "the internet has set a new dark standard for the expression of strong opinion, which some politicians, activists and commentators are only too happy to meet".[101]

The lesson is that increased freedom of movement, in people, finance, goods and services, is good for the mobile, for the educated, and for those willing and able to show initiative. The role of the state becomes more, not less, important in ensuring that the benefits of these increased freedoms are shared across the whole population because there is no doubt, looking at the long-term statistics, that across Europe and in North America increased trade has benefited all, but that the tide has raised some boats higher than others. We forget, we forget, we forget. Remember, remember, remember. Where we have come from, and how we arrived here. Remember in Europe's case how we have maintained peace for the last 70 years in an area that was awash with blood not so long ago.

The values that Europe espouses are the values of Thomas Paine, and the foundations of democracy in Greece 2,500 years ago. Literally, the word "democracy" means people-power, but of the 300,000 people who lived in Athens at this time only some 30,000 were eligible to vote – all men born in Athens, and of these only 6,000 were allowed to act as jurymen. In the Gettysburg Address on 19 November 1863 Abraham Lincoln said that democracy meant "government of the people for the people by the people", and this built on the idea of the rule of law as enshrined in the three treaties between the king and the barons that all individuals have equality before the law in the Magna Carta in 1215 – and 1225 and 1297. The EU tried to expand its four freedoms towards the idea that equality should also be applied to economic matters – that labour could move just as capital does, and that everyone has a right to work just as investors have a right, in a capitalist economy, to invest and see a return.

I meet a German hotel owner in Switzerland, who represents many in Europe in telling me that "Europe will always be at war: it's part of our history." When I plead that we have had 70 years of peace he seems to have forgotten this completely, so present are the wars of last century, this century. Had Europe run out of ideas in 1945 to such an extent that it was ready for the Americans' taking? Or was it the Marshall Plan and the US militarization of Europe that provided the impetus for Europe's change? Both Britain and Japan became "offshore aircraft carriers" for US forward projection and both benefited from US rebuilding loans and access to US markets. But the US benefited more, becoming the world's default currency, the world's largest military power and cultural superpower led by the car, fast food, cigarettes, Hollywood, rock 'n' roll and "democratic freedom", regardless of the fact that it had a lot of fixing to do back home. When I was living in Japan in the 1970s, assaults by men on US and European women were common. Why? Because in Hollywood films women ended up so easily in bed with men, so all Western women must be easy, right?

The US and the UK share a history, in that neither has been invaded in the recent past, they share the same language, and they share some of the same culture – films, music and obesity. The other thing that the US and the UK share is the death of social mobility, which has all but stopped for the bottom 20% of these two countries, unlike much of Europe and countries like Australia, New Zealand and Canada.[102] India has never had social mobility, and China's is managed by the government not by the individual.

1976 saw the introduction of monetarism by a Labour Chancellor, Denis Healey, when Britain had to ask the IMF, largely financed by the US, for a loan. This set in train the global movement towards monetarism, neoliberal economics and liberalization and privatization steamrollered by Prime Minister Margaret Thatcher and President Ronald Reagan. This set the two countries apart from the European continent, although Thatcher could not shake off the baggage of health and welfare institutions in the UK that link the UK to Europe and not to the US. At the end of World War II, both the US and the UK retained their sense of nationhood, and this is one of the major cultural disjunctures between the UK and the EU. Apart from the war, the other movement that has helped to integrate Europe is, ironically, Americanization – music, films, and, in some countries, food. Europe has been bound together by a sense of social democracy and geography, but these attributes are now ironically threatened by the democratic principle: many people across Europe, including in the UK, feel threatened by their own freedoms and so are voting against those things that have given them peace, stability and prosperity for so many years. They do not, as we observed before from Eric Hobsbawm and Niall Ferguson, have a sense of the long view.

Sitting in the piazza, a very common human-focused feature of most Italian towns and cities, I wonder what it is that makes Italy similar to Britain? The Italians don't seem to have heard about health and smoking – everyone smokes all the time. They dress much better than the British, even when they're not trying – it's the way they walk as much as anything, with style and pride. They speak a different language, and their food and coffee is uniformly of a higher standard than in Britain. And their weather is much more pleasant! So the EU could be seen as a territorial convenience and a memory of what seem like distant wars to many people. For the EU to progress and for the euro currency to work requires political union and the natural distribution of wealth rather than debt repayments, as in the case of Greece. They need to think like federalist Australia or America and see Greece as Missouri needing annual support not punishment.

So in search of a single form or a unifying theory we may have to turn to people like me: the peer group, i.e. horizontally rather than vertically.

As the author Michael Morpurgo and the academic Timothy Garton Ash cried after the Brexit vote: "We are Europeans." They say that what strangely binds Europe is the war and the consequential Americanization – what an irony. The post World War II benefits are closer union and peace. Just as Northern Ireland doesn't war any more, so too Europeans, and so the blessed peace. But in both the USA and Europe rightwing populists averse to expertise whip up hysterics and forget the past. Europe had been trying another route, the feminized negotiation route, where talking leads to agreement rather than appeasement and war. And tells us the world is angry.

No, the EU is a high-value and -values proposition and the people have forgotten, or have not been reminded for a while. On such stuff America does well in principle and badly in practice, and on such stuff Europe does well in practice, but less well than it did, and not well in selling the principles. Why has the EU stumbled? Is it because the Germans adopted monetarism and neoliberalism, benefited enormously from an undervalued euro, and lent their surpluses to poor countries within Europe like Greece, Italy and Spain who could not repay and would be forever in Germany's debt? Or is it because the EU has been edging too slowly towards a federal model, similar to Australia and the US, but has failed to go the whole way and cement the deal? Or is it that countries like Britain and the former Eastern bloc members have diluted the European social dream of France and many other founding members by embracing a more neoliberal economic model?

After the UK's vote to leave the EU, the reactions of those with a longer view say most. Kazuo Ishiguro, born in Nagasaki, Japan, but living in London most of his life, said that he was "Angry that one of the few genuine success stories of modern history – the transforming of Europe from a slaughterhouse of total war and totalitarian regimes to a much-envied region of liberal democracies living in near borderless friendship – should now be so profoundly undermined by such a myopic process as took place in Britain."[103] Ian McEwan, another bestselling, award-winning author, wrote, "Our country is changed utterly. Unless this summer is just a bad dream."[104] And so some of the people, 37.4% of the possible total, in "this sceptred isle" voted by a small majority (52% to 48%) to leave the EU and float off into a sunset and join the Flat Earth Society.

> This royal throne of kings, this sceptred isle,
> This earth of majesty, this seat of Mars,
> This other Eden, demi-paradise,
> This fortress built by Nature for herself
> Against infection and the hand of war,
> This happy breed of men, this little world,
> This precious stone set in the silver sea,
> Which serves it in the office of a wall,
> Or as a moat defensive to a house,
> Against the envy of less happier lands,
> This blessed plot, this earth, this realm, this
>   England . . .

William Shakespeare, *Richard II*, Act II, Scene 1

The vote to leave the EU by the UK changes everything. It was a renunciation of expertism and also a reiteration of Dean Acheson's comment from 60 years before. Those who voted to leave rejected the recommendation of all main political parties represented at Westminster, voted against all expert opinion, separated the intelligentsia and the elite from the masses, and was led by people who claimed to be anti-elitist but who came from the most privileged parts of British society. More than anything, the vote exemplified the growing social media trend of people listening and talking to people who are like them. How do you book a restaurant or check out a film? You read other people's comments. How do you vote? You read like-minded people's comments. We trust our "friends" on Facebook or Twitter more than the government, the IMF or the Institute for Fiscal Studies.

There is a global citizenship movement taking shape composed of people who think, eat, have sex, work, travel, wear similarly. Their meeting place is the modern airport where they mingle, share, eat, wait and do their messaging. They don't mind each other and they know that they are secure; hey – they even have machine-gunned police patrolling along the corridors of power, commerce and privilege. If McLuhan was to imagine the global village, it's here at the airport and replicated in the hubs of the grooviest cities where there is youth, opportunity, wealth, diversity and plenty of art – culture writ large as part of what it means to be alive. These are the people of East and West Coast America, of Tokyo, Melbourne, London, Liverpool, Reykjavik, Copenhagen, Stockholm, Shanghai and Toronto. These may be the people of the airports of Cape Town, Nairobi and Delhi, but not of those cities outside the airport for they are not safe, secure and fair places to be. Some 2.7 billion people live way below the poverty line, on subsistence, on scraping a living, on getting by, on insecurity, without the health and welfare support that the rest of us have come to expect and enjoy.

But the global citizenship movement's joys and excesses can be accessed very easily via the cheapest of handsets, and, just as television brought Dallas into every living room in the 1980s, now football's fabulous fortunes and the Williams sisters' wealth is in everyone's heads, rich or poor, for the internet has liberated everyone to want whatever they haven't got. How do we reconcile the difference and satisfy the desires? Identity is a hot topic now as we merge into one but retain our local identity. The most successful societies are open, but retain a sense of themselves. The Japanese have been partially successful at this taking of ideas, foods and institutions and turning them Japanese. Will the world embrace human rights, civil liberties, sustainability, democracy, accountability, transparency and feminization, or will it close down, turn inward, parochial, despising, jealous and afraid? Most of all, will it understand and embrace history: its own, its regions, and the world's? Now more than anytime we need the long look back and the long look forward. Will the unifying principle, the theory of our undivided past over thousands of years, allow us to see the stars as the Aboriginal peoples of Australia and the Kalahari bush people of Africa have been doing for years? Or will we become more unknowing of each other and more myopic in our view of "the other"?

One of the most striking aspects of the terrorist attacks on trains and buses in London in 2005 was the diversity of those who were affected and how, regardless of gender, race, ethnicity, age and language, they all helped each other. The same was true of the attacks in New York in 2001. These melting-pot cities have always been that way, and most people now and for the future live in close, dense, complex, environments. Are they a hope for the future? They tend to exemplify love, hope and art along with collaboration, negotiation, cohabitation and cosmopolitanism, for how else can they work?

The cosmopolitan, sharing, tolerant living environment represented relatively by New York, London, Paris and Tokyo is challenged to distil its wisdom nationwide. How, many will ask, can one London Mayor, a White man with the most elitist background, Boris Johnson, be replaced by a Black Muslim man, Sadiq Khan, from a modest background? Part of the answer lies in their origins: Johnson's parents were American émigrés and Khan's were from Pakistan. Khan grew up in social housing and his father was a bus driver. Johnson was born in New York and has a Turkish, French and German background. What does identity mean in an age where many, many people are mongrels? In 2010 Barack Obama described Americans as a "mongrel people", particularly African Americans, in answer to a question about his own background – White mother, Black father, Kenyan, Indonesian, American background. While the US, and many other countries, have yet to come to terms with their racist past – and present – the growing divide globally is in economic inequality, between the educated and the uneducated, between the skilled and adaptive and the unskilled and immobile. And of course Winston Churchill had mixed parentage, an American mother and a British father, while the Queen of England's back story is largely German, and she has a Greek husband.

The cosmopolitan global citizen is expressed by Christiane Amanpour, when she told the BBC:

> My mother and my father taught me that you can
> be from East and West, you can have a tolerance

of different ethnicities and of religions – my father was a Muslim and my mother was a Catholic – you can live in these disparate environments and learn about tolerance and "can-do", and my mum, even when we lived in Persia, never intimated, and neither did my father, that as a girl any route was closed to me.[105]

Chiwetel Ejiofor, a Black British Nigerian-born actor and star of the 2013 film *Twelve Years a Slave*, has talked of the shock realization that many British people have no experience or understanding of multiculturalism: encountering difference in life is transformative – it was for him and it is for all of us. "Until you meet people who didn't have a multicultural experience, you don't realise how different an experience that is. It's taken me really all of my life to understand that."[106]

And we have to look at the way senior professions are composed, in business and in other organizations, because they are often made up of talent regardless of ethnicity, race, colour, gender or hair colour. On 24 June 2016, the day after the UK's vote to leave the EU, consultant urologist Dr Junaid Masood posted a picture of his NHS operating team in the UK: consultant urologist, British Pakistani; radiographer, Irish; consultant anaesthetist, German; scrub nurse, Spanish; urology specialist, Greek; scrub nurse, Spanish; scrub nurse, Spanish. Latest DNA research shows that, given the relatively short time-span of humanity's time on Earth, and given the churn around the world and particularly in Europe, we are mostly mongrels anyway. This research makes racism ridiculous, and reinforces the melange that is humanity. Is there also something about the cosmopolitan elite that thinks, eats and behaves the same wherever it is? Another doctor, this time in Sydney, Australia, says that in Glebe Point, Sydney, a new bakery has opened which mills the flour you buy right in front of you, which is "just as likely to be found in Williamsburg, Brooklyn, New York City, or the Shoreditch neighborhood in London".[107] She also notes that her medical team and patients in Western Sydney are from everywhere – patients from Australia, Sudan and the Pacific islands. And at lunchtime her colleagues share a Halal snack.

But it isn't a global elite that we are talking about. The Swedish home furnishing company IKEA is everywhere and homes worldwide have IKEA products dotted about; the Japanese design company MUJI is in most cities and every airport; McDonald's and Starbucks are everywhere good food and coffee are not; the French hotel chain Accor allows me to book worldwide from dirt-cheap to super-luxurious; we all drive German Volkswagens and Japanese Toyotas; America's Apple is the dominant mobile phone, but being chased by Korean Samsung and Chinese Huawei; and the two most trusted English-language news television stations globally are the UK's BBC and America's CNN. Is this homogeneity, or just the economies of scale, national strategic advantage, or imperialism by corporation rather than nation-state?

Despite the revolution in civil rights in 1968 in the US, that country still has to come to terms with its racist past. This is also more true of the UK, because although some would argue that the UK has done rather better at integrating its Black and minority ethnic communities into society as a whole, there is an almost complete denial of Britain's colonial past and the legacy of inhumanity, genocide, human rights abuse and resource theft. The UK, Japan and the USA could learn a great deal from Germany which has been forced to confront its past – and it has done so with firmness and alacrity. To a certain extent, South Africa also began the task of reflection and reconciliation with the Truth and Reconciliation Commission chaired by Archbishop Desmond Tutu, but this has stalled as the fruits of democratic capitalism have yet to trickle down to most South Africans.

I once asked Gerry Adams, President of Sinn Féin, a former IRA commander and since then a leading member of the peace movement in Northern Ireland, if a truth and reconciliation commission was possible in Northern Ireland. His answer was: "Yes, if it was chaired by someone from outside, by a foreigner."

It is not possible or sensible to do more than Prime Minister Tony Blair's apologies in 2006 and 2007 for the transatlantic slave trade – Britain cannot hold a truth and reconciliation commission at this late stage – but it would be possible to make sure that all schoolchildren are taught the truth about Britain's empire. This would go some way towards revealing the concealment of the unpalatable truth, that while Britain may have had a beneficial effect in terms of nominally promoting the rule of law and democracy, especially in the decolonization period from 1945 onwards and in leading the Commonwealth, the ways and means she deployed at the height of the Empire were appalling. In Tony Blair's words,

> It is hard to believe what would now be a crime against humanity was legal at the time . . . the slave trade was profoundly shameful . . . we condemn its existence utterly and praise those who fought for its abolition . . . but also express our deep sorrow that it could ever have happened and rejoice at the better times we live in today.[108]

A good start would be to go against Britain's natural aversion to transparency and openness and release all the files relating to the governance of former colonies. Apparently, they are kept at GCHQ, the Government Communications Headquarters in Buckinghamshire.

What started as a South African campaign at Africa's top university in Cape Town spread to Oxford University. In Cape Town the statue of Cecil Rhodes was successfully pulled down in April 2015; and at Oxford a much smaller statue remains despite the "Rhodes Must Fall" campaign, but the exercise has ignited a debate about Britain's colonial past, a debate long overdue. David Priestland, Professor of Modern History at Oxford, whose interests are communism and neoliberalism, pointed out that no one said that free speech was being stifled when Lenin's statues were pulled down across Eastern Europe. Timothy Garton Ash, Professor of European Studies at Oxford, said the statues should stay but were useful symbolically for lighting the fire on a long overdue debate: "The British memory of empire is, I think, quite woolly . . . unlike in Germany there is little agonising about what your grandfather might have done. In a very British way we just don't talk about it." He thanked the Rhodes Must Fall people for "violating my safe space".[109]

By contrast, Chris Patten, the last Governor of Hong Kong, when part of the British Empire until 1996, and former Chair of the Conservative Party and now Chancellor of the University of Oxford, epitomized the postcolonial problem using aggressive language and a combative tone in defending the university's postcolonial attitudes in an interview on the BBC. He also pointed out that there were 28 African students as part of the Rhodes scholarship in 2016, without mentioning their skin colour.[110] Cecil Rhodes was a mining magnate who left his money to Oriel College, Oxford, when he died in the 1870s. He thought that the English were a superior race and began the process of apartheid in South Africa. As much as anything, the campaign sought to start a debate and flush out the denialists:

it was always an attempt in the best spirit of free speech, and in this regard it succeeded.

Britain's elite have always had it good, and most of their institutions are still going strong despite many decades of social reform in other areas of British life. Many people visiting the UK are surprised that the British are still talking about the class system, but for most people it is a daily reality. It is based first of all on a private, elite, fee-paying education system; second on access to the best universities; third on access to the networks and clubs that count, that get the best positions and money in life; and fourth to power and privilege. At the apex is the Royal Family and at the base are the small number of schools that produce the majority of people for senior positions in public life. The system is very long-standing – centuries old – and was adapted and adopted to provide "leaders" to run the Empire; now it continues to run the world's fifth largest economy (falling fast after the vote to leave the EU).

It is far from being Michael Young's meritocracy:[111] those at the top will not give up what they have to make way for those at the bottom. The same is as true of Whites in South Africa as it is for private-school-educated people in the UK. But there is a further problem with meritocratic social mobility: from 1945 to the 1990s expanding economies needed more managers and senior people, but now we are in an era where that need is decreasing, so social mobility is made more difficult as the pyramid gets sharper.

The 93% of children who attend state school in Britain are 55 times less likely to gain entry to Oxford and Cambridge than privately educated children – the remaining 7%. That flows through into later life, a fact that has not changed for 100 years. Research shows that, if children are told they are either bright or not so academic too early, this has a direct effect on the rest of their lives; and the UK segregates these two groups in terms of type of school, ability and subjects earlier than any other country in Europe. Finland has the best-performing education system in Europe and has no private schools in any meaningful way, and does not select or separate children until they are sixteen. Also, the UK is the only country in Europe, apart from Estonia, where class sizes are larger at primary level than at secondary level. The glass ceiling starts early in the UK. The 7% of British children who go to private, fee-paying schools in 2015 will take the top jobs: 71% of judges; 62% of senior military officers; 60% of senior posts in financial services; 55% of senior civil servants; 54% of senior journalists and broadcasters; 54% of CEOs of FTSE 100 companies; 53% of senior diplomats; 51% of senior medical personnel; 50% of the House of Lords; and, in both Labour and Conservative cabinets, about one-third of positions.[112]

The vote against the EU was also a vote against globalization, as it was perceived, and against obvious excesses at the top of British and global society. It is manifesting itself both on the left and right across Europe and North America, and in Australia. This is despite the fact, and there is no denying this, that life is dramatically better in these countries than in 1945 and also since the UK joined the EU in 1973: a 103% increase in average per capita income; absolute poverty is very much lower; life expectancy has risen; crime is down; teenage pregnancy is down; more than 40% of people go to university; everyone has an inside toilet; and the price of cars and petrol relative to income is much lower. Against that, property to rent or buy is much more expensive; the streets are dirtier and the potholes bigger; obesity is a pandemic; and, since 2007, income has not grown for most people in the UK, and for people below 30 it has actually fallen 7%. The award-winning film director

Ken Loach, who came to fame through his 1966 BBC play on homelessness *Cathy Come Home*, and whose 2016 film *I, Daniel Blake* won the Palme D'Or at the Cannes Film Festival and a BAFTA in the UK in 2017, captured the way many people in the UK feel after more than 50 years of neoliberal economics when he said: "People weren't [in the 1960s] imagining zero-hours contracts, agency work, food banks. Who would have thought in the 60s that it would become acceptable and normal to starve unless you got charity food?"[113]

If the British have shot themselves in the foot over their vote to leave the EU and have to find a new identity; if they have a lack of social mobility; and if they have a similar pandemic to the USA when it comes to obesity, there is also much to recommend this small green Atlantic island when it comes to looking at the themes of this book as the basis for political economy.

The UK is one of the safest countries in the world to drive in; it has the only free-at-the-point-of-delivery healthcare system, creaking at the seams but relatively cheap by comparison with other countries; its crime rate is dropping and is safe and secure to live in by comparison with other countries; its people live a long time; and people across the board are relatively happy. And they have the best broadcaster in the world in the BBC (not without its critics), along with one of the freest and most diverse print media in the world, albeit biased towards the right.

I have lived in Australia where the press is owned by Rupert Murdoch, and I've spent a lot of time in the USA, where the rest of the world doesn't exist, so I know what a dearth of diverse, honest media looks like. And this is increasingly the worldwide trend. Facebook, which sorts and transmits other people's news stories and in 2015 had 1.6 billion users, has become the most usual way for people to find the news – and Facebook's profits are over US$6 billion a year.[114] Two-thirds of British people use Facebook regularly. Here's a powerful analogy which has yet to be addressed by the men who bestride today's Western media world, particularly Mark Zuckerberg from Facebook, Sergey Brin and Sundar Pichai from Google, and others: "Facebook has a responsibility to society beyond servicing shareholders and investors ... Just as a water company has a duty not to poison the supply, so Facebook has a responsibility to use its significant distribution power for better democratic and civic outcomes."[115]

But the area that is most challenging to the UK, and more so now it will no longer be part of the EU, is its relationship with the US. Apart from Syria recently and Vietnam from 1961 to 1975 (when it had Australia as its willing buddy), Britain has been alongside America in every war. Britain has a nuclear deterrent – based on the Trident nuclear-armed and -powered submarine – but is reliant on the US for technology and targeting, so it is not an independent nuclear deterrent. Indeed, the theme of interdependence, which runs through this book and is contrary to the populist isolationisms current in the US and UK, is exemplified by the next generation of the UK's Trident submarines where the finance will come from international borrowing, the iron from France, the nuclear propulsion and cooling systems from the US, the sensors being largely Italian, and the sonar systems French.

In 1945, at the end of World War II, the USA reneged on an agreement to share nuclear technology, despite the fact that much of the knowledge came from the UK in the first place. The then British Foreign Secretary, Ernest Bevin, part of the postwar Labour government, said that Britain must have a nuclear deterrent or it would "send a British Foreign Secretary naked into the conference-chamber" and so Britain secretly started its own nuclear programme without full cabinet discussion or approval from Parliament, such was the agreement with the US and fear of the Russians.

Since 1945 all British prime ministers, with the partial exception of Harold Wilson, who refused to take the UK into the Vietnam War, have been in the US pocket, and the US has worked hard at seducing the UK into believing that it is a credible big power, and will be if it works alongside the US. The seduction has had many climaxes but perhaps the peak was when Tony Blair joined US and other allied forces in taking the UK into Iraq in 2003, despite all the advice being against him and facing significant opposition within the country and from some senior colleagues. Thirteen years after the war, a government-commissioned report chaired by John Chilcot and involving several senior war professors was damning in its criticism of the way Blair had conducted himself, the denial of normal discussions within government and his distorting of the truth to parliament. Overall, the report was an indictment of the way government and Whitehall works: it should serve as yet another wake-up call – more checks and balances are required for the UK's prime minister, who has far more authority and patronage than a US president.[116] But most of all it highlighted Britain's umbilical relationship with the US – which is the case in every sphere: military, diplomatic, cultural, and in language and economics. Blair wrote a note to President W. Bush in 2002: "I will be with you, whatever." This was before UN weapons inspector Hans Blix had finished his investigations of Saddam Hussein's weapons of mass destruction, before all the UN avenues had been tested, and before Parliament and the British had been told. After the Chilcot Report had finally appeared, the *Guardian* published the following letter from me:

In the wake of the Chilcot report, I thought I would add to the evidence that the UK was largely impotent when it came to influencing the events that led to the invasion of Afghanistan and Iraq. A month after 9/11 I was invited to attend and speak at a meeting of senior business leaders in New York. The meeting went ahead as a show of defiance to the terrorists. Members of the group came from North America and the UK and were chairs of Fortune 500 companies or held a similar rank.

On the final day of the meeting, we were addressed by General Wes Clark, then very senior in the Pentagon and to become a Democratic presidential candidate in 2004. In this closed-door session we were given the details of forthcoming invasions of Afghanistan and Iraq by US and other forces. We were told outline strategies, troop numbers and dates which were being rapidly set in place. We were told that there were no contingency plans for what would happen to Iraq after the invasion, except that US policy was to leave it unstable and chaotic so that it did not pose a powerful threat in the region, and the US could control the oil assets and establish a large forward military base in Iraq.

At the end of the briefing the room was silent apart from one question on the effect on oil prices from the chair of one of the world's largest oil companies. It was clear that these two invasions would go ahead and that discussions that might take place in wider society, local or global, would be minor distractions to the plan, which already had enormous momentum in terms of planning, resources and support across the political-military establishment in the US. The seduction of UK prime ministers by the US has been the norm since the end of the Second World War, and Blair was just the latest

victim. The only PM not to be quite so seduced was
Harold Wilson.[117]

Dr Malcolm McIntosh, Author,
Managing Britain's Defence

Around 1995 I was asked to draw up a plan for the Greenwich Millennium Exhibition which was to be a showcase of
British talent and industry and give some sense of the past, the
present and the future. My task was to integrate all three, and
I set about building a four-dimensional map for the exhibition.
In the event, the exhibition was a damp squib of lacklustre
photographs presumably arranged by people unaware of the
import of the occasion and the space. It was a failure.

My plan had three themes: place, people and resources. It
was located in Greenwich on a time-line that runs around the
world, in an area that had been one of the hubs of world trade
and the British Empire and was now being redeveloped in a
post-industrial state. Under "place" I emphasized the merid-
ian, global links, and the new millennium. Under "people"
I had three connected subthemes: celebration (success, fun
and happiness); human needs (subsistence, protection, affection, understanding, participation, creation, recreation, identity and freedom); and the human experience (being, doing,
having and interacting). And under "resources" I thought the
exhibition ought to be exemplary and talk about reclamation,
post-industrialism and global trading, along with the idea
of global commons: public space, amenity and accessibility,
rights and responsibilities, and land, air, water and biota. And
it should redefine wealth for the twenty-first century: human
resources, social capital, produced assets and natural capital.
The fourth dimension was to ensure that the past, present
and future were clearly signposted. The whole exhibition

would be linked by two overarching criteria: relationships and stakeholders.

I was paid handsomely and you can see why I failed! It was far too ambitious to be managed by a rather narrow-minded government led by Tony Blair, and instead they outsourced it to some children in a "creative" advertising agency. What it needed was the sort of creative force and risk-taking that characterized the opening ceremony to the London Olympic Games in 2012, designed and mounted under the direction of the very experienced film director Danny Boyle, who was supported by then UK Prime Minister David Cameron.[118]

The UK continually fails to live up to its own image, or fantasy. In this regard, I reference both the "independent" Trident nuclear submarine programme and the Millennium Dome fiasco. It is a country run by an elite, for an elite, which denies access to the majority. And it is not a particularly liberal elite either: it has maintained power by throwing just enough scraps to those below to keep them happy – until now.

The Japanese conundrum

I first came to live in Japan in 1978 and remained there for two years. I have returned time and time again; it is a country I love. It looks and feels almost exactly the same today as it did in 1978. The minor changes are that taxi drivers and street sweepers no longer wear white gloves and smart sales ladies at the entrances to department stores and supermarkets have in some cases been replaced by recordings.

Depending on where you stand, the Japanese economy is still the third or fourth largest in the world, just overtaken by the

Chinese. But the Japanese are some 127 million, and declining, while the Chinese are nearly 1.4 billion, or nearly 20% of the total world population. The Japanese archipelago comprises about 6,000 islands but 75% of the land mass is comprised of largely uninhabitable mountains. This makes Japan one of the most densely populated and urbanized countries on the planet. Like the Chinese, the Japanese can feel 4,000 years of history despite volcanic changes in their lifestyles in the last 200 years. Their post-war "pacifist" constitution is slowly crumbling and they are coming to terms with a rapidly escalating situation in the seas between them and China.

In terms of wealth, Japan is one of the most equal countries in the world, and is certainly one of the least obese. It has an excellent publicly funded healthcare system, and a public transport network that is as safe, cheap and accessible as anywhere in the world. It also has the lowest crime statistics in the world, with virtually zero gun crime. It is in the top few countries when it comes to educational attainment, and its social mobility is as good as the best. Declining population growth coupled with an ageing population means Japan is dealing with these issues in ways that the rest of the world should watch and learn from. There are now some 60,000 centenarians in Japan and their diet is rated in health-giving terms as second only to the Mediterranean.

Two examples serve to make the point that we continue to rank countries against indicators that do not serve their peoples well or fail to appreciate local resilience and determination to retain historical cultural identities. In *The Rise and Fall of Nations* by Ruchir Sharma, a Wall Street analyst,[119] measures of success include the number of billionaires a country has. He comments that Japan has very few and says this is because they have not accumulated enough wealth. But he fails to realize that ostentatious wealth in Japan is disapproved of, and indeed the issue of executive pay is a hot topic in a country where being seen to take too much from the country is very much frowned upon. Also, Japan is one of the most equal countries in the world, in terms of wealth. And Japan's debt-to-GDP ratio of 230% (2016) is one of the worst in the world, but the difference is that Japan's debt is owed to her own people, not overseas banks. Japan is not America, or Russia or Greece. And no account is taken of the fact that, despite Japan's debt, its current account surplus in 2014 was $45 billion.

In 2015 the Economist Intelligence Unit (EIU) published its *Long-Term Macroeconomic Forecasts: Key Trends to 2050*,[120] in which it said that by 2050 national GDP would be led by China, the US and India with individual income per capita much surpassed by the USA and Germany, followed by Japan, China and Mexico. India's per capita income would be half that of China, and less than a quarter of the US's. The figures, although this was not the EIU's intention, say nothing about quality of life, inequality of income, longevity, infant mortality, healthcare, obesity, transport infrastructure, the role of migrants in the economy, carbon loading or air quality.

Earlier when discussing Greece I referenced the export of tuna from the Mediterranean by air to Japan on a daily basis in the early twenty-first century. The king of tuna is the bluefin, who in the open sea can roam for thousands of kilometres and grow to over 400 kg. The bluefin is a threatened species on the IUCN's Red List, and Pacific stocks are down by 97% over the last 60 years – hence the exports from the Mediterranean, which have now stopped as the tuna have been fished out. The Japanese eat 80% of the total global catch: some 40,000 tonnes.

But why can't the British run railways like the Japanese do?! I'm standing on a draughty British platform and the sign says "go to the front", but no one knows where the front is. On the 15-minutes-late train the first-class table is dirty. In Japan in 1978 all trains ran on time and were spotlessly clean, and these things are still true. And public and private run alongside each other, often in the case of subway trains in large cities running into, and as part of, department stores taking customers to and from shopping and work. Every ticket on every long-distance train in 1978 had an allocated seat as standard, but in 2015 the Friday-evening trains from London to Bristol are twice over-sold with no explanation or apology. Why do the British put up with this? And what does it tell us about culture, capital-ism and productivity in the UK, especially when Japan is being written off in the press?

From the window of my Tokyo hotel room, Japan's post World War II success passes me by every ten minutes on the dot. That's the frequency of the Shinkansen that's now been running for more than 50 years between Tokyo and Osaka: on time, in time, quiet, fast, safe, polite, reliable, every time all the time. It is a beautiful hymn to liberating technology. And on the train it tells us "not to rush for the train" and "to switch your mobile to silent". How civilized that the use of mobiles is banned in public unless set to silent. You can only send mes-sages, the phone mustn't ring, and you mustn't speak into a phone in public. This is a sign of the good society! How I wish for that in the UK, China and Australia.

However, the railway station plays the sound of the calling cuckoo and the local café has piped birdsong: such is the work-ing of the world's largest city where the average person sleeps just four or five hours a night and mass alienation leads to sui-cide. But on other issues it's better than most cities. I leave my bag containing my MacBook Pro laptop computer in a café: it's still there later in the day. It's safe to walk all streets at any time of night or day – for anyone. The cost of this: agreement and conformity – you are my neighbour, I am you, there are social rules, I know what you are thinking: language and gesture are glue not dividers.

From the lobby of the Park Hotel, Tokyo, on today's clear day, I am staring directly at Fujisan and the mountains that surround the world's biggest city. The lobby is adorned with artwork: vast soft stuffed parrots in red and white climb the walls and perch on the internal balconies. Tokyo waits for its next earthquake, but they are ready and when it occurs this 50-storey building will sway 3 m either way – and stay upright. If it's a vertical quake, it'll drop like a stone and remain upright.

Japan's success is its problem. Not just affluence but more importantly the conformity that raised it out of ashes in 1945 is now stifling its development. As a senior Japanese academic and advisor to the government tells me: "Japan is still glorying in the success they found in the 1970s, and they refuse to move on." It benefited from a post-war industrial strategy between government and business that focused on specific areas of growth, particularly electronics and cars. It also benefited from pragmatism, which has always been its strength beyond Shintoism and Buddhism, and the US military forward projection which saw Japan, like the UK, become an offshore aircraft carrier. What non-Japanese people fail to understand is that this affluent and equal society has problems but it does not see growth as a major necessity because this is a country that in international terms works well, despite 20 years of apparent economic flatlining.

The trains run on time and safely, it is largely crime-free for most people apart from corruption in politics and in areas like prostitution and gambling. They have a universal healthcare system that is one of the best in the world and caters for

MALCOLM McINTOSH

everyone. Everyone pays an insurance premium for health and
social care. Perhaps there are issues of what has been called
"affluenza", but most countries would envy having such problems; Chinese people I have spoken to say privately that their
model of a successful China is Japan – but only privately! As
some commentators have said, "if this is austerity and lack of
growth bring it on – future capitalism!" Japan has retained
its economy, kept its social cohesion and only borrowed from
itself: its government debt is from its own citizens.

It is also very polite with excellent service, has enormous
efficiency in many areas, is socially cohesive and has some of
the best food in the world. If you see a fat person they will not
be Japanese, they will be Western – Australian, American or
British in the main. It has vast wealth. It is very clean and tidy.

But there are a number of serious issues that Japan is failing
to confront and they show institutional failure on a significant
scale. We have already mentioned smoking as an issue that
doesn't seem to have affected public policy, but then the same
is true in Italy and France. There are some other issues that are
just as important.

Conformity in an economy that needs greater diversity and
creativity is a major problem, especially as some see the suicide figures, particularly among young men, as very alarming
– and are some of the highest in the world. Twenty-thousand
Japanese people a year commit suicide. This is put down to
alienation, saving face and disconnection in a modern world
of connectivity. A highly educated workforce does not have
enough outlets for its creativity and Japan has failed to create
Googles and Apples, despite leading the hard- and software
revolution from the 1960s onwards. Social media can be seen
as alienating: friends but no friends.

A couple of anecdotes help unpack the issue of conformity. I am in a café where I buy a cake but the drink I want has sold out. I sit at a table but am asked to leave because I haven't bought a drink! Taking a side-trip during a stay at a university I am fined for not sleeping in the accommodation they have provided! And a third story: I arrive one minute before opening time in a hotel restaurant and have to wait with the waitress outside in the freezing cold until the clock hits the exact spot. I love Japan and smile, but some would see this as intransigence in an international world of movement.

Japan still sees itself as the centre of Asia because of its historical "uniqueness" and having been the first Asian Tiger and the model for all others. This is a problem as it has lost its competitive edge, which was based on miniaturization, social cohesiveness, hard work, a US democratic model, and innovation in electronics – it was an intelligent nation.

Now it is one of many intelligent South East Asian nations but without the cheap labour and with the encumbrances of its past history in World War II with its near neighbours, and with an education system that rewards rote learning at the expense of innovation, challenge and creativity in the social space. It does not reward change, women or being not Japanese. At worst, arrogance, inertia and misogyny are its characteristics. At best, social cohesion, fairness, equality, low crime, excellent public transport and healthcare, and cleanliness are its characteristics.

Prime Minister Abe has called for more women to enter the workforce, but Japan is a very misogynistic society and the masculine hierarchy does not support women's advancement. Much of the cartoon Manga is violent and abusive to women. The *Japan Times* reports that 51% of Japanese men think women should stay at home, and only 7.9% of the new House of Representatives is made up of women, which makes for one of the lowest gender representations in the world.

Despite stagflation, Japan does not have an employment problem. As its population ages, its workforce has dropped by 10% over the last 30 years and its unemployment rate is less than 4%. The West, which is addicted to growth, particularly in employment, sees this as a problem, but Japan has a policy to reduce the population. This in turn reduces environmental stress and increases the availability of accommodation so that housing prices have remained steady for the last few decades. This is such a contrast to the UK and London in particular, and other countries in the West. But also, because of fewer planning restrictions and an increasing density on individual housing plots, in 2014 there were 142,417 housing starts in Tokyo versus 137,010 in the whole of the UK. The ageing population – in 2014 there were over 60,000 people aged over 100 or older in Japan, and women have the highest life expectancy in the world at 86.8 years – coupled with a dramatically declining birth rate means that in 2014 there were three million empty homes.[121]

Serious commentators say that Japan is resting on its laurels and if it is not careful it will be overtaken by its near neighbours with whom it has difficult relations because of its inability to come to terms with its role in World War II. Half-hearted acknowledgements of abuse and torture of Chinese, Korean and other citizens has not led to full apologies, and, unlike Germany, Japan has spectacularly failed to face its own history. This is not helping in its relations with the country that threatens to dominate Japan for the rest of this century, but the Japanese right seems to be intransigent in its resistance to change.

Over the centuries, Japan has been very good at rapid adaptation in the face of external threat and indeed is built on the belief that it could be destroyed by the next earthquake or volcanic eruption. When the 2011 Tōhoku earthquake and resulting tsunami struck, many people thought that this would provide the jolt to force Japan to see the world afresh, and engage in another revolution, as they did in 1868 with the Meiji Restoration and in 1945 with post-war development. But it has not happened.

The current period in Japanese history is called Heisei, and in this period wealth has plateaued and economic uncertainty has become the leitmotif. But in this period many Japanese product names have become ubiquitous worldwide and synonymous with reliability and quality: just think about Sony, Toyota and Honda. Japanese designers, computer games manufacturers, food and authors have become globally recognized and feted, not forgetting the plethora of brilliant Japanese classical music artists. Even their football team has impressed.

The earthquakes, or tremors, are as frightening as ever but, as testimony to an advanced industrial economy, they only destroy cities when they are large and accompanied by tsunami as in Tōhoku. Large tremors in Tokyo make the buildings sway but there is nothing comparable to the damage seen in countries with corrupt and/or slack building practices.

As one eyewitness to the 2011 earthquake said:

> I was on the twenty-fifth floor and one moment you could see the sky, the next the road. The chairs on wheels became missiles, the workers carried on working, the first burst lasted about four minutes, the second, after a 30-second lull, about three minutes. Only then did panic break out, but there was no escape. But the building, being modern, was absolutely fine. There was no panic in the streets despite most electricity being down. Most people walked home many kilometres.

As a country, Japan mobilized late for Tōhoku, but it was not that they were chaotic or fell apart. They were so composed that they still waited at red lights to cross the road even when the traffic was gridlocked. But what else was there to do? This sense of fatalism and order is at the heart of Japanese society.

Only water became a problem. Most Western governments organized emergency flights out, and the UK finally reluctantly did so, but with the British ambassador and the Irish head of Unilever remaining in the country making them exceptions. Radiation was the greatest fear but the British embassy in Tokyo had all the monitoring equipment on the roof so they knew what was happening.

Japanese people see the tsunami as just another example of living on Earth, and it fits with their sense of harmony between people and planet. It is because of this, I am told, that it has not had the same effect as the Meiji Restoration or World War II, both of which were human acts. In Japanese this is called *kyosei* – living and working together for the common good. There is also a sense of fatalism in Japan and, as one senior commentator told me, "the focus on ecology and *kyosei* is a diversion from thinking about bigger, international issues like human rights: for instance, look at the treatment of Indigenous people and Koreans in Japan".

One irony of this crisis relates to the US and post-war Japan, where the US had used atomic bombs on two cities. The Tōhoku tsunami caused so much damage and spread radiation because Japanese nuclear power stations were built partially underground, on US insistence, to make them safe from typhoons. But this meant they flooded and stopped running when hit by the wave of tsunami water. One of the reasons for building them in the first place was to supply plutonium for the US military. Now Japan, if it goes nuclear, has enough plutonium for about 1,000 warheads.[122]

Kyoto, near Osaka in the south of Japan's main island Honshu, is a UNESCO World Heritage Site. Now a city of 1.5 million, it was Japan's capital from the eighth to the late nineteenth century. In front of me is the juxtaposition of old and new: the Karasuma-dori Starbucks looks out through plate glass at Rokkaku-dō Temple. Americano coffee and espresso are mixed with the spirits of old in this online free-wifi culture. The comfortable leather armchairs look out and the women, for they are mostly young women here, look down into their machines floating in virtual worlds of make-believe as they sip coffee from happy faraway lands – Tanzania, Ethiopia, Peru and Papua New Guinea. The smiling-people posters say so. Way before the internet, Carole King sang in 1971 "so far away, doesn't anybody's head stay in one place any more?", and she is being played now. There is piped muzak and there are security cameras. There are flags outside around the ancient temple, and there are flags inside around the coffee temple. And here I am drinking Starbucks and worrying about eating McDonald's in Japan. But why should I worry, apart from the health issues, when the world drives Toyotas and watches Sony TVs?

One final thought crashes into my head as I ponder Japan and why it represents so much of what is the good society, and why there is much to emulate here for the rest of the world. I have just been to India where there is a deliberate attempt to keep the poor poor and to maintain the caste class system. Yet both Japan and India believe in ancestral spirits and an afterlife. But when it comes to the structure of their political – as opposed to their religious – economies, Japan wins hands down. It is possible to believe in the spirits of the dead, the living, and the future, *and* build a society that works for all, now.

India

Twenty and more years of significant economic growth in India have only increased the country's wealth inequality and not improved government efficiency. The tax take is some 2–3%, and yet, while the US still dominates the world super-rich, India has the largest disparity between the rich and the very poor. This is in contrast to China, which now has the largest proportion of rich middle-class people, and Japan, where their post-war economic development has ensured the best overall universal income and wealth distribution in the world. India has followed neither the Chinese nor Japanese models of development, and yet it is the world's largest democracy. Understandably, it does not feature anywhere near the top half of the Human Development Indices, or the gender disparity rankings, or any of the other many ways in which the good society is now understood in relation to crime, infant mortality, pollution, educational opportunity or attainment . . .

More than 50% of the world's population now live in cities and this century *most* people will live in cities in developing countries. But will these cities be like Delhi, Nairobi and Rio de Janeiro or like Tokyo, London and Stockholm?

Cows are sacred in India as domestic cats are in the UK, but cows disrupt the traffic and sit where they like. India is the world's biggest democracy, with 1.2 billion inhabitants. Stephen Hawking says that the universe is expanding, but in 40 years this country has made little movement from bullock cart to engine. And here, like Greece and so many places, the Honda is the Hero, by name and by use. Maybe Francis Fukuyama was correct: some business products have become ubiquitous, and the Honda Hero is a good example.

I am asked by everyone how the country has changed since I first came here 40 years ago. I reply diplomatically that smoking seems to have stopped – unlike Italy, Japan and France – and that the traffic has increased and some of the vehicles, but by no means most, have got much larger. In reality, for me the destitution on the street has not become more bearable. And yet India is one of the fastest-expanding economies in the world – 7.1% for 2016 and now the seventh largest economy in the world. Only between 1% and 2% pay any income tax due to corruption and government inefficiency and, although it now has 84 billionaires, it is one of the most unequal countries in the world on a par with Brazil, Mexico and South Africa.[123]

John Kenneth Galbraith, the Harvard economist who advised numerous US presidents, famously talked about inequality in the affluent society (which was also the title of his 1958 book from which this book's title draws) pointing to "private wealth and public squalor". This is exactly how I saw India in my twenties and how I see it even more so coming up to the twenty-twenties.

In the 1970s, in my twenties, as an affluent post-hippy European student, I found it romantic, with the smells of patchouli and turmeric rubbing up against the praying and the dying. It was what I had been looking for in what I saw as an old-fashioned Britain. But now in my sixties I am no longer romantic about death on the streets and the sight of children begging. I felt very guilty writing this paragraph, but note that the *FT*'s travel correspondent felt the same in not recommending Delhi as a destination for 2017: "what a nightmare India's capital has become. The city is smothered in acrid eye-stinging smog . . . it is choked by every sort of wheeled vehicle . . . the once wonderful Chandni Chowk market is full of tat, while Connaught Place has been hijacked by bland western designer stores . . . I fled . . .".[124] This is the end-game, this is ubiquity, this is the end of history, this is globalization's failures writ large.

Stepping out of my hotel I am beset by sharp smells and noise, an onslaught of vibrancy around my failed attempt to cross the heaving six-lane carriageway. I cross a busy road dodging the traffic – tuk-tuks, lorries, diesel-fume-spewing buses – and arrive safely on a traffic island between the lanes and realize I have landed in a family home, for, amid the traffic on the central reservation is a family of women, men, children and old folk. There is a shout and the children are mobilized – poor begging urchins, human beings pulling with their hands and eyes at my soul. How do I look in their eyes? And yet I know if I give I will be besieged: the knowledge will travel far and wide, such is the lifestyle and the desperation. Although the caste system, with the Dalits or untouchables at the bottom, was formally abolished in the new 1947 independence constitution, in India today all caste groups know who they are. Not dissimilar to the UK and its class system, lower castes have been given some notional benefits to distract them from poverty protesting. The fact that this is still an issue resonates with social mobility issues in the USA as well: how elites hang on to power even in the proudest of democracies and how the meritocratic dream is still to be realized in a world where expertise, education and high skills are in demand.

Delhi: one forgets the assault on the senses. The thick dust, the rubbish everywhere, the men in groups, the women (if out at all) in lovely clothes looking beautiful in groups of three, not staring but chatting, the poverty in the streets and in the eyes of passing men, shuffling past: going where? The endless roadside enterprise, with piles of nuts and fruit and rows of bicycles for sale, and the mending, mending of this and that and everything. How do we build – and how do we destroy – the beauty of the fair society that tries to live within the Earth's limits?

I'm speaking at a conference and am told that in India "this is reality". There doesn't seem to be an appetite for change – even in this change community. I think about the normalization of and indifference to pain, which I have seen in the White community in South Africa where they drive past the informal settlements every day, and I remember Jared Diamond talking about "landscape amnesia". How does it happen that we accept such a lack of humanity in this life?

I hear things here, even among enlightened people, that defy credence: "women are innately genetically liking stitching and colours" in a session run by UNDP. Another attendee tells me she now lives in the world's most liveable city, Copenhagen. She says that when she steps off the plane in Delhi it's back into the Indian world of "chaotic dysfunctional collapse". Copenhagen is wonderful, she tells me: "You can walk free, unmolested, and it's safe and women are equal". Being so naïve, I ask: "Why not in Delhi?" "It's the reality here. It's karma. If you can make them happy in the moment, now, that's enough, because you cannot change their path or karma. The caste system is historical and scientifically based on evidence." I am stunned. I must rethink my ideas on collectivism – on life on Earth now, versus karma and inevitability.

The reality is that, overall, poverty in India has fallen by about 25% since the early 1990s, and that for Dalits (the former untouchables in the caste system) the improvement is higher, but this doesn't hide the massive wealth inequality and attitudes towards this situation.[125] Quite simply this is about the culture of the political economy and about policy decisions: elites have to give something up for others to benefit. Social mobility and wealth distribution means movement both ways, both within countries and internationally.

India is a disparate continent held together by the idea of nationhood. Democracy and government are veneers covering fixed hierarchical inertia-led institutions: caste, wealth, misogyny and karma. I wonder is this true for China too? Here in India people have low expectations of the state because for most people it doesn't deliver and is corrupt. Between 80 and 95% of employment is informal. Corporate responsibility is philanthropy-based. I'm told: "We inherited a bureaucracy based on compliance and a neo-communist state – from the British!" But that was in 1947, and economic liberalization was as long ago as 1991.

And the magic of India comes to me again as I eat lentils and rice, the daily basics for all Indians. Here I am again listening to a raga with a sitar and a tabla player playing just for me . . . it's very soothing and meditative after a traffic jam. Perhaps if they all have this music in their DNA, then all things must pass and flow – karma – what will be within you and without you.

I am confounded by the urge in India to enterprise, to trade, to buy, to sell, and I think of Amartya Sen again and his understanding of enterprise as part of what it means to be human. These are kind people, loquacious and happy to commune; they are gentle and kind. But I remember that Indian-born Sen wrote in the *New York Review* that if you were interested in social justice and sustainability in the world's two largest growing economies, India and China, then he, even as a Bengali, would look to China, not India.[126] He upset many Indians.

I'm on the road back from Sikri and Agra to my hotel in Delhi. The journey out took just over an hour. So far on the way home one hour has become three and we've been sitting in the dark, stationary, for an hour. The disorganization and chaos for each individual carries into this traffic jam and we are all in cars vans tractors buses bikes heading nowhere no one knows people are cross it's dark and very dusty loquaciousness rules on this dark night somewhere and the air's worse and the plastic overwhelming dystopia, dystopia. I see no progress. Men on bikes, women in saris. Conrad talks of the heart of darkness, "the horror" "the horror" Kurtz and Marlow the destroyer and the enquirer both seekers after truth everyone has turned their engines and lights off now it's dark and just the sound of Hindi in the night and even the dust settles a little as we wait, how long, how long? And yet there is no anger, not even really raised voices. If I were to construct the end-game for libertarian economics, I would use Delhi as my model. As Galbraith said: "Private wealth and public squalor".

And the West wants India to change. One idea is to push, like Prime Minister Abe in Japan, and make women part of the measured economy, to commoditize their work and therefore liberate them from men. According to the consultancy McKinsey in a 2015 report, $700 billion could be added to the India's GDP by 2025 if women had a greater role in the workplace.[127] The report said it would mean "upping India's annual GDP growth by 1.4 percentage points and bringing 68 million more women into the labor force". In a country where most business is not registered and where most business does not work to any international standards and the subsistence economy relies on unpaid work and where most men's work is not registered, is this another example of misthinking?

One man who is registered, and does receive holiday pay, sick pay and some sort of pension, is my waiter at the five-star Hyatt Hotel, where I've been put up. He lives in a hotel dormitory and works six days a week, twelve hours a day for 1,500 rupees a month – or £18/US$22. My room costs £150 a night. The minimum wage in London would gross him approx-imately £570 a week, and in Australia about A$1,300 a week, although in neither country would he be allowed to break the ILO's workplace guidelines as he does at the Hyatt in New Delhi.

How shall we maintain our standards of integrity, social cohesion and tolerance in the face of the onslaught of globaliza-tion and the race to the bottom, yet without military interven-tion, gated communities, armed militia and a denial of human rights for the most vulnerable – women, children and the old?

The China ascendancy

China has three economies for its 1.3 billion people. One-third live at a subsistence level on less than $2 a day; the middle third live on about $10,000 a year; and the top third (that's the same size as the total European population) live at the same level of income as the average European. This last third constitute the largest and most affluent middle class in the world. The Chinese Communist Party knows that to stay in power it must continue to lift the bottom into the middle and keep the affluence dream working. Despite some 50 or so riots or demonstrations a day across this vast geography, it is a stable country at the moment with a relatively cohesive population and a conscientious work-force. Given the vast disparities between the rich and the poor, it is no surprise that its overall Human Development Index (HDI) rankings are as low as India's, but with the very significant dif-ference that the number of people lifted out of poverty in the 30 years between 1980 and 2010 was just below 700 million, and the number in extreme poverty went from 84% to 10%.

By contrast, about 70% of Indians don't have adequate toilets, and 80% of villages don't have secondary schools, while half the country lives on less than $1.25 a day. And this is with 9% annual economic growth, similar to China's.

I first went to China in 1978, and in the following few years travelled extensively without a visa incognito around the country on trains, buses, canal barges and on foot. Since then, I have been a frequent visitor, with the correct visas, and I have watched this vast country and its varied people transform itself over nearly 50 years. At first, the only clothes were uniform green and blue Mao suits; now they are some of the most stylish people in the world, not that the Mao suits weren't stylish. Indeed, I wore a blue Mao cap in my teens when many of us misguidedly found the Little Red Book inspirational. I never felt frightened or alarmed when in China and I don't now: they are a gentle people with an enormous loquacity. I feel more nervous in an American city than I do in Beijing, Shanghai or Xian.

Comparing India and China is an interesting exercise, and the West, particularly the British because of their colonial domination over many centuries, has a romantic fascination with India and a slight fear of China. I feel the other way round.

This is how the CIA describes first China and then India in its *World Factbook* for 2016: "For much of the population, living standards have improved dramatically and the room for personal choice has expanded, yet political controls remain tight." "Despite pressing problems such as significant over-population, environmental degradation, extensive poverty, and widespread corruption, economic growth following the launch of economic reforms in 1991 and a massive youthful population are driving India's emergence as a regional and global power."[128]

Eating is something the Chinese do in company – all the costs and the experience are shared every time. Even now, it is so cheap because of the economies of scale, the speed and efficiency of delivery and instant cooking in hot water or oil (which also kills the bugs). It's a happy, noisy experience often with too much grease and salt. Opium has been replaced by coffee a century or so on, and, following the incumbency of Deng Xiaoping from 1978 to 1989, the talk is of efficient supply chain management and global trade.

If, in Shanghai, you walk up to the Henan Road from the Yunnan Gardens towards the shiny new metro station you will pass a UK Tesco supermarket and a Starbucks coffee shop. Starbucks has taken off in China; Tesco is struggling. In Starbucks I am told, via wall posters, about "the shared planet" and how "we all crave simple human connections". Apparently, this is a place for "communities to meet", but at 07.30 am it's just me and the smiling staff. This Starbucks could be anywhere in the world with its homogenized product, the same signage, the same coffee and donuts, and the same music. This morning it's Ella Fitzgerald and the Fleet Foxes. Why do I think this is weird, given that sixties pop music is played wherever I stay?

Large signs announce that the coffee comes from exotic far-away places full of smiley people working in the sunny fields of Nicaragua, Papua New Guinea and Tanzania; as in Kyoto, London and New York, the same smiley faces: globalization works for all. Ella sings of her man always having an "ace in the hole" – I'm not sure how that translates or if the Chinese censors are on to that one. But censor they do: I can no longer access either my email or Google. My Chinese hosts tell me that I can if I go in via another country's servers. Will I get arrested? It's easy getting arrested here and then disappearing.

The last thing this state-run capitalism wants is any disruption: harmony is all. Not that I'm disapproving of a system that has lifted millions out of poverty in two decades, where spitting and smoking has almost totally disappeared in the last five years, and where everything and anything can be discussed as long as it's not disruptive. What's not to applaud? Well, the treatment of outliers like Tibetans, democracy in Hong Kong, and human rights in Africa.

I pick up a Starbucks feedback leaflet which invites me to let them know "if there's anything else we could be doing better?" and "what makes you really happy?" I decide to send them some feedback; a year and more later and I'm still waiting for a reply, so that doesn't make me really happy. I praise their friendly staff and ask the following questions: "Does all your coffee really come from PNG, Tanzania and Nicaragua, and does China grow any coffee? Is the Californian lifestyle appropriate to Shanghai? When you play Frank Sinatra's 'My Way', is it easy for Chinese people to do it their way? Does Starbucks pay taxes in China?" I sent it to the President of Starbucks China in Shanghai and I remain in expectation of a response.

The Chinese government officially says its policies are to "globalize", open up, "regard innovation as the fundamental force to improve growth quality", improve the balance of technological breakthroughs *and* "mobilize society to innovate". It should "strengthen the rule of law to use the laws to ensure the market plays a decisive role in allocating resources while making better use of the government's role". China has a mixed economy with only one party in power, and "China will combine the market's 'invisible hand' and the government's 'visible hand'."[129]

There are as many motorists here now as cyclists, but the cyclists must now keep to cycleways as the car is taking over.

In 1978 the bicycle ruled, but the air quality was as awful as it is 50 years later, because of the burning of brown coal in all homes. In the last few days the authorities have told people to stay inside as the pollution levels have reached dangerous levels: 254 ppm of PM2.5 (particulate matter). Air quality is a public health issue and the greatest leaps a developing country can make are in the delivery of public goods: air and water quality, street safety, public healthcare, the rule of law, transparency and accountability. In 1978 it was smoke from millions of brown-coal-burning homes; today it's brown coal burning in hundreds of power stations.

On a recent visit I entered a friend's apartment in Shanghai through double-sealed doors. His family live in a building that is akin to a gated community, even if the security controls are to keep out the pollution rather than thieves.

Starbucks, who pay few taxes anywhere in the world, trade on the delivery of public services while they trumpet their caring coffee procurement and community spaces. "One shared planet", as long as someone else pays for the police. Also here in China, Tesco is struggling: there are piles of raw meat stacked up in the bargain section of the meat department which would never be allowed where Tesco is domiciled in the UK. They can show us happy farmers sifting coffee beans on the ground and pigs strolling across idyllic countryside in some faraway mythical land, but we're not supposed to see the unsanitized product, piled high as if in a local market.

The Hyatt Hotel at 100 Century Avenue, Shanghai is a millionaires' hotel, and on the top floors the restaurant dishes start at 250 renminbi (£32/US$37) but the same can be found in the basement restaurant for 12 renminbi. This is as it always was in Chinese restaurants, but writ larger now that the wealth divide is so vast.

Is there a crisis of identity here? Does the public matter? There are rules everywhere: to control the masses. According to Oxfam, 85 individuals have as much wealth as 50% of the world's population, and according to *Forbes* a growing number are Chinese. On a night cruise down the river in Shanghai, I asked one of them how he felt about China, the wealth divide, democracy and the Communist Party. This wasn't a dangerous conversation as everyone will discuss anything in private. He said that the Party was democratic and new ideas and leaders could and would grow in the Party "organically". Rather than democracy being represented in parliament or in a multi-party state in China, that democratic discussion takes place in the Party – people in the West don't understand this.

China's wealth has been created by bringing millions of young people in from the country to work in manufacturing facilities in the cities. This has denuded the countryside and left the old to fend for themselves in the villages, and created a very significant and dangerous (for the Party) divide between richer urban and poorer rural communities. Since the early 1980s, China has transformed from being a largely rural country with less than 20% of the population living in cities to more than 55% urbanized now. This movement of people has lifted more than 700 million people out of poverty, meaning that when we talk of global poverty alleviation in the last 50 years more than 90% of this has occurred in China: in a country with a single party and a mixed economy but with a rigid application of planning guidelines. It's not quite the neoliberal dream of small government, and it was learnt from the Japanese in the post World War II era, the Germans and the British (in a different era) that there is nothing more effective than targeted business working hand in hand with government, and vice versa, for the good of the country.

One of the most striking differences between talking to British and American people and talking to Indians and Chinese is that the latter two countries have a sense of history reaching back some 5,000 years. India and China dominated world trade up until the fifteenth century when first the Europeans and then after 1900 the USA started to take control of world trade and global exploration. The 500 years of overseas domination will not be forgotten in a hurry, a mistake that the West really does not understand when it comes to trade, global governance and terrorism emanating from outside Europe and the USA.

In an acknowledgement that these are issues of international importance, in 2015 the Chinese President Xi Jinping reminded "the mother of parliaments dating back to the thirteenth century" (Britain's) that China embraced the rule of law and "putting people first" 2,000 years ago.[130]

In 1978 when I first visited China I was on my way to live in Japan and found that the Japanese had Japanized their Western imports and not lost their own identity. So, as in China today, 50 years ago, superficially, Japan looked as if it was understandable through a Western lens, but it was only superficial. By 2025 66% of the world's population will live in Asia, with only 5% in the USA and 7% in Europe. Since 1945, one of the ways the West has maintained some sense of hegemony in Asia is through US military spending and superior technology. But even the US National Intelligence Council, which coordinates all US "intelligence", has said that "Pax Americana – the era of American ascendancy in international politics that began in 1945 – is fast winding down."[131]

In 2014 China joined the World Trade Organization, and countries and companies have been beating a path to what they think of as highly lucrative internal markets. In some cases they have been successful; in most cases the Chinese have the upper hand gaining control of essential infrastructure around the world and denying companies real internal access. Google, Amazon, Uber and Facebook have withdrawn their full-frontal assaults and where they have stayed they have gone into partnerships with Chinese state-owned or partially private companies. And they have had to accept controls on content and ways of doing business that would not be accepted in the West. The same is also true in India, Singapore and Hong Kong, where mostly US companies have had to contort themselves in order to remain in the market, mostly because they have been initially insensitive to local markets. A bit like trying to sell alcohol or non-Halal meat in an Arab country or pork in Israel.

Just as Japan fails to recognize the way South East Asia still feels aggrieved about its role in the 1930s and 1940s, so it is failing to reach a real rapprochement with China which is flexing its muscles in the South China Seas. This is challenging US client states like Japan, the Philippines and South Korea. Peace in this area seems within reach but only if these countries and the US have some sense of 5,000 years of history and not just the last 500, or the last 100.

Perhaps a sign that China has changed eradicably is when it comes to the dramatic turn-round in the one-child policy, which has not led to a rush to have more children. Urbanization, improved healthcare and wealth has changed the lives of hundreds of millions of people. In 2016, of the 11 million people eligible to have two children, only 1 million had applied to do so, and yet there will be 400 million people over 60 in a decade or so. The numbers, in the context of smaller countries, are managerially unimaginable.

In 2017 the world's bestselling mobile phone, America's Apple iPhone, is made in a free trade area of China, Shenzhen, in the Foxconn factory which is owned by Hon Tai Industry, a Taiwanese company. The USA has recovered technological innovation from Japan and also become the software innovator, China is currently the manufacturing heart of the world, and other countries act as intermediaries between the USA and difficult working conditions, as in the Foxconn factory.

Suicide rates at this factory can justifiably be favourably compared to other operations around the world and, despite very bad publicity in the last few years, they compare very well with most India and Pakistan factory deaths and with the average suicide rate in Chinese mainland factories. And international suicide rates prompt a whole range of questions. Why are former USSR countries and affluent countries like Japan and South Korea so predisposed to suicide? Generally, lower- or middle-income countries have the highest rates, with the above exceptions. In other words, because of cultural variations, unified explanations – the one-size-fits-all, homogenized and "end of history" theories – are not necessarily helpful. Just so with China.

The rise and fall of the American century: we share the same planet

In "The Fiddle and the Drum", written in 1969 by singer-song-writer Joni Mitchell, she sang "How did you come to trade the fiddle for the drum? . . . You raise your sticks and cry, and we fall . . .". This is normally heard as an anti-war song, but it gets to the heart of the conundrum that is the United States of America. A country with the highest of ideals, the epitome of freedom, justice and personal liberty, is also the country of poor universal health and social care, the highest obesity and gun ownership in the world, and a military budget that dwarfs the world. And yet Canadian Joni Mitchell, like many others around the world, wishes this country well: "But I can remember all the good things you are . . . O, America my friend . . .".

As a Special Advisor to the UN's Global Compact, I accepted an invitation to speak at the University of Minneapolis on the subject of corporate responsibility and the UN's Global Compact. Thankfully, it never occurred to me that one of the thousand or so people who turned up to listen to my talk might object to what I had to say and shoot me. One man did come up at the end and say, "I thought a lot of what you said was rubbish, but then I looked up your figures on the internet and you're right – thank you, I learnt a lot." Some relief on my part.

The university put me up in the Hilton Hotel in Mankato, just outside Minneapolis where I was to speak. The university staff were very kind and I was shown the Scandinavian houses and the local area – just like Sweden where I had lived, with lots of cold, snow in the winter and red houses. Waking up in the morning, I went down to breakfast and picked up the local newspaper and read that a new law now allowed the carrying of concealed weapons by citizens. But I was still surprised over breakfast to see a man cycling down the road with a rifle holder under the cross bar, and, when I went and made the mistake of walking – nobody walks – to the local cash machine, I was stunned to see signs outside both the church and a supermarket asking customers to leave their guns at the door. At breakfast a man was wearing a shirt with the letters W.R.A.N.G.L.E.R.S running vertically down. Running horizontally was the following: Western; Rangers; Against; No; Good; Lowdown; Environmentalist; Shitheads. On Fox News I heard a man say that environmentalists were pagans because "they love the planet more than people".

I am from another planet.

Perhaps the best example of American twentieth-century superiority, and a lack of international diplomacy and tact in a country where only 30% have passports, was an advertisement from Coca-Cola in the 1960s which featured pictures of Adolf Hitler, Lenin, Julius Caesar, Napoleon Bonaparte, Emperor Hirohito, and a Coca-Cola bottle with the line: "Only one [of these] launched a campaign that conquered the world. How did Coke succeed where history's most ambitious leaders failed? By choosing the right weapon. Advertising."[132]

Coca-Cola's main ingredient has been sucrose and sweeteners, and in the 1970s sucrose derived from maize became almost free as President Richard Nixon, down in the polls because of the Vietnam War and desperate for the farming vote, decided to subsidize high-fructose corn syrup (HFCS), a technology developed in Japan, as a way of buying the rural farming vote. It is now the basis of all US-exported fast food from Coke to Macs to pizza to muffins and is at the heart of the world's obesity epidemic, as HFCS replaced fat in these products[133] – but more of the link between wealth and health later in this chapter. Obesity has to be one of the new ways we rank (un)successful societies, and on that basis Japan, Italy and Sweden rank well above the USA, the UK, Mexico and South Africa.

On world obesity rankings, the Pacific islands come top by a long way, not as was thought for genetic reasons but because of a very unhealthy high-fat and -sugar diet. The same is also true of Mexico and South Africa, who are followed closely in the rankings by the whole of North America and much of Europe, but with the extraordinary exceptions of Sweden,

France, Denmark, Switzerland and Italy where high-carb diets are not packed with saturated fat and sugar and US portion size has been resisted. Overall, on an average basis, the least overweight countries are India, China and Japan.

The story of the world's biggest business, defence and war spending continues, with the global consultancy Deloitte triumphantly announcing

> A return to growth in 2016 is expected to be fueled by increases in the US defense budget, a resurgence of global security threats, and growth in defense budgets of key nations around the world ... The global aerospace and defense (A&D) industry is expected to return to growth in 2016 with total sector revenues estimated to grow at 3.0 percent ... This positive signal follows years of declining revenue growth ...[134]

According to Deloitte in 2013 revenue in this sector reached US$706 billion, earnings were US$63 billion, the operating margin 8.9%, and the return on invested capital 17.0%; the number of employees was 2,042,252, which does not include the number of people in uniform worldwide.[135] According to the Stockholm Peace Research Institute, total spending in 2015 rose as the US under President Obama sought to increase its capabilities, and the total global spend was US$1.7 trillion.[136] President Obama agreed an upgrade to the US's nuclear capability during his tenure – arguing that the risk of nuclear attack has increased – which will take until 2045 to deliver at a cost of some US$1 trillion. This is of great significance as he would like his healthcare reforms to be his legacy, but he may instead be remembered as the president who wanted to talk down a war on terrorism while dramatically increasing death from a distance through the use of drone attacks. While some defence spending is always necessary against the warmongers, the immoral, the tyrant and the unexpected, war is always a failure especially as, since the 1940s, it has almost always caused untold damage to civilians who have been used as collateral. And, despite rhetoric to the contrary and the Treaty on the Non-Proliferation of Nuclear Weapons, the number of nuclear warheads held by the US and other nuclear powers has increased not decreased.[137] What hypocricy that Obama is reported as saying of North Korea that "they are not very good at feeding their own people, but they invest a huge amount in their weapons". The US has an obesity epidemic with one-third morbidly obese and two-thirds overweight, and many North Koreans suffer from malnutrition and starvation.

If China's twentieth- and twenty-first-century development challenges other models of economic development and social progress, and Japan offers us lessons that remind us of the way in which the British formed a partnership between the state and corporations to build world-dominating businesses in previous centuries, then the USA offers us another divergence.

The liberalization of banking that began in 1979 with the ascendancy of President Ronald Reagan in the US and Prime Minister Margaret Thatcher in the UK, with copies of Friedrich Hayek and Milton Friedman in their pockets, saw a transformation of global capitalism that led to the credit crash in 2008/9.[138] These are the interpretations of avowed capitalists, not just mine. The 2008/9 crash united Alan Greenspan, US Federal Bank Chairman, 1987–2006; Paul Volcker, US Federal Bank Chairman, 1979–87; Warren Buffett, investor and the third richest man in the world; Andrew Haldane, Executive Director of the Bank of England; and Martin Wolf, chief economics commentator on the *FT*, in saying, to use Volcker's words, "the bright new financial system has failed the test of the marketplace".[139]

During the 30-year experiment in liberalization and privatization, the gross debt of the financial sector in the US rose from 22% of GDP to 117% and in the UK to 250%. The risk during this period was transferred to those least able to manage it, as has been the trend during previous crashes in globalization such as in the 1930s. In the twenty-first century the dominoes started to fall with sub-prime mortgages in the US, Northern Rock Bank in the UK, and all banks in Iceland. Had we learnt nothing from previous crashes where private debt became public debt? Had we not learnt that allowing markets to rip and credit to get out of control leads to depressions that cause great hardship to ordinary people and often leads to the rise of right-wing populist demagogues, as we are now witnessing across Europe and in the USA? As that unelected head of state and head of the Commonwealth, the British Queen, famously asked at the London School of Economics in November 2008: "Did nobody notice?"

The US has an obsession with what it calls small government, and yet the US military is the largest employer in the world with 3.2 million employees and a budget of US$523.9 billion for 2017 – the largest in the world. The UK's defence budget is about one-tenth of that. The US maintains the largest defence (war) forces in the world, with those 3.2 million personnel costing 3.3% of US GDP in 2015. This is four times that of China who spent 1.2%, and ten times that of the UK at 2%. It is no surprise given these figures that US airports are full of people in battle fatigues: this is a country at war, with a war economy.

In 2016 the UK spent about 8.5% of GDP, or £116.4 billion, on what is still the world's only free-at-the-point-of-delivery healthcare system. The US spends about twice as much as any other "advanced" economy on healthcare, but only half of this goes to front-line care, and even then it fails to cover 20 million people. What has come to be called "Obamacare" in the US would save about 45,000 premature deaths, but not the 13,000 killed by handguns or the 38,000 in car accidents every year.

When it comes to differences in political economies and the way the cake is sliced, most Europeans are shocked on visiting the US for the first time. The US is somewhere between Europe and India when it comes to social service provision and healthcare but is in a league of its own when it comes to gun control – or the lack of it – and attitudes to obesity and social care.

One of the great paradoxes of the US is the balance of nationalism and individualism. It is a well-known truism that one way to pull a nation together is to talk up external threats and make citizens fear "the other". And yet the US, more than many other countries, is a nation of migrants, but this means that it has had, and has, to bang the drum for what it means to be an American. Henry Kissinger, a former controversial Secretary of State, when returning from a visit to post World War II Europe, paraphrased J.K. Galbraith in speaking about New York: "alongside excessive wealth, unspeakable poverty. And then this individualism! You stand completely on your own, no one cares about you, you have to make your own way upwards."[140] Even "the world's most famous whistleblower", Edward Snowden, living in Moscow in 2016, said that his allegiance is still to the US despite a desire among many Americans to put him away for a long time.

Others have commented that President Barack Obama will be remembered as an intelligent adult in the White House, but more importantly that he was the first US President to have been a cultural outsider, with a backstory in Kenya and

Indonesia – and as a Black American. Obama also trained as a lawyer and did community work before entering politics. US individualism is also the basis of US exceptionalism, but, as Obama said, with a smile on his face: "I believe in American exceptionalism. Just as I suspect that the Brits believe in British exceptionalism, and the Greeks believe in Greek exceptionalism."[141] US citizens *are* exceptional in that only 30% hold a passport and anyone visiting the US is struck by the national myopia and the lack of media reporting from around the world except when it's about war, violence or terrorism, which makes the Americans among the least aware of how the world works.

One of the issues that confounds those who do not live in the US, and confounds many of my numerous US colleagues and friends, is the US obsession with guns. For someone like myself who has lived in the UK, Sweden, Japan and Australia, the idea of individuals carrying guns seems bizarre, like some throwback to medieval days, the dark ages. A personal recollection comes from London's hosting of the Olympic Games when visitors were amazed that police officers did not carry weapons. "How do the police work, without guns?" I was asked by an American on the first day of events – which, ironically, was fencing. The answer is that policing in Britain is based on the premise that the best policing is by the people, for the people, with the people. It has been commented that a British police officer is able to stand and talk to a crowd, or wade in, without fear of his or her weapon being taken, unlike in almost any other police force in the world.

Although overall crime is down over the last 30 years in the US – as it is in the UK – the perception of it being a more dangerous place has increased. I suspect in both countries this is because of the increased demand for dramatic, violence-related news and instant media images on social media platforms. So it is that a beheading becomes instantly available in our distraction economy. So crime and gun violence are down in the US, but gun ownership is up. The National Rifle Association says that the former is because of the latter – a self-fulfilling circle: "an armed society is a polite society". The right argues that most gun crime is "Black on Black", which marginalizes the problem as specific to one group within society rather than seeing it as a national issue. Gary Younge, who I came to realize was Black only after having seen him on television, points out the nervousness of living as a Black person in the US. In Chicago, the city the Obamas hail from and to which they return, some 30% of school students have witnessed a shooting. Younge is British, lived in the US for many years as a writer, and now lives back in the UK which he finds less polite but less deadly.

Australians would argue, after a mass gun tragedy in Tasmania in 1996, their amnesty, which netted 650,000 guns and significantly raised gun ownership rules, that their commonsense, humanity-based approach is what has significantly lowered gun death statistics. And this was from a right-wing prime minister, John Howard. The government gun buyback cost A$35 million in 1996. Since then, there have been no mass shootings (there were only 13 in the 20 years before the Tasmanian shooting), and, in the ten years since 1996, suicides, using any means, were down a staggering 74%.

There are many studies of gun control, homicides and police action from around the world, and it is another area where the US stands out dramatically from other countries that one might want to emulate – or cite as examples in describing successful political economies. For instance, the best gun control in the world is in Japan where there were just six handgun-related deaths in 2014 – much to the country's horror! There are six a day in the US. There were a total of 100 homicides of any category in London in the whole of 2015.

More people were shot by children in the US in 2013 than by terrorists. Between 1983 and 2013, 66% of all mass shootings (78) in 25 similar economies occurred in the US (the next highest is Germany with seven); there is direct correlation between gun ownership and mass shootings. If the controls that are exercised in Australia had been used in the US, most mass shootings would not have happened. In the same period, 3% of deaths from mass shootings occurred in the UK. There are 6.2 guns per 100 people in the UK, and 88.88 per 100 in the US.[142]

Fear in America escalated after the 9/11 attacks. The sanctity and exceptionalism of America had been penetrated. It was an horrendous attack which was shown live on television around the world. Just as I remember when John Kennedy and John Lennon were assassinated on the streets of America, so will we all remember 9/11: 2,996 people died and around 6,000 were injured in the bombings of the twin towers of the World Trade Center in New York and on the Pentagon in Virginia on 11 September 2001. For Americans, the inviolability of the country was a given, and the shock of the attack being organized from inside was as great as the attack itself. For Continental Europeans, one of the reasons for their tolerance, and the origins of the European Union, is because none of them feels territorially inviolable. For the British, it is different as they haven't been invaded since the arrival of the Normans in 1066, and this partially accounts for the vote to leave the EU on 23 June 2016. Travelling around Europe, one hardly notices moving from one country to another apart from the language on the road signs and the type of food on offer at roadside restaurants. I was recently waved through France, Italy, Germany and Switzerland in a single day without showing any identity papers.

Seventy years after the end of World War II, Europe is still rebuilding after the bloody first half of the twentieth century, and by rebuilding I mean building on the lessons learnt from the first decades of the Community. Driving across parts of Europe is to drive past numerous Ground Zero memorials, and, for the British, being vigilant became a way of life because of bombings from the IRA for some 30 years from the 1970s to 2001.

Immediately after 9/11, *Time* magazine talked of America's cathedrals being attacked – the World Trade Center. They published a piece by Lance Morrow in which he said

> hatred will not . . . be a difficult emotion to summon. Is the medicine too strong? Call it, rather, a wholesome and intelligent enmity – the sort that impels even such a prosperous, messily tolerant organism as America to act. Anyone who does not loathe the people who did these things, and the people who cheer them on, is too philosophical for decent company.[143]

Some would see this as a reasonable immediate reaction to such an awful act of terrorism, especially in America, but, reflecting on E.M. Forster's writing of tolerance while London was being bombed during World War II, it is possible to replace loathing and hate with sorrow and pragmatism. Morrow also said perhaps America had become complacent because of the good times since the mid-twentieth century: "Good times sometimes have a tendency to make Americans squalid . . . This is the moment of clarity. Let the civilized toughen up . . .".[144] As power slips away from the USA and Pax Americana slowly comes to an end and Russia challenges and China rises and India expands, the question is worth asking, as the *New Statesman* did:

> Americans would do well to ask themselves why, despite what should be an enormous propaganda advantage in beaming their way of life to every corner of the globe, their ideals and values have signally failed to inspire the Third World young in the way that Marxism did and Islam now does . . . The answer . . . is that American values too easily come over as shallow and hypocritical.[145]

The pictures of people running terrified from the collapsing Twin Towers in New York in 2001 seem reminiscent of pictures we have all seen of people running from warfare in Vietnam, Iraq, Syria . . . from American and British bombs. But President George W. Bush in his televised address to the nation after 9/11 said that America had been attacked "because we're the brightest beacon for freedom and opportunity in the world". This exceptionalism has some truth but is also seriously deluded with a large touch of myopia. But he may, like UK Prime Minister Tony Blair, who, against all the intelligence advice, followed America into Afghanistan and Iraq, have believed his own rhetoric when he said, "When we act we create our own reality."[146]

In the 1980s I wrote my doctorate on the relationship between parliament, government and defence decision-making, essentially about transparency and accountability. We also made a major BBC TV series on defence management which was broadcast in 1986. One of my key interviewees later rose to be very senior in intelligence, and in the aftermath of the Iraq invasion he told me that Blair was "deluded" about WMD (weapons of mass destruction) in Iraq. I said that "deluded" was a very strong word to use about a prime minister. He affirmed his use of the word by saying that there was no definitive evidence of WMD in Iraq but Blair was unmoved by evidence.

Away from mass shootings and bombings, the world today is generally fearful, as I report in this book from encounters in Greece, Switzerland and other countries. Some have said that the US is having a collective nervous breakdown; in the wake of the 2008/9 credit crash, and in the case of the 9/11 attacks in the US, this is true across the globalized world. Simon Heffer, a UK columnist for a right-wing newspaper, reports that he found "an exceptionally unhappy country: polarized, introspective, angry, disappointed, and, above all, fearful".[147] Columbia professor and Pulitzer Prize-winning novelist Richard Ford says "America is getting nuttier and nuttier." He comments on the fact that Texas allows students to take concealed weapons into college "to prevent mass shootings". He says this has "some blunt logic, especially for people who fantasize infantile, action-figure scenarios as their primary uplink".[148] He says he declines speaking at Texan universities in case he says something that offends a 21-year-old member of the audience who might shoot him: this puts the debate in Europe about freedom of speech on campuses in perspective. Ironically, Ford and his wife now carry guns because of fears for their safety. They join the world's most heavily armed militia, larger than any of the world's armies: 8.2 million assault weapons in personal possession.

Perhaps new US President Trump reflects the view that Americans have of life generally when he said, after his election in reference to waterboarding as torture, "Anger? There's plenty of anger right now. How can you have more? The world is a mess, the world is as angry as it gets. What, you think this will cause a little more anger? The world is an angry place. The world is a total mess . . . the world is a mess."[149] His view of life is also that of commentators like Pulitzer Prize-winning author and *New York Times* columnist Thomas Friedman whose view of everything is also whizz, bang, wallop, and aggressive. We must apparently fight everything all the time. Life is a war, not negotiated, and certainly not feminized.

And then there's the obesity, which is a shock. So many people not just fat but morbidly obese, feasting on awful high-fat, high-salt, high-sugar food. And, apparently, because of portion sizes – the amount of food that Americans routinely put in front of themselves – 50% of food in the US is wasted while obesity nonetheless escalates; it's almost as bad in Europe at 30%.

This divided country – where I feel very safe in making my frequent visits to New York and Boston to talk to "the liberal elite" at the UN or among Boston's 31 superior academic establishments – is different from other advanced industrial democracies in other ways: in other, very exceptional, ways. The UK may be heading in the direction of the US on many counts, but not on gun control, the death penalty or incarceration. These two countries' wealth distribution differs greatly from almost all other members of the OECD, especially when it comes to those things that make a civilized society: healthcare, housing, welfare support and education. Talking about exceptionalism, the US writer Teju Cole points out that poor White working-class people saying they feel disadvantaged is ironic because, as he says, quoting James Baldwin, "To be a negro in this country and to be relatively conscious is to be in a rage all the time."[150] African Americans have mostly felt disadvantaged most of the time, and yet they are being disparaged by those who feel they are newly disadvantaged. US journalist

Ta-Nehisi Coates, author of *Between the World and Me*, points out that the US is always saying it needs to have a conversation about race, but has no idea where to start.[151]

And Americans need to have a conversation about aggression, violence and death. Some 38,000 people are killed in car accidents a year, and about 13,000 by guns. The lowest risks of death come from refugees, asteroids, hornets, sharks and earthquakes. The highest comes from all accidents, chronic disease and walking. Americans are 129,000 more likely to die of a gun assault or 407,000 times more likely to die in a car accident than to die at the hands of a refugee. And in 2016 there were 740 people on death row, but you are much more likely to be killed by the police before trial than by state execution.[152]

As previously noted, Gary Younge, a Black Briton, who lived for many years in the USA, feels safer in the UK but "public drunkenness is far more common [and] the culture feels both far more violent and less deadly".[153] Hanna Rosin, a White *US* author, commenting on books by White *UK* author Ruth Whippman, who has written about living in America, and not always sympathetically, was coruscating when talking about the French. Apparently, they are unfriendly, boring, eat the same food . . . and she says the French would describe her as a stupid American. *Vive la différence*! US President George W. Bush once said that Europe is "a museum" and, famously, that the French "don't even have a word for 'entrepreneur'"! How we laughed. And now we have Trump . . . and we're not laughing.

Security and insecurity: "I am not a goat"

We are at a point where we can become proactive and seize power for common global good or where we can turn inward and seize power for parochialism, fear and probably increased violence between nations, tribes and individuals. As the US peace activist John Paul Lederach says, at the moment we are reactively running around correcting the consequences of violence,[154] even if we have managed to stop a major global conflagration as witnessed in the first half of the twentieth century. Is it possible to make peace on Earth, now for this generation, or are we forever to be cursed by those religions that claim salvation in the next life? Those in the USA and the UK who claim that the poor are feckless and lacking in motivation display a thought pattern like that of many Indians I have met, who tell me that street-begging families must go through such a stage in order to ascend to a higher caste in the next life—which is a delusion similar to the one held by those who kill for the Taliban or the Islamic State in order to gain a place in heaven.

On one occasion, in the small Italian town of Fano, having been approached a dozen times by beggars in the street, my wife and I are sitting having coffee. A man approaches and asks for money, and I say "Sorry, but no" and gesture with my arm. He goes away but at once returns and straight to my face says, "I'm not a goat ... I'm not a goat to be waved away like that ... I'm not a goat." I am humbled beyond belief, and remain so. I must be careful how I reject pleas to the rich and comfortable from the rejected and the poor.

What story should we tell for the twenty-first century? That it was the best of times or the worst of times? "It was the best of times, it was the worst of times, it was the age of wisdom, it was the age of foolishness, it was the epoch of belief, it was the epoch of incredulity, it was the season of Light, it was the season of Darkness, it was the spring of hope, it was the winter of despair."[155] It depends where you have found yourself in the world today.

I'm sitting here writing this in a converted barn in rural Italy with the warm Mediterranean just a few minutes away. I've just listened to the BBC news on the internet. Soon I will contact friends and children by text and Whateversup and by email. Children, you couldn't do this when Daddy and Mummy were children: out of touch meant out of touch. The aerogramme thin blue paper would arrive sporadically, postal service permitting, and the sighting of a newspaper from back home was a cake-like treat, to be devoured slowly over the following week. The times they have a-changed.

This week the Paris Agreement on climate change has all but been ratified as the EU sends its formal support, and the UN Security Council has appointed António Guterres as its new Secretary-General. As Christiana Figueres, who negotiated the Agreement, tweeted "Bittersweet results #NextSG. Bitter: not a woman. Sweet: by far the best man in the race."[156] Guterres's appointment highlights what is and will continue to be one of this century's crucial issues: the population churn of refugees from war and despoliation, and economic migrants and asylum seekers from oppression and genocide. As I write, the top five countries of origin for refugees are Syria, Afghanistan, Somalia, Sudan and South Sudan, and the countries that are hosting the largest refugee settlements are Turkey (2.5 million), Pakistan (1.6 million), Lebanon (1.1 million), Iran (1 million) and Ethiopia (0.75 million). The countries with the greatest capacity to host refugees but with the smallest settlements are the USA, the UK, China and Russia – all members of the UN Security

Council that has just appointed a new UN Secretary-General who was previously in charge of the UN High Commission for Refugees and sees this as one of the greatest challenges for the UN.

The outgoing UN Secretary-General, Ban Ki-moon, has talked about managing the representatives of 193 member countries, 15 agencies, 12 funds, 40,000 people and a budget of $5.5 billion (2014–15). I have experienced his quiet but smiling style at first hand, and it was in contrast to his predecessor Kofi Annan who had a quiet but authoritative presence when he walked in the room. All UN Secretary-Generals would agree with Ban Ki-moon when he says "time is limited: I am dealing with 193 nations . . . There are almost unlimited actors who I have to have harmonious relations with."[157] The difference that Kofi Annan made is in relations between the UN and business through his sponsorship of the UN Global Compact, which was also supported by Ban Ki-moon. Annan was the first UN Secretary-General to have an MBA. As a Special Advisor to his initiative, I had first-hand experience of the way all but the most enlightened businesses treated this attempt to ameliorate the downside of a rapacious model of capitalism and make boardroom concerns of human rights, labour issues, environmental protection and transparency. But just as important was observing the tribal workings of the different UN agencies who wanted to protect their special interests and, with a few exceptions, were largely uninterested in a transdisciplinary or complexity approach.

All those who know the UN's work understand that quietly, in the margins, without recognition, it has made significant changes in the areas of communications, medicine, food distribution, conflict resolution, education, and support for marginalized people including women.

A number of commentators on the UN have called for greater cross-agency approaches to problems, and in particular bringing together civil society groups and the private sector. Indeed, some have called for the UN to be reinvented based on its charter, which talks of "we, the people".

Migration and refugee issues have been exploited by populist right-wing individuals and political parties who have spread fear and misinformation in the USA and Europe. It is an important issue, and the action that needs to be taken is in two areas: preventing the wars, genocides and oppression that cause people to abandon their lives in search of new ones, and correcting the misinformation that abounds in the USA and Europe, in particular about the differences between refugees, asylum seekers and economic migrants. Votes in affluent societies against migrants are as much votes against the economic globalization process as they are about fears of "the other".

Building on the UN's work in the area of human security, begun in 1994, a group of independent thinkers in the UK have produced a report which begins by highlighting how they think the world is now perceived:

> We all want to feel safe and secure in our beds at night, but the news is dominated by tension, conflict and violence across the world. At home, financial worries and concerns about our changing society are widespread. Internationally, the horrifying violence in the Middle East and beyond is a source of great alarm, while global perils, such as climate change, are deepening a common sense of uncertainty about the future.[158]

Their remedy is based on thinking of security as:

> the extent to which we strive to treat ourselves, our fellow human beings, and the planet on which we depend with respect and care. This is an "ecological" approach to security, because it invests faith in the possibility of building sufficiently healthy relationships at every level of our societies worldwide. It is distinct from a "militarist" approach, in which the state reacts to "threats" as they emerge, gravitating towards armed force.[159]

Redefining security in this way accords with the themes of this book of rethinking political economy, and the structure of society, as going beyond formal, informal and institutional structures and better understanding the expressions that bind people together. However, we have to come to terms with, and face head on, the model(s) of capitalism that dominates most people's lives. While the Ammerdown Report, quoted above, makes significant reference to the military-industrial-financial economy, it does not offer solutions to the necessary corrections that need to be made to today's capitalism, although one of the report's authors, Paul Rogers, briefly covers the economics of change in his book *Irregular War*.[160]

The report makes reference to the public's concern on climate change. The problem with this major twenty-first-century issue is that for most people it is slow-moving and difficult to pin down – and the science is complex. When talking about climate change, reference should be made to a number of other understandings, including work at the scientific level by the Stockholm Resilience Centre on the nine planetary boundaries that control our environment. These concern ozone levels, biodiversity, chemical use, climate change, ocean acidification, freshwater cycles, land use, nitrogen and phosphorus inputs, and atmospheric aerosols.[161]

The Sustainable Development Goals (SDGs) were launched in 2015 to replace, or update, the Millennium Development Goals (MDGs). They included reference to the private sector through instruments like the UN Global Compact. However, the intellectual gap between the goals of the United Nations and the idea that "responsible business", as a form of voluntarism, can achieve them, makes delivery of the SDGs via these means an unlikely prospect. What the UN Global Compact refers to as "business engagement architecture" makes the right points in linking the SDGs and long-term business goals: revenue growth, resource productivity and risk management. The same document says that "companies realize that their ability to prosper and grow depends on the existence of a prosperous and sustainable society, and that social deprivation and ecological destruction can have negative material impacts on supply chain, capital flows and employee productivity".[162] Not yet, and not enough. And many companies make money by trading on these adverse conditions. There are many companies that exist because they exploit labour, despoil the environment, abuse human rights, and openly play on the weaker points of human nature. To think otherwise is naïve. The areas of possibilities and priorities in the same document in reality consist of major systems changes and innovations: educational reform, women's empowerment and gender equality, energy and climate, good governance and human rights. The most realistic policy proposals made by the UN Global Compact are for increased transparency and disclosure, encouraging public–private partnerships, and creating incentives for "more responsible corporate behaviour". But the required cultural change and adaptation of capitalism is immense and not at all likely to come about through a mixture of enlightened leadership in business, voluntarism, and nudges towards morality.

Quite apart from the notion that there are divergences and different "cultures of capitalism", it is clear that the various corporate social responsibility initiatives over the last few decades have failed to stop the growing wealth inequality, CO_2 emissions and child labour. And this is precisely because these trends have been abetted by good people with strong moral compasses who do not recognize that, as US economist Michael Sandel says, the direction of global of capitalism is away from "*having* a market economy towards *becoming* a market society" and the commoditization of everything.[163]

So, for example, Facebook has sought to quantify and capitalize on social relations, but by contrast Wikipedia has remained non-profit. In the UK all blood donations are given freely as an altruistic act, while in the US some donors are paid as a contractual exchange. How also can I quantify the differences in culture – which is clearly linked to how we see all social relations including those that are economic?

In the car-free Swiss Alps town of Zermatt I was confronted with differences in the culture of everyday exchange, and they forced me to sit back and think. I was due to catch the early-morning train down the mountain to Visp where my car was parked, a journey of about an hour. I chose too large a takeaway coffee cup for my espresso and the woman at the counter didn't believe it was a demi-tasse, so she insisted on looking inside. In broken English she told me that nowadays people are so dishonest and so stressed that they can't be believed and they even start fights. How things have changed in the last few years. It's not the coffee, she says, it's because people are much more stressed. The disruption across Europe because of the population churn is palpable. People are friendly when you get them to engage, but initially suspicious and fearful. I have seen this in Greece. And now here in

Zermatt. On the train, the German mountaineering lad has his dirty shoes on the seats, and on the seat opposite me an older Japanese woman opposite me is massaging her bare feet using shiatsu. *Vive la différence*! But my sensibilities in both cases are affected.

Michael Sandel worries that, in discussing the morality of markets, public discourse may not be up to the task because of "the persisting power and prestige of market thinking" and, referring to the USA, "the rancour and bitterness of public discourse".[164] For UK Marxist commentator Terry Eagleton,

> the modern period in particular has made moral questions hard to handle. It is not only because in a complex society there are too many answers rather than too few; it is because modern history makes it especially hard to think in non-instrumental terms. Modern capitalist societies are so preoccupied with thinking in terms of means and goals, that their moral thinking becomes infected as well.[165]

Modern capitalist economics, often referred to as neoliberalism, tends to take love, hope and art as givens to be exploited rather than acknowledged, fed or nurtured. And so it is that it often debases public goods such as our natural love and concern for each other, or our democratic processes, which it overpowers with financial influence. Max Weber, writing in the late nineteenth and early twentieth centuries, said that culture was a combination of beliefs, values and dispositions. It is to this understanding that we need to return if we are to reform discussions on political economy; but how many politicians are willing to talk of love, or of art as messages – and make reference without fear of ridicule to the founders of sociology and political economy: Max Weber, Émile Durkheim and Karl Marx?

There are many who argue that the left, or progressive politics, has not found the language to articulate the obvious fears, frustrations and grievances that concern people across all democratic societies – and therefore we endure the rise of populist, right-wing xenophobes, homophobes and misogynists and what are called far-left leaders who seek to capture this protest without articulating a modern politics that will deal with the world as it is today. And yet there are societies that can articulate, live and embrace most of what we need to think, do and live the good society. It is these positive differences and divergences that need teasing out.

In putting forward an argument for an acknowledgement of diversity in different political economies and some sense of a unifying body of thinking and practice in what constitutes the good society, I am not going down the Francis Fukuyama route of the end of history. His vision was based on a rather boring, certainly hegemonic, world in which a particular model of economics had triumphed. No, I am pointing out that, while I believe in liberal democracy, its ambassadors and exemplars on Earth are dynamic, diverse, interactive, interdependent – and they range from Japan to Sweden to Greece. They are very different places to live, work, eat, play, make art and watch a play. I agree with Pankaj Mishra that it is *not* true that "bourgeois democracy has solved the riddle of history, and a global capitalist economy [has ushered in] worldwide prosperity" except that it *is* true that a combination of factors, which include capitalism, democracy, collectivism and civil rights movements, have raised most people's standard of living significantly over the last 70 years.[166]

The reason so many people in OECD countries around the world are angry is partly because they are not beneficiaries, partly because they do not believe in this model or in progressive modernism per se, and partly because they hold hundreds of years of resentment about the oppressive nature of colonialism. Without seeing this as a complex issue with very varied perspectives, we will not be able to formulate a progressive agenda that raises the tide for everyone and comes to terms with the current modes of terrorism, from Al Qaeda to Isis to Anders Breivik and to the US. What seems most important is to recognize that any progress that we have made is not just because of trade, markets, management, technology and economic organization, but also because of the development of ideas, and art, and expression and humanity, most particularly the feminization of decision-making. It has been a balance between individualism and collectivism: between liberty and control, and between freedom and choice.

Let me make a brief argument for international bodies, apart from the UN, which we have already discussed, that ostensibly promote global public goods. There has been much criticism in recent years of corruption, a lack of accountability and megalomania in sports bodies such as FIFA (the Fédération Internationale de Football Association) and the IOC (International Olympic Committee). It is clear that they need fundamental reform, and it is possible to write them off as not worthy of their ideals, run by madly corrupt men with Trumpism as their defining way of life. But sport is the lifeblood of many people, and, despite corruption at the top, these festivals of sport, whether in football or athletics, have provided highs as well as lows. Nowhere have I seen accounts that contrast the lows of corruption and incompetence with the highs of World Cup finals or athletic triumphs on the track, in the pool or on the road.

Just like the argument that the UN is an organization that has failed to live up to its mission or obligations, the notion of disbanding FIFA or the IOC is cowardly. The aim should be that, having got this far, we should work hard to reform them, to remove the petty dictators and grand egos so that these organizations can be better. The dysfunctional and the sociopaths will always seek power and prestige, so it is essential to ensure that constitutions have checks and balances run by people whose highest ideal is to maintain the organization's integrity.

Tofu, Boeing and democracy

I am in Japan and a good friend has taken us to eat in a Matsumoto restaurant which sells only food based on tofu. The owner is in his eighties, and he and his wife are doing what they have done all their lives and what their predecessors did for a thousand years before them, using the same cooking, preparation and processing methods as ever, starting with the soya bean. It's a successful business, too, and supplies most of the restaurants in this Japanese spa town with their many *onsen* where for many happy hours I have lain naked in near-boiling water with my friend discussing the world and business, and the Japanese view of it all. Tofu has become ubiquitous around the world as a healthy form of protein, even if it's not always appreciated – unlike sushi, another Japanese export. Japan is still the third or fourth largest economy in the world even if we don't hear much about it, apart from its stagflation, concentrating instead on its near neighbour, China. Japan has managed to maintain ancient traditions like *onsen* and tofu while pushing ahead with innovations in electronic and motor manu-facturing and creating one of the world's most affluent, peace-ful and egalitarian societies.

I have been struck by other examples of technology that has endured, albeit for nothing like as long as tofu production. In Greece I was reminded of the Honda 50 ridden by our hotel owner to get around – it was only 50 years old. Launched in 1958, the Honda 50 motorcycle is an icon of the twentieth cen-tury: some 90 million have been sold so far and supported per-haps a billion bottoms. Similarly, the Land Rover was phased out in 2016 after 2 million had been sold around the world to farmers, the military and, latterly, deluded city folk who liked a basic but very reliable ride. It started production ten years before the Honda 50, in 1948.

And since 1970 I've travelled the world on the successor to the B-29 that bombed Hiroshima and Nagasaki: the Boe-ing 747, which has now sold over 1,500 in its original version and carried millions of people around the world. During its millions of passenger-miles, only 3,718 lives have been lost in B747 crashes – a figure that makes it safer than being almost anywhere else on the planet. Certainly, travelling by car is potentially more life-threatening than the likelihood of cancer or a heart attack, and dangerous driving is the largest single killer on the African continent. As a BA crew member told me: "If it's a Boeing, it's going!"

I wear Church's shoes, a product that started production in 1873 in Northampton, in northern England. Five thou-sand handmade pairs are produced every week from natural materials. Their shoe research institution began what has now become the University of Northampton.

These are examples of the rich tapestry of life, and very much part of the love, hope and art that makes up the culture of society. My life has been as much Church's, Boeing, tofu, Land Rover and Honda 50 as it has representative parliament, education, my family and friends, and the freedoms I have enjoyed as part of an energetic, renewing democracy.

As the world faces a revolution in manufacturing and working practices, and a meltdown because of perceived and real inequality, it is often technology that changes everything – and causes revolution. Take the current debate around climate change and the use of fossil fuels. As the world releases coal seam gas through what is known as fracking, it is worth remembering the revolution that was the *Industrial* Revolution. In 1756 Scottish engineer James Watt had an idea for a condenser that would make steam power much more efficient, by three times, and therefore make coal stocks, its fuel, go much further. This technology revolutionized industry and started the machine age, just as computer information technology has revolutionized life in the last 50 years and computer manufacturing is beginning to revolutionize life again now.

Love, markets and democracy

It is more than ten years after the end of apartheid and I've been taken to the opening of a women's enterprise centre in one of Stellenbosch's large informal townships where most of South Africa's population live. The last 20 years post-apartheid have provided some political freedom, and a ground-breaking constitution because of the embedding of sustainability and the recognition of the different language and ethnic groups in the country; but economic apartheid is still the rule in this mostly one-party state. Much as I want to, I cannot eat the celebratory

dish presented to me at this auspicious event. It's grey and rub-
bery and is made with tripe: sheep's stomach. The ladies are
very considerate and, when they have stopped laughing kindly
at my discomfort, they take it away and we continue with the
ceremony. The point about the food is important because,
under apartheid, Blacks were not allowed the main meat of
animals, only the offal and parts that the Whites would not
eat. This means that, even today, sheep heads and tripe are
common celebratory meals. With reference to Weber's descrip-
tion of culture, there is as much to celebrate in South African
townships as there is in Japanese towns. When the men were
sent away to work in the largely Anglo American mines, the
women and children supported each other in subsistence lifestyles making the most of whatever resources became available. Love and hope were the métier and the art was obvious
in the music, graffiti and street festivals between the hard work
and striving for freedom.

There is no less love and hope in a South African informal
settlement, in a Turkish refugee camp, in a Paris *arrondisse-
ment*, on the streets of New York, or in the bars of Beijing: but
the measure of the pudding is in the mix of mutual trust across
the whole of society, the distribution of wealth, the feeling of
belonging and commonality, and the physical structures and
institutions that provide the everyday background for people's
everyday lives to be free, fair, secure and worthwhile.

As the economist Partha Dasgupta wrote in his *Economics: A Very Short Introduction*, his (and our) economics has to
deal with two ten-year-old fictional grandchildren: Becky in the
affluent USA and Desta in Ethiopia who, by contrast, lives on
a subsistence basis. Becky's parents are professional people and
highly educated. Desta's parents are professional farmers but
they're illiterate and innumerate.[167]

What fails at the moment is the link between the economics that dominates the current round of globalization (this being the seventh or so) and the delivery of wealth and the enhancement and protection of public goods. How to mend this dysfunction is the challenge for this century, and it will not be solved by voluntarism or appeals either to altruism or to the morality of business. It requires clear policy movement and distinguished intellectual thinking as well as real leadership that can take democratic society with it. The current model of capitalism is at the heart of the climate change crisis, at the heart of the world's biggest business – war materials (US$1,244 billion a year[168]), and causes much, but not all, of the increasing wealth inequality that now threatens the stability of all societies, rich and poor. The political denominations of left and right are obsolete. All economies are interdependent; all governments are interventionist; all policies rely on mixing public, private and third-sector interests; all governments have policies on working with global markets; and all governments have to manage their relations with regional and global institutions. The issues that face all potential political leaders and political parties are: managing turbulence and the new social media democracy; distributing public services and wealth and managing inequality; intervening during periods of market failure; increasing transparency, accountability and reducing corruption; managing in a multi-stakeholder environment; and decarbonizing manufacturing and consumption.

But at the global level there is often little discussion of ideas and politics. This is the testimony of Nobel economics prizewinner Joseph Stiglitz on joining the International Monetary Fund (IMF) as a Chief Economist from 1997–99:

> I discovered that neither good economics nor good
> politics dominated the formulation of policy ...
> Decisions were made on the basis of what seemed
> a curious blend of ideology and bad economics,
> dogma that sometimes seemed to be thinly veiling
> special interests.[169]

Similar comments have been made by Yanis Varoufakis when he was briefly the Greek Finance Minister in 2015. He commented that he never had a discussion about philosophy or ideas with the "troika" – the ECB (European Central Bank), the IMF (International Monetary Fund) and the EU Commission – involved in managing Greece's debt. This meant that there was never a substantive discussion on how Greece's debt had happened, and what it meant for global finance, and how global finance may be failing. He told the meeting that the Greek people were opposed to the stringency of the troika's austerity approach, and has quoted a senior IMF official as replying: "Democracy must not be allowed to get in the way of the market."[170]

If these commentators are not substantive enough, then consider former Bank of England Governor Mervyn King, or Martin Wolff from the *FT*, or the financier Warren Buffett, or the historian Paul Kennedy, who have all made serious suggestions on reforming capitalism – because the default position of the current model is unstable and needs state intervention, at an international level. Neoliberalism is an ideology. As Terry Eagleton wrote in *After Theory* in 2003: "Ideology is around to make us feel necessary; philosophy is on hand to remind us that we are not." The plea in this book is to look beyond ideology and accept the need to think philosophically about the future. It is love that binds us, hope that is our daily experience, and art that gives us the ways and means to see the past, present and future differently. And it is populism based on hate, fear that is manifest in racism, misogyny and xenophobia.

In June 2016 the IMF acknowledged the evidence – and the arguments of people like Stiglitz and many others – and published an article that in terms of global financial structuring was momentous. In the article, headlined "Neoliberalism: Oversold?", three of the IMF's lead economists said that, while neoliberalism had been beneficial in increasing wealth globally by freeing up world trade, lowering trade barriers and diminishing the role of government in economic planning overall, it was now seen as an impediment to growth and had significantly increased inequality. Their realization was that the creation of too much credit, often by private banks, has led to what the Bank of England's Governor Mark Carney has called "a low-growth, low-inflation, low-interest-rate equilibrium"; the Bank of International Settlements says that "the global economy seems unable to return to sustainable and balanced growth".[171]

It is welcome news that the IMF has recognized that the evidence does not support the narrow strictures that the Washington Consensus has imposed on large and small economies globally, often with disastrous results; but the authors' failure to link the imposition of their policies with the politics of action seems to lack a moral perspective. For instance, they use Chile as an example of a country that, they say, benefitted from liberalization but has now had to develop a more nuanced approach introducing increased state involvement in the economy and the distribution of wealth and welfare benefits because the market has failed to do this. But they do not comment on how their policies were enacted, and how it took a military coup to overthrow an elected government with support from the USA and the CIA to effect this. And there is no reference to the 30,000 or so people who exercised their rights to free speech and whose whereabouts are still unknown.[172] The CIA's comments at the time of the Chilean coup that brought Pinochet to power are the same as those made to Yanis Varafoukis: "Democracy must not be allowed to get in the way of the market."

While the IMF, at a theoretical level, in 2016 acknowledged the limitation of the market as god, it will take much more time to correct the way global financial markets operate and to deal with the flood of cheap money desperately looking for quick, and often instant algorithmic, gain. It is also notable that the other two parts of the troika negotiating Greece's debt, the ECB and the European Commission, have not noted publicly the limitations of their policies. This is mostly because the ECB is tasked with recycling German surpluses, an economy that has a natural fear of credit. For the US the opposite is true because it floats on other countries' credit, particularly that of Japan and China, and the US economy remains buoyant as a self-satisfying high-growth one. Even at the height of the credit crash in 2008/9, investors still sought comfort by investing in the USA, because where else could they go?

Economics is about life and thus should take direction from a moral compass, however much some economists may want to deny the idea. That is why this book is concerned about discussing ideas not usually linked to economics: love, hope and art.

3

Health, wealth and social progress

> I took my shoes and socks off and left them on a
>   rock,
> I know not where,
> And walked home barefoot alone.
> I stood with one foot in the Atlantic and the other
>   in the Pacific,
> I know not how,
> And walked forever happily to my home.
> The icy water and the burning sun tore at my
>   body
> and ripped asunder my flesh,
> And I was in heaven as I walked home.
>
> MM, Cape of Good Hope, South Africa, 2015

I've chosen to focus on a mixture of countries around the world in this book, and they are a mixture of developing, emerging and developed economies: China, India, Japan, the USA, the UK, Sweden, Italy, Greece, South Africa and Australia. Two perspectives are necessary when linking health, wealth and longevity. First, for developing countries the least they need to do is provide housing, clean water, security (personal, tribal and national), education and transparency. Second, much of the literature on longevity derives from developed countries where the basic bar of living long enough to die of old age has driven both an academic interest in living long, happy lives and an economic drive to sell pharmaceutical and other products to an ageing population.

With these caveats in mind, it is possible to link health, wealth and longevity – and the answers are not obvious and contradict some commonly held nostrums. For instance, obesity is not necessarily causally linked to poverty, and longevity is not just the preserve of rich countries and affluent people.

My interest in health not only derives from it being a fundamental element of the good society, but because at the time of writing I am a cancer survivor, or thriver. At least three times in the last six years I have been told I have months, or at worst weeks, to live. I have had a survival plan which I have tried to adhere to for the whole six years. Everyone wants to see this. But the greatest assets are research, a plan, a positive attitude and consistency: follow it every day. My lessons are built into this chapter, but the principles are no-brainers, even if following them is tough. *Every* day be consistent on diet, sleep and rest; exercise (*every* day, even when on chemo); and have something to do: be useful to society and to yourself.[173]

The last 100 years have seen a dramatic change in attitudes to, and our experience of, mortality. Until recent times, death came swiftly as a result of illness. Today this is rare; with the exception of gun deaths, car accidents and heart attacks, most people die slow, lingering, uncomfortable deaths, thereby consuming vast resources in healthcare. Humans have had about

100,000 years on Earth and for most of this period the average age of death was about 30. Even in 1900 world life expectancy was 31, and 2,000 years earlier, in Roman times, it was 28. By the mid-twentieth century in Europe and North America it was 65 and now it's in the mid-eighties. So, as recently as 100 years ago, most people died before they got old. For us this is an affluent luxury; just think of the 1965 song by The Who, "My Generation", which contains the line "Hope I die before I get old". The writer, Pete Townshend, aged 70 in 2015, said he was just joking.

We are the first people to live life with surplus energy: never before have humans had enough. We have adapted over millennia so that we survive and so that we can have as many offspring as possible. As human evolutionary biologist Daniel Lieberman says: "As a result our bodies don't do the right things in the environment we live in today."[174] For instance, to stigmatize people who are obese is to fail to recognize that their environment contains far too much stuff to eat: fattening "food" is far too cheap and portion sizes are abusive. These people are products of evolution and simply following their basic biological urges. It takes training, willpower and public policy to change the food environment and curb corporate excess.

One day I'm lying on my trolley at the end of a five-hour chemo download when suddenly the air is filled with the smell of rancid fat and burnt chicken. The woman next to me, also on an expensive drip, has been provided with a nourishing meal from the hospital café of fried chicken and chips. She is morbidly obese, and, like the smokers who stand outside the hospital entrance puffing away, the hospital turns a blind eye; yet in both cases the hospital should simply ban fast food and smoking from within 50 metres of anywhere.

My oncologist tells me, when I discuss this with him, that patients understand when he talks to them about the deleterious effects of smoking and alcohol but not when he talks about obesity, let alone simply being overweight.[175]

One of the first things you learn when mining the literature on health, wealth and longevity is that genes affect your body size and shape but not necessarily your life expectancy. If your parents are tall, there is a very good possibility that you will be too, but in most cases if they both died aged 30 there is no reason why you shouldn't live much longer. Second, attitudes to life and death, at the beginning and end of life, are the same all over the world: we all want our loved ones near us, and we all prefer comfort to medicine and technology. Third, it's best to think positive: you can override genetic predisposition and your life chances by how you think, and what you do with your life, and how you live your life. So education and the control of advertising become crucial factors in determining health outcomes if not necessarily standards of living.

Humanity's greatest killers have in the past been pestilence, famine and pandemics, along with our predisposition to annihilate one another. But even this fourth factor has receded since 1945 and most people now die of degenerative or human-made diseases. Success breeds dissatisfaction. Population increase is as much because we are living longer as it is because of increased fertility and declining infant mortality; and, as we grow richer, we have smaller families if we have access to birth control and women are empowered. So, once again, education and universal emancipation are fundamental issues in linking health, wealth and longevity.

Just as with the internet and social media, we forget our evolutionary past at our peril when it comes to health issues: we must not forget our prolonged development as human beings in attempting to engage with innovations in science and technology. Just as our brains have developed "fight or flight" protection, particularly in men, so too our bodies can absorb fat as a buffer against scarcity. The social-media-driven distraction economy grips us, as do high-fat, high-sugar foods – and the avaricious know this. And populist, unprincipled politicians know this when they feed us fear or hope.

Lessons from longevity

Watching the world go by in Tokyo, Beijing, Milan and Stockholm, you wonder why there is so little obesity in these four cities; doing the same in Los Angeles, Delhi, London and Sydney, you wonder why there is so much obesity. The link isn't poverty: it's political economy, or capitalism.

It is possible to argue that a propensity to obesity is genetic, but this is a cop-out, because the blame lies in targeting poorly educated people in exactly the same way as the tobacco industry used to target people globally but now confines its immoral marketing to developing countries. A 2016 US report said that most Americans saw obesity as a greater threat than cancer, and that the problem was a lack of willpower. In reality, it's a mixture of willpower, the power of advertising, the availability of cheap sugar- and fat-rich foods, and the normalization of the sight of obese people. In Italy, France, Switzerland and Japan you very rarely see obese people, whereas some one-third of American, Australian, Mexican, South African and British people are not just overweight, they are clinically obese. An Australian GP once said to me that Australia would be fitter in every sense – emotionally, physically, economically and socially – if everyone lost three kilos (seven pounds) in weight.

Sitting, waiting for the doctor who will tell you if you are to live or to die, to have hope or to slowly succumb, has occupied many hours and weeks over the last six years. Three times I have lain post-op, coming round slowly through the fog of morphine, descending from the ceiling, pumping the button to ascend again, and truly believing in transcendent drugs. Bliss. I have come close to death many times, and once nearly fell over the edge in 2016, before a heart procedure to drain my pericardial sac of 1.7 litres of cancerous effusion saved the day – and me. Cancer. Starting with bladder, and a nephrectomy, then a tumour radiated near that site, followed by a total of 36 weeks of chemotherapy over a five-year period, and since then being told "there is nothing more we can do" – go home and die, you have "a matter of weeks", checking in to a hospice, making funeral arrangements, putting my affairs in order, saying goodbye to my family. And then, nine months later, writing this paragraph and feeling fine, with the friendly experts confounded, nay, dumbfounded.

Waiting rooms are rarely bright and cheerful, however much nursing and admin staff do their best to be uplifting; and, throughout the world, they have screens pumping out the lowest level of commercial television replete with ironic ads for life insurance and drugs that will save my life. How many people have died inside, waiting in these morbid places? I have found waiting rooms in palliative care hospices and funeral parlours more uplifting.

And I ask the question: Given that most people die at the top of the bell curve and I'm at the sharp right end, what research has been done on survivors? And the answer: very little because there's no money to be made out of those who survive that long, but there is money to be made out of those on the upward curve and at the top of the bell curve.

But this isn't wholly true. While very little time, attention or money has been devoted to looking at those people who survive cancer, significant research has been carried out on those communities of people around the world who live longest, and have the lowest rates of those chronic diseases that kill people in Western societies: cancer, heart disease, Alzheimer's, and Parkinson's. Many years ago, while attending a UN conference in New York, I chanced to spend time with a man who had carried out research on this topic for the World Health Organization (WHO). He told me that often it was not whole populations that had significant longevity, but groups of people living in specific communities. After extensive field trips and in-depth scientific analysis, his team had concluded that there were three important factors in the low incidence of disease and the high incidence of longevity in these communities. The first two are relatively obvious, and they are diet and exercise: a poor diet and a lack of exercise kills people. Secondary contributors to these two indicators are obesity, poor sanitation and housing, and war. Wars kill people, and increase stress for those who experience them but survive. Poverty also kills.

Failing to remember our evolutionary past – that we are animals with the explicit need to exercise regularly and keep our soft-skinned selves well oiled, sleek and supple – is a determiner of early death. Some one-third of the world needlessly suffer from malnutrition, insecurity, war and poverty; but here we are interested in those two-thirds of the world's population who have choices, or whose governments have choices through public policy to make or break the link between health, wealth and social progress. It is clear that it is possible to make choices that ensure that most people have long, healthy and relatively happy lives but that at the moment the healthcare business is as much a corrupt racket as the military-industrial complex, international finance, and the fast-food and sugar industries.

Returning to the WHO study, the third category, after diet and exercise, is where things become really interesting. My WHO researcher said the terminology they eventually settled on was very contentious, and linguistically difficult. He said that some referred to this third area as happiness, others as well-being, and others as lifestyle, but they – the commission – wanted to call it "usefulness". This means how people fit into a community, how they feel valued, and how the community values them. None of the communities with the highest longevity statistics discarded those who stopped work, or retired, in the way neo-industrial societies now do where, when you retire, there is often a tendency to scratch around for something to do, to make yourself useful. The good society recognizes your talent and wisdom and says, "We still want you: you are useful, and we want you to feel part of us."

One of the greatest challenges in countries across the whole world this century – in all five continents – is the changing demographic distribution. Improved healthcare, female emancipation and empowerment, and rising incomes have produced a significant increase in two groups: young people who need jobs and purpose, and elderly people who need purpose, to be wanted and social care.

The three essential components of longevity are therefore seen to be: a good diet, plenty of exercise and being part of the community – "usefulness". Then the breakdown of these three components becomes interesting, and complex. And the politics becomes entwined with economics, and the issue of entitlement becomes paramount because it is clear that some societies do not tend towards caring for all, but to caring for individuals who can pick themselves up. Longevity is an issue of collectivism and community. It is clear that longevity is an art, and involves loving all members of the community and hoping that they will all prosper together.

Interestingly, none of my 20 or so oncologists, urologists and other medical experts, academic, private and public, in Australia or the UK, have pointed me in the direction of a dietician or a lifestyle expert. And none of them have mentioned the research on those groups who lived long, relatively healthy lives. Why not? The answers lie in two areas: the structure of knowledge that denies complex linkages; and the fact that the healthcare business is an industry driven by profits and pharma companies. The literature on both sides of the Atlantic, and in other parts of the world from Africa to Australasia to Japan, is concerned with costs, the science of new drugs, ageing populations and the profitability of drug companies. Very rarely is there a celebration of what is known as positive deviance: in other words, those people that live longest. The fact is that healthcare is at the centre of the current model of global capitalism, and, like banking, is broken and in need of fundamental reform.

That elites know how to keep healthy seems obvious: that's why they're elite. For instance, England's chief medical officer, Dame Sally Davies, takes exercise early every morning. She knows that it reduces cancer risk, improves mental health and improves quality of life. She recommends everyone takes 150 minutes of exercise a week, that they cut down on alcohol, and she knows that the misuse of antibiotics will "kill us off before climate change"[176] If Davies in her position knows this, why does nothing happen? Is it because the alcohol, fast-food and pharma industries are too powerful, or that politicians are either ignorant, lacking in bravery or complicit in what is a moral indictment of public policy? I ask my oncologist, and he replies that for anything to change in the UK's NHS takes a long time, but that what I am talking about is long-term and systemic – and that's not on the table. He is also slightly defensive as if I'm suggesting that his practice is bad, which I'm not. On reflection, and in other conversations, he says he knows that we could reduce cancers in the UK significantly if we followed the points in this chapter and the following appendix. But these are matters for political economy not the siloes of health "care", or as he calls it the "national illness service".

The Somme, Beveridge and public healthcare

Franklin D. Roosevelt's New Deal introduced between 1933 and 1938 in the USA presaged an understanding that society did exist and that government could and should have some control on public events through the use of judicious interventions and targeted public infrastructure spending. These initiatives were driven by the Great Depression and provided support for the unemployed and poor while attempting to restore the economy and reform the financial system that had led to the depression.

In 1916 the Battle of the Somme killed or wounded some one million men over a six-month period, many of whom on conscription were found to be suffering from numerous ailments and malnutrition. The war to end all wars was followed just a few decades later by World War II, and just a few kilometres away an Allied force landed in Normandy on the D-Day beaches, and again many of the best and brightest of men from across Europe died for freedom and solidarity. And again they, and those they left behind at home, were determined that this should be a war that redefined the good society, that shook up the old order, that mixed and matched wealth creation with wealth distribution. So it was that the 1945 UK General Election threw out the prime minister for war, Winston Churchill, and gave the Labour Party, led by Clement Attlee, a thumping majority which allowed them to manage the peace.

But it was a UK report that took a real leap into a space not heretofore entered by government to any great extent. It argued that society had a moral commitment to care for *everyone* "from cradle to grave" by tackling (the report's capital letters): Want; Disease; Ignorance; Squalor; and Ignorance. William Beveridge was not a socialist, but a liberal in both senses, who had been a senior civil servant and a director of the London School of Economics (LSE). Like UK Prime Minister Clement Attlee, he had had a privileged upbringing and had worked at Toynbee Hall, a university settlement in London where future leaders worked with people living in poverty and acted as a think-tank for ideas and policy. Just as Karl Marx said that he was never a Marxist, so William Beveridge was never a socialist, and yet both provided some of the foundations for a good society – a sound social democracy. Beveridge was following in the footsteps of the Liberal government from 1904–14 which had introduced unemployment benefits and old-age benefits. Chancellor Lloyd George had introduced social insurance and significant redistributive tax initiatives between 1908 and 1911. Both Beveridge and Attlee were disciples of Sidney and Beatrice Webb, founders of the LSE and the Fabian Society and authors of a 1909 report on the Poor Law. Like Beveridge, Attlee had taught at the LSE, where they first met.[177]

In the second decade of the twenty-first century it is important to note that all members of the OECD and many others

– all those countries with the means – have adopted some form of *universal* public health and social care provision, with the exception of the USA.

It is also worth noting that the Beveridge Report was published two years into World War II. The first and second World Wars had thrown men and women together and into jobs that had mixed and matched talent, opportunity and necessity rather than operating under Britain's outdated class and trades system. Alongside this churning milieu was the fact that, on recruitment, many men were found to be unable to perform active service due to illness and malnutrition. For once, Britain was one country together facing two scourges: fascism and welfare inadequacy. The 300-page report sold 635,000 copies, including a cheap copy distributed to all the armed forces. It united left and right, and the momentum it created was unstoppable – even though some on the right thought it too invasive of the state and corrupting of the poor, and some on the left at first thought it too means-testing and not supportive of trade unionism. But the left quickly adopted the report's recommendations and ran with it held high, as if it was their report, which it wasn't. And, 60 years later, a Conservative prime minister was to describe the report's off-spring, the National Health Service, as the nearest thing the British had to a religion. So significant was the report that a copy was found in Adolf Hitler's bunker with a note saying that it was a good fit with Germany's national socialism. The key distinguishing point, however, is that *universal* welfare provision has to be universal: for all, forever, without attachment to gender, class, level of affluence, religion, skin colour, sexuality or ethnicity. It was based on love and hope, whereas Nazism was based on fear, anger and hate. Beware those who peddle division.

If this was a revolutionary time, Beveridge certainly embraced the need for radical change:

> A revolutionary moment in the world's history is a time for revolutions, not for patching.
>
> Now, when the war is abolishing landmarks of every kind, is the time opportunity for using experience in a clear field.
>
> ... organisation of social insurance should be treated as one part only of a comprehensive policy of social progress.[178]

Many commentators have pointed out that the British were fighting, in both World Wars, on two fronts: against Germany and fascist tyranny, and against want, fear and against the tyranny of a capitalist system that had seemed hell-bent on perpetuating old divisions of poverty and affluence, struggle and privilege.

The Labour victory in 1945, at the end of World War II, came as a complete shock to Winston Churchill, and the world, not least because the new prime minister Clement Attlee was many things that Churchill was not. He was modest, quiet, and not a good speech-maker, but he had great integrity and moral authority, and experience in government as deputy prime minister during the war, and he bestraddled the various tribes of the British Labour Party. Churchill said that Attlee was "a modest man, with much to be modest about". Churchill may have won the war, but Attlee won the peace. The various Labour factions spent much of his highly successful period in office from 1945 to 1950 trying to remove him. Attlee's Minister of Health, Aneurin (Nye) Bevan said of Attlee that "he brings to the fierce struggle of politics the tepid enthusiasm of a lazy summer afternoon at a cricket match". But perhaps the art of the successful leader is being quiet and firm, sure and resolute, a listener and a decider, a unifier and a bestraddler. Churchill is for war, Attlee is for peace: must we always be at war?

At the end of his tenure, Attlee's government had introduced the National Health Service and free-at-the-point-of-delivery universal welfare provisions "from cradle to grave"; provided unparalleled educational opportunities for demobbed service people of all ranks and classes; established the National Parks in the UK; nationalized the railway and many other industries; helped enable the foundation of the United Nations and NATO; triggered the decolonization of India in 1947; and given the UK an independent nuclear capability: not a small list for a five-year period. He said he was a "supporter of World Government . . . Impractical, they say, but not so impractical as trying to run the world of sovereign States equipped with hydrogen bombs . . ."[179]

As a man with an imperial background in birth and education and links to the East India Company, he had not recognized Britain's geopolitical demise, but he had provided the greatest opportunities for social mobility that the country had ever seen and confounded the Americans with an Anglo-European model of the good society founded on egalitarianism, redistribution and liberal ideas. The division with the US is perhaps best shown in two issues which now dominate political affairs worldwide. During the war the US and the UK had agreed to share all their knowledge on atomic issues, but the US reneged on this at the end of the war. In 1945 the US had extended the UK, in its penurious condition, a loan, but now the Americans were endeavouring to prevent it from being used for health and welfare support, as they saw this as "financing socialism". In both cases it was the US not Albion that was being perfidious.

The revolution in support, opportunity and equality in the UK was to reach its height under another Labour prime minister, Harold Wilson, in the late 1960s. It has been in decline ever since, while still maintaining the broad provisions of the welfare state brought about by an Act of Parliament in 1948. Churchill was to accuse Attlee of being influenced by European socialists, but Attlee's retort was that Churchill was high on Austrian economist Friedrich von Hayek's *The Road to Serfdom*, published in 1944 and later adopted even more biblically by Margaret Thatcher and Ronald Reagan in the late 1970s.[180]

Clem Attlee later wrote that his transformation from patrician to socialist and from Tory (i.e. Conservative) to Labour Party member meant renouncing his Christianity and his *noblesse oblige*: as he put it: "I had been ready to do anything for the poor except get off their backs."[181] The welfare state gave everyone equal opportunities without the stigma of means testing: it was a citizen's entitlement.

Four Acts of Parliament came into force in 1948 covering national insurance, industrial injuries, free school dinners, health and welfare. By the end of the year almost 100% of GPs (general medical practitioners) had joined, and 75% of the population had made a visit and signed up. Attlee described it as "the most comprehensive system of social security ever introduced into any country". But these acts, and the Beveridge Report, did not turn Britain into a socialist paradise; rather, they emphasized collectivism and the need for everyone to make a contribution through national insurance payments *and* "The State . . . should not stifle incentive, opportunity, responsibility."[182] Britain has remained a relatively prosperous country with a capitalist ethos, entrepreneurship and creativity, as well as having a significant safety net since that time.

At the heart of this brief dip into the historical origins of what is certainly one of the most significant achievements in the history of humanity – as significant as agriculture, the Industrial Revolution, the development of nuclear weapons and the internet – is the fact that the good society based on love, hope and art must have as one of its foundations the collective, publicly funded, universal provision of health and social care from cradle to grave. How else can we call ourselves civilized? If we do not care for those who cannot help themselves, how should we sleep at night? What matters is the quality of the healthcare delivered and its universality. In the good society, looking after the sick, the young and old, and the infirm is a fundamental along with civic squares, crime-free communities and beautiful parks.

The world's first free-at-the-point-of-delivery universal healthcare service stumbles on in Britain, much beloved by its population and much assaulted by neoliberals who want to get a hook on its financial flows to make a quick profit. Comparing percentages of GDP spent on healthcare tells you little, as the US apparently spends some 17% of GDP on healthcare but only 50% of this reaches the front line, putting it in line with France or Germany, and leaving some 45 million people with only emergency provision. The UK's NHS is the world's fifth largest employer at 1.7 million employees, a table that is led by the US Department of Defense (3.2 million), China's People's Liberation Army (2.3 million), Walmart (2.1 million) and McDonald's (1.9 million).[183]

Britain continues to spend proportionally less of its GDP on healthcare than most other OECD countries, and under all Conservative governments since 1984 spending has fallen. Yet it continues to deliver extraordinarily well, despite its curtailment, such that it is recognized globally as one of the most cost-efficient health services in the world. Its figures on improvements in chronic illness continue to match most other countries with universal public healthcare, despite the fact that Britain now ranks as being the third highest in relative poverty in the OECD; and its infant mortality statistics, while much better than the USA, are not keeping up with the highest-ranking countries such as Germany, Japan and France. As the twenty-first century proceeds, Britain currently gets its health-care on the cheap.

What does this tell us, if anything at all? Perhaps that providing a universal healthcare system on a national basis is akin to running a well-resourced military, or a global retail and fast-food operation. It certainly requires similar management perspectives and skills, and it is easy to see how the neoliberals eye it eagerly. It is a wonder that it consistently scores extraordinarily well for its delivery-per-pound as it struggles to administer to an ageing population, to those who sometimes abuse it without thinking first, and in an age of rampant medical equipment and pharmaceutical cost increases from a rapacious global industry.

Before we look further at comparative healthcare statistics, it is worth noting that universal free-at-the-point-of-delivery healthcare is not only possible in affluent countries but has been achieved in a number of developing countries. Cuba, with 11.2 million people and an economy smaller than most UK cities, has achieved better outcomes than the vast majority of countries worldwide. Under Fidel and Raúl Castro, most people have lived frugal lives, often at subsistence level, but all the research shows that they have lived happier lives than many other people around the world and that they have better literacy and numeracy than people in their tormentor country, the USA. They also have a lower infant mortality rate than most countries at 4.3 per 1,000 live births, and life expectancy comparable to much richer countries. Their rankings on chronic illness are also among the world's best. So, for the good society, what can be learnt? An almost 100% literacy rate means that the population are well informed and active participants in healthcare, where Cuba spends 10% of GDP. The emphasis has been on primary care, preventative care and public health across the whole community (unlike the UK, for instance) – it is universal. Not surprisingly, obesity is almost non-existent. Each community has a local physician and a nurse, and all households are visited by a physician annually. Cuba has also trained so many medical experts and developed so many pharmaceutical products that medicine is a significant earner of foreign currency.[184]

Trawling the data on healthcare reveals a paradox: there are some very clear immediate lessons and, after that, at almost every level, complexity kicks in. There are a few straight lines, or direct causal links, but then the overlapping circles yield ambiguities and anomalies galore. This is another lesson for those who want to write healthcare policy.[185]

Once again the hard research data only throws a partial light on the minutiae of difference and diversity. For instance, why is it that US *public* healthcare spending is the highest in the world and yet they have some of the worst health outcomes in the OECD, and far worse than countries like Cuba and Costa Rica? Why is there a high obesity cluster of the USA, New Zealand, Australia, Canada and the UK, and a 50% lower obesity cluster of France, Denmark, Italy, Netherlands, Sweden and Switzerland? And why is Japan's obesity rate one of the world's lowest at 3.7% against one of the world's highest in the USA of 35.3% (using BMI [body mass index] categories), when both countries have personal incomes that dwarf most other countries? Why do Americans see their GPs much less than most other countries and the Japanese average more than 12 visits a year? How does the UK consistently outperform almost every other country in terms of value for money when it "only" spends about 8% of GDP on healthcare and the US twice that amount? Why is infant mortality higher in Denmark, New Zealand, Switzerland, France and the UK than in Japan, Norway and Sweden? And, of course, why is US infant mortality nearly twice the OECD median? And why are cancer care outcomes so different in various countries?

We might look more closely at US healthcare, because in this area it is aberrant (as it is in others, such as gun control, capital punishment and incarceration). A number of reports, but most particularly by the Commonwealth Fund (an independent US health think-tank), make the following points. Within the OECD it is the only country not to have a publicly funded universal healthcare system and it also spends significantly less than other countries on social care; its costs are driven by medical technology and care prices for like-for-like treatments across the OECD. Why, for instance, does it cost twice as much to have an operation in the US than the next most expensive OECD country, Australia?

The US spends 17.1% of GPP on healthcare, versus France's 11.6% and the UK's 8.8% but with significantly lower universal outcomes. The US also has the highest private medicine costs and by far the largest out-of-pocket costs. The US spends twice as much per patient on its *limited public* healthcare as the UK with *universal* provision, but with worse outcomes. The US, along with New Zealand, spends more on pharmaceuticals than other countries, and the US relies on expensive diagnostic technology more than most countries. There has been vast expenditure on MRI (magnetic resonance imaging) and

CT (computerised tomography) scanning technology as ways of extracting wealth from customers (known as patients elsewhere). But, as we know, increased testing does not necessarily lead to better outcomes, and prostate cancer testing is a good example. At the age of 65, 68% of Americans have at least two chronic conditions, whereas the British score only 33%. Is this because the US health industry runs on fear and over-diagnosis while the UK's NHS waits for symptoms to appear? Whatever the reason, early mortality rates are better in the UK than in the US for most chronic conditions, if not for cancer.

The Japanese do not die of heart disease, while New Zealand tops the table on this indicator. Germany, Denmark and the US leave others far behind for amputations due to diabetes – but perhaps in those countries they do not see this intervention as a last resort? Or sales of mobility scooters are higher?

Through the fog, the literature does produce some clear lessons for policy-makers:

- Health *and* social care outcomes are always a mix of issues, uppermost being diet, exercise and "usefulness" – they are indivisible.

- Measures to reduce obesity and increase exercise follow through on all chronic diseases – heart disease, diabetes, respiratory problems, mental health, cancer and arthritis.

- Warnings, advice and pricing are important in changing dietary patterns.

- It *is* possible to change national diet and exercise behaviours within a ten-year period.

- Controlling costs in all areas from medical professionals, medical equipment manufacturers and pharmaceutical companies is absolutely crucial.

- Primary education on diet and exercise as well as *universal* early diagnosis of symptoms is essential.

- Primary healthcare, illness and social care are the same thing – all part of a complete package.

- Free-at-the-point-of-delivery universal healthcare works *if* a nation is inclusive and wants to raise all its citizens' health outcomes.

Returning to the UK in 1940, at the outbreak of World War II, a direct link can be made to wartime conditions and progressive health policy in the twenty-first century. From inauspicious origins, Frederick Marquis rose to become a leading retailer, Minister for Food under Winston Churchill in the wartime coalition government, and after the war Chair of the Conservative Party. He had an interest in retail distribution and logistics as well as knowledge of health and diet. During the war, when a significant proportion of the nation's food had to be imported, he prioritized nutritious items over sugar and fats. In the period 1940–45, cultivated land in the UK rose from 12.9 million acres to 19.4 million and the number of tractors from 55,000 to 175,000; and, by 1944, 66% of food was produced in Britain.

John Boyd Orr, post-war head of the UN Food and Agricultural Organization, said that, under Lord Woolton – as Frederick Marquis had become – the UK had produced

> for the first time in modern history a food plan
> based on the nutritional needs of the people, with

> priority rationing for mothers and children . . . the
> rich got less to eat, which did them no harm, and
> the poor . . . got a diet adequate for health, with
> free orange juice, cod liver oil, extra milk . . .[186]

Sugar rationing continued until 1953 and, given the current obesity pandemic, this seems salient. I was born in 1953 and had a ration card: eight years after the end of the war and five years after the introduction of the National Health Service. This generation in the UK, or those that survived, were some of the healthiest people on the planet, walking everywhere, picking blackberries in the country lanes and growing their own potatoes and brassicas. They are the generation that is now living into its eighties, nineties and beyond, unlike the current generation who show declining levels of health due to high-sugar diets and sedentary lifestyles.

During World War II everyone felt useful, even if they were opposed to the war by virtue of conscientious objection or had lost loved ones (and almost all fell into this latter category because of the two World Wars), and most people in cities lived in a state of fear that the next bomb had their name on it. When I watch the bombing of Syrian cities now, I am reminded of my mother taking me to bomb sites in London and saying, "This is what war does: it destroys all our hard-earned efforts."

Both my parents were conscientious objectors and Quakers – in that order – and my father taught throughout World War II and ran summer camps in the Cotswolds for orphaned kids. He argued that this war was to be expected given all previous wars, and he cited the punitive conditions of the Treaty of Versailles forced on Germany at the end of World War I, which would inevitably lead to a reaction among the German people – which produced a fascist leader and World War II. Many have compared the ascent of facsism in 1938 to the xenophobic backlash of 2016, and are fearful of the rise of the far right in the US and Europe in coming years.

We can learn, we can learn; we can remember, remember, remember, if we so wish. But so often we forget and repeat our mistakes. But life does *not* have to be "a tale told by an idiot, full of sound and fury, signifying nothing"[187] – if we can learn and progress. And progress we have, overall – between the wars, genocides, famines and disease – by learning, collectivizing and overcoming the worst fearful natures of ourselves. As T.S. Eliot wrote, "... the end of all our exploring / Will be to arrive where we started / And know the place for the first time."[188] And in this exploration we must get back to asking: what does it mean to be alive, to be human? Recently, in the BBC Reith Lectures, Atul Gawande asked the same question as I am asking in this section on health, wealth and social progress: "Lacking a coherent view of how people might live successfully all the way to their very end, we have allowed our fates to be controlled by the imperatives of medicine, technology and strangers."[189]

I am, as I've said before, a cancer survivor. Being told you are going to die in the very near future, as I have been three times in the last six years, is akin to being told that there's bad weather about: you either survive it or you don't. I echo the story told of the palaeontologist Steven Jay Gould who lived 20 years after he had been told he had about eight months to live. Like him I have noted the long tail of those who survive *and*, most importantly, how I might perhaps learn from research and experience and "rage, rage against the dying of the light".[190] Except that anger is a worthless emotion in this situation: what is required is calm – persistent, consistent attention to changing one's lifestyle to help one's immune system to help itself. *If* you are lucky, and I take that element on board, then my motto is: if "they" give you one month, you can make it two; if "they" give you one year, you can make it two; and so on. Nelson Mandela said that one of his management maxims was "know when to quit"; so too Atul Gawande quotes Plato's Laches in which Socrates is discussing courage. Courage is being knowledgeable about both the constraints of life and our biology, and how to rest our souls. That is courage. And I would accord with Gawande, and my current oncologist, that the real job of medicine is not just to ensure health and combat illness but to "enable well-being".[191]

You think I'm going to die, and I'm not. I think I'm going to live, and I won't. But these are not different positions: they are different dispositions. How many near-deads do you see every day? How many people do you try to give hope to every day?

Near death

My wife drives me to the NHS hospital at 00.17 on a Monday. We arrive in Accident and Emergency and I say, "I can't breathe." Immediately, a team springs into action – it's not Friday night. Over the next few hours I am assessed for every possible possibility. The first nurse conducts test after test, calmly, clinically, calculatedly. There's no chair for my wife, but that's a minor detail as some nights they probably don't want relatives hanging around. A woman in another cubicle is screaming at everyone: "Don't take my baby", "You bastards" and "Fuck off." Later, it turns out she didn't have a baby for anyone to take . . .

Katy, the doctor, tells me to be quiet and just answer yes or no to her questions. She's done this before. Been here before. Doesn't know I'm not drunk or mad. Again, she's looking at every possibility for my condition, and I'm impressed at this whole-person approach. Why, then, has my hospital experience been siloed into one or another category? Cancer, coronary, urological? Katy goes away for my test results and comes back relaxed and smiling (what has happened en route?) and makes a few jokes. She says that, like me, she also wears odd socks because she can't be bothered to sort them. I want to tell her I do it in a deliberate manner every morning matching the colours and thinking about the process – a sort of meditation. Katy's much more straightforward: no pretentious bullshit. She calls in Richard, a junior coronary doctor, who is also good at talking to patients. They are both so lovely – and seemingly so young, but then I'm 63 and they're in their twenties – that I want to hug them. If I could breathe, that is.

Richard shows me my heart pumping away on an MRI scanner. Look, he says, it should be here but instead it's all the way over here. Indeed, it now fills up a space where my left lung ought to be. Instead of my heart sitting in a small sac of juice, it's swimming in a large bag of fluid. He'll have to phone his boss to ask his advice. It's three in the morning, I say. He says, "That's his job!" Dr Rob Lowe is woken and he advises that I be admitted, with no treatment until the morning, and no drugs whatsoever so they can monitor my heart which is going like a steam engine uphill.

Five hours after we entered the hospital, I'm admitted to the coronary care unit. My wife's still on her feet, bless her. I'm now not allowed to walk: I have a driver, a night-shift hospital porter. Like all the others, salt of the earth, as good as it gets, except he can't drive a trolley and we crash our way across the hospital. "One of the wheels is stuck," he says. This seems to be the least of my problems.

I haven't paid any money and I haven't been asked for a health insurance card. It's all about entitlement in a civilized society – in the good society.

Later they all tell me, "You should be dead. We don't understand why you're not." My oncologist gives me weeks to live, and when I live another year he writes that I have defied all medical knowledge. Against this backdrop, I have written this book, this year.

Mindlessness

And, finally, searching for happiness does not work. It's like good art – it comes up on you unexpectedly. Indeed, there is good reason to live life mindlessly, not mindfully, as this will encourage you to wander around and take more exercise, vary your diet, and meet new people ... these things are part of the good community and difficult to legislate for – or are they?

On a sunny day under the trees, I'm sipping my coffee in a car-free square, dipping my brioche for breakfast, watching the children play, listening to the chat around me, talking to my wife about the play last night and today's weather, and knowing that we've all pulled together this last week, and that, should we need them, the services of life are but a call away.

And the bells are calling, calling us away, for redemption and ritual on Sunday morning. But first the espresso, before praying to whoever your god is. Then to break bread and drink wine around the flowered-bedecked tablecloth that my grandmother used on special occasions, wiping the last of the ragu from the plate and smiling across at friends and family opposite. It's a scene from a Swedish Carl Larsson painting or an Italian square or a restaurant in China. And, after, a nap, or sex. Or both. It's a wonderful life.

4

In search of the good society in the post-human world

This book's title is a reference to the esteemed and much-awarded economist G.K. Galbraith's 1996 book *The Good Society: The Humane Agenda*.[192] In that excellent book he lays the groundwork for a good society operating within a capitalist economy. As a self-declared liberal, he was denounced by some in the extreme USA as a Communist, and yet all he had said accords with how most Europeans, Australasians and Japanese see the good society. He talked of the redistributive necessity of taxation, of the absolute necessity of good education for all for the sake of democracy, social mobility and mental well-being, and concern and care for the environment. He was not hot on examples, and his was a theoretical perspective that has stood the test of the last 20 years. He saw the need for competition, creativity and innovation, along with equality and a lack of discrimination, to create a meritocratic society that would be fair for all. What was not to like? Well, there were some, and still are today, who saw and see as false targets his emphasis on equal education for all, his highlighting of racial discrimination in the USA, and his concern for the environment.

Perhaps his inability to find examples of his good society is best summed up in an interview he gave to the BBC in 1982 in which he said that "music has largely passed me by". Does this tell us more about him as a dry academic rather than a man living life to the full? I find it difficult to imagine a good life without the sound of music, a love of art, and brioche and coffee, but these essences of a wonderful life are absent from his books. Perhaps he might be forgiven, as a piece of music that hadn't passed him by, and which he described as his favourite, was "Oh What a Beautiful Morning" by Rodgers and Hammerstein from the musical *Oklahoma*: a song as optimistic as *The Good Society*.

Bombs, climate change and men

I was born eight years after the end of World War II in 1953, and I had a wartime ration card which limited our sugar purchases. My father taught at Birmingham University and my mother was a full-time housewife. We kept chickens in our back garden and grew most of our vegetables in an allotment provided by the local council. At the age of five, it was perfectly safe enough for me to be taking the bus to school and home by myself. We acquired our first car (second-hand) just before I was born, our first television when I was 12, and I didn't experience central heating until I was in my twenties.

We were beneficiaries of the National Health Service and my three siblings and I and our mother all survived childbirth and grew up healthy and protected. We had one telephone in the freezing hall.

I remember, aged 11, singing "She Loves You" in my primary-school playground; in 1967 the Beatles sang "I admit it's getting better / A little better all the time / Yes I admit it's getting better / It's getting better since you've been mine". It's true that the 1960s were the most productive, most egalitarian and more expressive period in the whole of British history. It also turns out that people were happiest at this time. In 1957, when Prime Minister Harold Macmillan, from a patrician perspective, said "You've never had it so good", he was correct, and most people in the UK felt happy with their lot.

The USA continued to expand economically and most Americans felt richer. The USA continued its involvement in wars – the Korean War from 1950 to 1953 and the Vietnam War from 1955 to 1975. From the end of World War II until 1991, the USA was also engaged in a Cold War with the Soviet Union.

Out of the ashes of World War II came many of the issues that are now in need of re-examination and reassessment. They could best be described as trends, and will be seen in historical terms as important developments in social progress. It does not underplay the seriousness and failures of this period, of which there are many, to argue that generally and globally this period was a period of peace, development and human betterment. For some, this is attributable to growing economic expansion under the mantle of capitalism and increasing world trade, but this is as simplistic a view as arguing that it is only the checks and balances against unbridled capitalism that have led to social progress. What is true is that it was a combination, or an integration, of all aspects of an open society that have led to what we refer to as progress, and that this was aligned with significant developments in science and technology. Clean water and penicillin, television and safe food, the internet and the internal combustion engine, democracy and international air travel, have created the liberal world that we now all share. Those who do not live in democracies (about 50%) or do not have access to mobile phones (about 5%) are affected by all those who do.

This period of globalization, which is by no means the first, started in 1945 with America's bestriding of the planet both commercially and militarily. Globalization can be thought of as having its origins several thousand years ago in terms of the movement of individuals, goods and ideas. The period of globalization since 1945, and particularly since the birth of the internet, has exponentially increased the churn of images, ideas, information and virtuality.

The establishment of the UN in 1945 and the 1948 UN Declaration of Human Rights set the tone for a period where negotiation was the norm, even if it was often hard-won, tortuous and has had tenuous outcomes. The fact that humanity had discovered how to destroy itself through nuclear conflagration had concentrated even the most warlike minds, as did two lengthy bloody World Wars. The main threat in the West was now thought of as the challenge to capitalism through badly managed centrally planned economies where the state and the people were the only shareholders. While this threat has now been diminished, the threat to capitalism now comes from extreme financialization and bank deregulation which will destroy our ability to control public and private policy. The post-1945 battle was between capitalism and communism, but it was also about global dominance, freedom and democracy.

Liberalism through an emphasis on individualism and human rights would win the day, and democracy would be played out across the world such that by 1992 Francis Fukuyama was able to assert that liberal democratic capitalism had won the argument and was the practical modus operandi for the world.[193] Nuancing this over-simplistic binary view that one set of ideas has won is one of the reasons for this book, but it is very much in the American way of thinking that life is a battle and that their model is exceptional – and exceptionally good.

In 1945 the UK was bankrupt and beholden to the USA for help in winning the war and for financial support as part of the Marshall Plan. The US had new markets to develop and exploit from Japan to Europe, and new places to place its strategic military forward projection. Both the UK and Japan became US aircraft carriers in return for open markets and being launch pads into Europe and Asia, commercially and militarily. And so the American century, which began as the UK and Europe declined, grew exponentially. It was led by products, such as Coke, Camels, Fords and the GI, and promoted by Hollywood, jazz, balladeers and rock 'n' roll. To the world it presented a bright new future of freedom, wealth and fast food – and Elvis Presley – but it had serious issues to confront back home: racism, gun control and inequality.

The greatest threat to humankind's existence is still unintentional or intentional nuclear warfare, with infantile sociopathic leaders in charge in a number of nuclear-armed countries, including the USA and North Korea. We should be very frightened that the clock is very close to midnight. Other nuclear-armed countries, such as Russia and China, are more strategic and still subscribe to MADness: mutually assured destruction. The *Bulletin of the Atomic Scientists* has published a Doomsday Clock since 1947, and in January 2017 it issued a statement saying that the clock had moved to two and half minutes to midnight, citing President Trump's "cavalier and often reckless ways to address the twin threats of nuclear weapons and climate change.[194] Similarly, the EU has said that the USA is now as great a threat to its existence as Russia.

The second greatest existential threat to humanity has again been created by us. Despite the small number of denialists, mostly in the USA, climate change, exacerbated by human activity, is undisputed by the vast majority of climate change scientists around the world. Denying climate change and its anthropomorphic origins is akin to denying the holocaust, an act not of interpretation but of Faustian evil-making.

In the National Portrait Gallery in central London is an iconic painting of the men who ran World War I for the Western Allies. Seventeen million people died and 20 million more were injured in that war. In "Some General Officers of the Great War" by John Singer Sargent, painted in 1922, the 22 assembled men in their khaki fatigues and riding boots stare blankly from the canvas into the past and future. But what is most striking is that they are all men. There are no women.

The masculine gaze is not as penetrating as it was in 1918, but it is still the leitmotif of the twenty-first century. In *Thinking the Twenty-First Century: Ideas for the New Political Economy* I discussed what I called "the feminization of decision-making". After the book was published, there was significant discussion of whether I had co-opted the language of feminism, or perhaps I had insulted a large number of men who already saw themselves as sensitive. The point I was making was largely missed. I was talking about the *masculine* gaze which has pervaded all our thinking because of the *male* gaze. I argued then, as I do now, that the masculine gaze prevents us from seeing that the future has to be negotiated, collaborative and collective in an interdependent world on a delicate planet. I said then, as I do now, that this view can be called the feminization of decision-making: the female rather than the male gaze. This is not based on the traditional divide between men and women, on what is unfortunately called "the gender war", but can be thought of much more interestingly as a discussion about masculinity. Since 1945, and the development of the art of negotiation, the world has seen the slow progression of the gentle man and the empowered gentle woman. This will take time, but it can be seen in Martin McGuinness, a Catholic and formerly an IRA Commander responsible for countless deaths in Northern Ireland, forging an alliance with his previously sworn enemy, the Protestant Reverend Ian Paisley, to form a stable cross-party government: a relationship that came to be referred to as "the chuckle brothers".[195] It can be seen in President Barack Obama singing "Amazing Grace" at the funeral of the Reverend Clementa Pinckney, shot by a White racist in June 2015.[196] It can be seen in President Nelson Mandela putting on a rugby shirt, the symbol of White South Africa, when the country won the World Cup in 1995.[197]

It is the day after the inauguration of a new president in the USA. On a bright, cold day in January 2017 I step outside the National Portrait Gallery in London into the crowd of some 100,000, mostly women but also many men and children. They have come to decry the election of US President Donald J. Trump with his hateful, misogynistic, xenophobic message. I am reminded of the Occupy movement: the collective desire for a society based not on hate but on respect, tolerance, human rights and continuing the post World War II work enshrined in the 1945 United Nations Charter and the 1948 United Nations Human Development Report. In cities around the world people have gathered with the same convictions, and in Washington,

DC the 500,000 people far outnumber those who attended the presidential inauguration. The White House issues a statement saying that the "media have lied" about the numbers. The BBC issues a statement saying that the photographic evidence supports their coverage of the different events. We are in a new Orwellian age. I am reminded of the metal slogan at the gates to Auschwitz: "Arbeit macht frei" – "work makes you free" – with those walking beneath it sent to the gas chambers. The truth turns on a sixpence. Then the new US president compares the CIA to "Nazi Germany". I wonder which planet I'm living on: certainly, we are talking about alternative realities. Trump's spokesperson talks about "alternative facts".

The posters at the demonstration today range from "Women's rights are human rights" to "We shall overcomb", "My pussy has fangs" and "This pussy grabs back", which reference Trump's abusive comments about women as well as digging at his ludicrous coiffure.

Of the 58% of Americans who voted, a slim majority went to President Trump's opponent, Hilary Clinton, but he won a clear majority in the Electoral College. In a White nativist stance, Trump offended Mexicans, non-Whites, women, China and the CIA. His "America First" message was reminiscent of, and a reference to, White America's neo-fascist movement; he was supported by the National Rifle Association and the Ku Klux Klan. Despite his offensiveness, of the women who voted in the election 42% voted for Trump, arguing that a change was necessary, that they didn't like Hilary Clinton, and that his vitriol didn't matter as much as not voting for Clinton. The writer Gary Younge wrote that Americans should perhaps understand that for the previous eight years they had had an adult in the White House. The multi-award-winning actress Meryl Streep echoed many people's feelings when in a speech that was broadcast around the world she said that "disrespect breeds disrespect" and "violence breeds violence".

The vote for Trump was similar to the vote for Brexit in the UK: older, White, working class, poorly educated, and non-metropolitan. And yet, as I write today, according to all the research, most people in the UK under 30 do not see difference – they do not see colour, ethnicity or even gender in the way these older people do. So we are at a turning point, and, as has been pointed out, if a few more people under 30 had voted in both elections, both results would have been different. The future lies with Barack Obama and Sadiq Khan. Barack Obama, the son of a Black father from Kenya and White mother from Kansas, was born in Hawaii, raised there and in Indonesia, and educated at Harvard Law School. In 2015, Sadiq Khan was elected as Mayor of London. His parents migrated from India to Pakistan following the partition of India, and then to England shortly before Sadiq's birth in 1970. He attended state schools before studying law at London Metropolitan University. His father was a bus driver for 25 years and his mother a seamstress. He is the first Muslim to be elected mayor of a major Western city and he had previously served as a Member of Parliament and as a government minister between 2005 and 2016.

By 2050 the USA will be more ethnically non-White than White, but this superficial distinction will have been significantly blurred by intermarriage. London is the most ethnically diverse city in the world and people voted for Khan because he represented a different future – and because he had good transport policies and represented moderation, negotiation and a non-racial future. How many people know that he had also previously been a stand-up comedian?

In a positive future where the post-human world meets the good society, Obama and Khan are the future – if the liberal collective progressive can defeat the divisive fear-mongering nihilists. The issue is about identity, and how people within communities feel about themselves – and about incomers. The research shows that it is not the incoming churn that is the problem, but the speed of that churn. America and the UK have always been mongrel countries with their cultures emboldened by incoming ideas, smells of cooking, new religions and ways of being to make them rich in every sense. But the pace at which they have been asked to change in recent years, or the perception that they are threatened, seem to be significant factors in skewing the reality about migration and "the other". This fear is played on by demagogic populists. Who are we, and who am I? Where do I belong? Am I threatened? And, at this juncture in history, the most threatened group is the White man who has always assumed he was on top. But the times they are a-changin' and the force is moving towards people who are everything, not one thing.

The good society: theory and practice

In this essay I have looked at the theory and practice of the good society through the lens of love, hope and art, always arguing that this is not utopian but based on decisions made through deliberate public policy. I have also pointed out that it is possible to deliver the good life to people within a global capitalist economy. As some 50% of people do not live in democracies, which anyway have a varied reliability for delivering the good society, it is also possible to highlight examples of progress in authoritarian regimes. I do not deny that, despite the evidence I have presented, there is much more that should be done to examine how the good life can be delivered. But, as is obvious from this discursive journey, some societies make active decisions to avoid progress, either because they do not see what is possible *or* because of false historical premises. Examples of this can be found in the USA where less than 60% turn out to vote, in the UK where voter turnout among people under 30 is very low, and in India where the world's largest democracy fails to fundamentally address injustice and environmental issues. All three countries are rich, and public policy could make the difference. In two other countries, Cuba and Costa Rica, there is no surplus of public money but lives are long, happy and fulfilling, with significantly lower environmental impacts on the planet than the USA and the UK.

I have highlighted health and social care, education and skills, inequality and social mobility as the keys to a good society. And I have argued that these are fundamental civil rights within a human rights mental framework. All societies that work for all share similar characteristics, whether they be big or small, resource-based or information societies: low discrimination in all areas and high social mobility, sound institutions and governance motivation and low corruption, and the universal application of the rule of law.

There are some interesting correlations that I had not expected. Declining wealth and declining equality of income correlate with increasing obesity rates. Regular mealtimes and resistance towards fast food are also equated with the lowest obesity rates. Low obesity rates provide for better distribution of health resources. The UK has voted by a very slim majority to leave the European Union, but since 1979 it has in many ways been less like the rest of Europe and more like the USA. Australia is more European than the UK in terms of social welfare economics and inequality. China will dominate the world not just because of its population size, which overshadows all other countries apart from India, but because, despite its male-dominated authoritarianism, the Chinese Communist Party knows that to stay in power it must promote wealth and egalitarianism unlike its rival for global dominance, India.[198]

I have highlighted several examples of the good society, or better practice, and I want to reiterate them here. They exemplify that good public policy on quality-of-life issues, executed with firmness and leadership, can transform a country.

- The Australian gun amnesty in 1996 netted 650,000 weapons and has led to a dramatic decrease in gun deaths, such that Australia now has one of the lowest gun death rates in the world. The best gun control in the world is in Japan where there were just six handgun-related deaths in 2014. More people were shot by children in the US in 2013 than by terrorists. There are 6.2 guns per 100 people in the UK, and 88.88 per 100 in the US.[199]

- In *First Bite*, Bee Wilson writes of two examples of significant changes in dietary policy and public health in the last 70 years. One is in Finland, which had become very concerned about obesity, where an experiment in one small town led to the whole country rethinking food policy and education. This led to a dramatic reversal of previous health concerns around obesity and the associated health issues, and therefore lowered the country's healthcare budget. Her other example comes from Japan where in the early twentieth century, and more significantly after 1945, many people were suffering from malnutrition. The government undertook a nationwide re-education on food such that the Japanese are now some of the healthiest people on the planet with very low levels

IN SEARCH OF THE GOOD SOCIETY

of the chronic diseases and obesity that affect many other affluent countries.[200]

- The world's first free-at-the-point-of-delivery universal healthcare in Britain spends less than most other countries in the OECD as a percentage of GDP but continues to deliver the most cost-efficient health service in the world, according to the US Commonwealth Fund.

- Since the early 1980s, China has transformed from being a largely rural country with less than 20% of the population living in cities to more than 55% urbanized now. This movement of people has lifted more than 700 million people out of poverty, meaning that, when we talk of global poverty alleviation in the last 50 years, more than 90% of this has occurred in China: a country with a single party and a mixed economy but with a rigid application of planning guidelines.

In the end, one of the primary measures of the good society in the twenty-first century is still how it treats those who can't take care of themselves: the sick, the old, the vulnerable and the dispossessed.

And now: public reasoning and the public intellectual

In this voyage it has been important to go and see for myself. Watching the wealth walk past in Shanghai is to remember that some 350 million Chinese live affluent lives. Crossing the road in Delhi is to be reminded that the 40,000 people who die every

229

year in the UK linked to poor air quality is dwarfed by the numbers in India and China. Lunching in Milan is to note that Italians still stop and pause and talk in the middle of the day. Walking through London is to wonder at how the country that first provided publicly funded healthcare can have so many people sleeping on the streets in sub-zero temperatures. Avoiding being assaulted in Los Angeles and stepping over the bodies is to deny one's basic humanity. Visiting Cape Town's informal settlements is to admire the human spirit, ingenuity and determination in the face of continuing deprivations in wealth and democracy. Brazil's favelas induce the same feelings. Talking to the Greeks, you know how they have been mugged from behind by avaricious debt collectors, mostly in German banks.

I have always wanted to visit places and people I believed to exemplify the future and who offer positive working models of how things could be. And so to Zermatt in Switzerland, supposedly a car-free city. But it is a confounding conundrum. It is car-free but not. It is full of electric buggies, all of which are powered by hydro-generated electricity; but, give a man a vehicle and he'll aggress with it. So it is that they drive their buggies around in just as threatening a way as they would any vehicle. And Zermatt reminds me of a modern airport – say Terminal 5 at Heathrow: there are acres of shops and electric buggies and lots of people wandering around aimlessly. Why do people need anything at an airport? Well, the same is true in a mountain resort. And the bottom end of town has cars. I did not learn what I expected. Ah, Utopia never looks like Utopia.

Utopia is a state of mind: hence Thomas More's 1516 joke – *Utopia* means nowhere. A bit like Dylan Thomas's Llareggub, "bugger all" backwards, the setting for *Under Milk Wood*. Norway tops most of the rankings for the good society, but some people would not like to live in a cold northern-hemisphere country with people who need warming up to chat, so they would choose the warm climate of Australia and its cheerily abrasive people, or the happy, slow amiability of the Costa Ricans. Myself, after enjoying the midnight sun and eating fish soup in Svolvær on the Lofoten Islands in Norway, I'd choose a beautiful Italian square and a good coffee and brioche, or a hot Japanese outdoor *onsen*, or a traditional Chinese Beijing duck restaurant full of noise and vitality and smells, or breakfast at Bathers on Balmoral Beach in Sydney after a swim in the warm sea, or "tossed salad and scrambled eggs" with my wife listening to *Desert Island Discs* on BBC radio at home. But in most of these cases I'd know that, should I need them, the fire, ambulance and police services would be at my door within minutes, that it was unlikely that my house would be broken into while I slept, that the water in the tap was clean and drinkable, and that my political leaders were relatively literate, intelligent and honest. Utopia is where your heart and mind are.

The coming of the post-human world has arrived: for how many of us can survive without connecting to a wider intelligence of ideas, knowledge and interaction via the internet? Our brains have been extended beyond the physicality of head and heart, and whether we like it or not we are becoming digitized. We have become part of an artificial intelligence. The discussions about AI are no longer whether we want it or not, but about how it now develops. But we forget at our peril our evolutionary development, whether that be Dunbar's number of 150, or that, despite mobile phones, most of us only call about four people most of the time, or that having friends on Facebook has led to greater alienation and lower empathy not more. The tendency has been for people to talk to "people like me", to live in echo chambers, as online media and sales departments connect us to items that relate to previous

231

purchases, whether of products or news. We need to remember that face-to-face is vital if we are to maintain the good society. Interpreting facial movement, gestures and sounds is at the core of brain development and human development from birth onwards, and electronic interfaces are no substitute.

Electronic connectivity does not necessarily lead to higher quality of life for most people. Of course, the internet, like Gutenberg, can be used for good or evil, but it is no substitute for communities that provide essential services and care for the sick, the old, the vulnerable and the dispossessed.

A friend of mine became president of one of the world's largest computer companies. When he joined the online sales department, it was losing money and customers at a time when online global sales elsewhere were booming. They had assumed the maximum efficiency – orders in, product out – but sales didn't grow; indeed, they fell. His job: to rescue the future of this global electronics company. He did this by remembering that customers are customers and are analogue even if the world is going digital. He was very successful, and his methodology, "think analogue: remember they're people", consisted of everyone in the company starting the day with yesterday's customer comments, criticism and praise – and then making sure every single one of these received a personal thank-you from the company. As president of this part of a larger company, he knew every one of the 200 employees by name, by job title and by history. He was so successful that he was promoted to president of global marketing and sales for the whole company. He went from being in charge of a large village-like community of long-serving, largely Japanese employees to being in charge of thousands of people from various diverse backgrounds with little sense of community, just a commitment to sales for the market-good. He hated it and retired after a few years. The company is still running success-fully but not expanding.

Much of the social media and internet hardware and soft-ware comes out of Silicon Valley just outside San Francisco in the US. Here, highly paid young men (and the figures show it is mostly young men) work for companies that pretend they are merely conduits for contacts, but in reality have become a com-bination of the world's largest marketing companies and media publishers. It is, for instance, through Facebook that Ameri-cans received 80% of their news in 2016, and this company has some 1.79 billion monthly users globally and growing. Even bigger is Google with 2.5 billion users: in 2016, of its US$74.54 billion revenue US$67.39 billion came from advertising.

A recent experience highlights the issue of how we have become subservient to algorithmic calculations with no human interface and zero explanation. I queried from my insurance company, Saga, a company in the UK catering to people over 50 years old in all services, the fact that two very different rates had been quoted on different days for my car insurance. I was told that they had no control over prices and it was done algorithmically online. They could not query the quote either. I wondered why I was using an interface company at all and was told by the employee that she didn't use Saga herself as it was easier and cheaper to buy online. I am so twentieth-century, I thought. But I now must think digital not analogue and never speak to a human again.

The robotization of so many jobs, including account-ing, insurance, medicine and shopping, using varying forms of limited and not-so-limited AI, is predicted to be the future for most people this century. This raises enormous issues with regard to managing the good society, especially if face-to-face communications become ever more remote. It leads to greater alienation, especially when there is a query, as with my car insurance premium, or when people feel that they are being traduced, manipulated or mismanaged to the extent that they understand, perhaps mistakenly, that "the other" is getting the better of them. The evidence from both the Brexit vote in the UK and the Trump vote in the US is that many people, particularly those with less of a handle on power – in other words, distanced from the powerful or decision-making processes – voted just to show they had some power. They were not just voting against the elite but also against one of the most important aspects of globalization: the digitization of the economy where the person has gone missing. Many people feel powerless and, in a democracy, some of them have revolted. It's a small majority of the total, but enough to tip the balance in favour of fear and lies. When the UK Minister of Justice said that people had had enough of experts he meant that they no longer wanted to be told what to think; they were happier to talk to "people like themselves" in their reassuring echo chambers. This has overtones of Germany in the 1930s. "People like themselves" does not include "the other".

And so we are led inexorably in the twenty-first century to linking democracy to 1930s Nazi Germany to George Orwell's *Nineteen Eighty-Four*, written in 1948, to Aldous Huxley's *Brave New World*, written in 1932. In *Nineteen Eighty-Four* the screen can be watched and it can watch you; and so it is now as every internet interaction records you. According to Yuval Noah Harari's positive prognosis, this mining of megadata will mean that the AI out there will know us better than we know ourselves; but of course through feedback loops we will be soon be more out there than we are of ourselves. In Stanley Kubrick's film *2001*, made in 1968, the central computer HAL tries to take over, telling the only living human left on the spacecraft "You can't do that" when he tries to switch HAL off. HAL doesn't, apparently, have feelings, so it doesn't have consciousness. Neither does the current model of AI, but, and this is crucial, the growing modelling of AI can read emotions by virtue of knowing what you like, where you go and when you're unhappy. In feeding this back to you, it will programme you.

According to most estimates, robotization will kill many traditional jobs, from accounting to manufacturing, leaving millions without work: especially those people who voted for Brexit or Trump – older, White, low-skilled and with poor education, hooked into echo chambers. The system wanted them as consumer-workers but now it just wants them as passive consumers. There is a sign in a restored nineteenth-century mill in northern England, at the heart of what was the Industrial Revolution, which reads: "The new virtues that the workers were persuaded to adopt were those requisite for a material civilization: regularity, punctuality, obedience, thrift, providence, sobriety and industry."[201] Now we want the majority to remain consumers – but to do what all day long? Harari says that "the nineteenth century created the working class, the coming century will create the useless class".[202] Part of the good society was the idea of work, of contributing to the whole good, but how shall we now collect taxes and distribute wealth if most people do little and if those who have wealth simply get richer?

If, as Nietzsche said, "God is dead", as Edmund Leach said, "men have become like gods", and, as Robert Oppenheimer, the chief scientist on the Manhattan Project which developed the Hiroshima and Nagasaki atomic and nuclear bombs, said, "Now I am become Death, the destroyer of worlds", then this is our final moment when we leave the state of consciousness that has allowed us to discuss the good society, for this has become irrelevant as we ascend into eternity and the machine age, self-replicating, self-destroying, self-satisfying, narcissistic, and self-congratulatory, spinning lies all the while because the truth is out there somewhere else. This, then, is the real end of history, not Fukuyama's end of history through economic exploitation or Einstein's unifying theory, but certainly the last man, for it is clear that, as nuclear conflagration and climate change make the planet unhospitable, most of humanity will become extinct and a few will fly on as machines escaping our febrile, tenuous grip on life on Earth.

But there is another, less dystopian, future. Thomas Friedman inadvertently presages the end of the American century, like the decline of the Roman Empire. This is in contrast to the Dalai Lama who is quoted outside London's Imperial War Museum: "We human beings are passing through a crucial period in our development ... May [the last century] remain as a symbol to remind us that human survival depends on living in harmony and always choosing the path of non-violence in resolving our differences." The Martin School at Oxford University has a similar perspective: "One of the greatest challenges in the 21st century will be solving the problem of how to get individuals and nations to set aside their self-interests and cooperate for the common good ... we should recognise that humans are the most cooperative vertebrates on Earth."[203]

In other words, we can choose our future and defy the determinism of both the biotech industry and the worst prognoses of Silicon Valley. But this means addressing and challenging what Otto Scharmer calls "the blind spot of our time". I share his diagnosis that we are living "in a time of massive institutional failure" which has created: "Climate change. AIDS. Hunger. Poverty. Violence. Terrorism. Destruction of communities, nature, life – the foundations of our social, economic, eco-logical, and spiritual well-being."[204] But my problem with his solution is, as I often feel about US solutions, that it is based on the US philosophy of psychology, individualism, libertari-anism and personal transformation rather than the collective, philosophical approaches of much of the rest of the world. I'm fine with doing up my boots and getting stuck in – it's what I've successfully done all my life – but I recognize that real positive change is always through collective action, even if it is often charismatic leadership that leads us up the hill to see the promised land. The real blind spot of our time is individualism and the atomization of society through the financialization of every aspect of life and the aggressiveness towards all aspects of change espoused by people like Donald Trump and Thomas Friedman: two sides of the same coin. I reject the model pro-moted through the last 70 years of Americanization: the death penalty; high incarceration rates; poor gun control; lack of universal health and social care; inequality; and the addiction to fossil fuels and the internal combustion engine. Despite the enormous strengths of the US Constitution and its separation of powers and reference to human rights and individual free-doms, participation rates are lamentable: at 58% the 2016 election was not a model for the participation that is required to create the good society in the rest of the world. Thomas Friedman says he wants "everyone to become an American". Please no. This will not deal with the anger that Pankaj Mishra detects around the world, in places that seek revenge for the hundreds of years of European empire and American strategy. It is very much a blind spot in the US and in Europe.[205]

We have challenges that must be considered carefully and tackled with quiet and earnest intent: reforming the global financial system to bring it back within our control; developing economies that nurture rather that destroy our natural capital; managing the development of biotechnology such that it provides solutions, and does not create problems; keeping control of AI such that, as with the development of writing and printing, we know where we are going and have some control; and turning our media tech companies into responsible publishers so that they are subject to the sort of social controls that govern our print media and daily libel and slander laws. If democracy is to work, and be more of a viable option for the 50% who don't currently have it, it must be based on what Edmund Burke, and more recently Amartya Sen, call "public reasoning". Burke said that "the only thing necessary for the triumph of evil is for good men to do nothing": add to that, in our time, "fake news" and "alternative facts". This requires the empowerment of what Pierre Bourdieu, and more recently Edward Said, call "the public intellectual" who through clear public engagement restores the role of the expert and dispels the propagandists that populated the Nazi regime and drive the Trump administration and the Brexiteers. Those who voted nihilistically against those they thought to be the elite, who were the elite, must be engaged so that they can see the wholeness of society, both locally and globally – or we are doomed. Rather than coasting on our laurels, we must re-engage with everyone, everywhere. We must win the argument with reason.

This "high-opportunity, high-risk" society is open to everyone, but also only those who have access to education and free information. As Antony Giddens says, "knowledge and innovation always cut both ways".[206] The future does not lie with nativism or isolationism. Indeed, such moves defy the tide of history, the interdependent nature of all our lives, what we now know about the science of the planet, and what Karl Jung called our collective unconscious, which holds the soul of humanity.

At the heart of the good society should be an understanding of what Jung called instinct, for these aspects are central to what it means to be human: hunger, sexuality, activity, reflection and creativity. And I count both art and science as forms of creativity.

Globalization, like its bedfellows trade and capitalism, is not dead: it just needs reforming. This is not binary: it has to be nuanced. A balance must be found on a global basis to forge what Sen calls a "democratic global state" through public reasoning. The forces of financialization, social media and consumption are out of control and have formed a model of AI such that we are beholden to their algorithmic vicissitudes. As Angus Deaton, 2016 Nobel prize-winning economist, has said: "I don't think globalization is anywhere near the threat that robots are . . . Globalisation for me seems to be not first-order harm and I find it very hard not to think about the billion people who have been dragged out of poverty as a result."[207] Deaton and his wife Anne Case have explained, through enormously useful and detailed megadata trawling both the Brexit and the Trump votes, that the ruling elites have been completely out of touch with White working-class people. For instance, they highlighted the fact that the only demographic group to decline over the last 15 years in America, because of "deaths of despair", were White, poorly educated, working-class men. This is the same group that I focused on earlier: in the UK and the US they have not only experienced zero social mobility, but the bottom 10% have gone backwards – they are poorer now than they were before. In the US they are now in the same position in which the African-American population have always been. Just as it took the Babbage Report in the village of Haworth in Yorkshire 150 years ago to highlight the appalling toll of poor sewerage and the need for clean water, so this may be a time for the elites – that's you and me – to take a look at what really matters for everyone: at the top and the bottom of society. China and parts of Africa continue to pull people up over the poverty line, while the UK, the USA and India continue to oppress working people. Japan and most of Scandinavia have virtually eliminated extreme poverty, while parts of Europe, such as the UK, seem to lack empathy for those who suffer most. In the UK this group voted for Brexit, and in the USA for Trump. In both cases fear and ignorance triumphed. The answer is not xenophobia led by elitists (Trump and the Brexit leadership – Gove, Johnson and Farage – all of whom are rich with elite backgrounds). And the groups that voted for Trump and Brexit shot themselves in the foot, like turkeys voting for Thanksgiving and Christmas.

It is not too late. All the statistics prove that globally we have made good progress over the last 70 years; we will look back and see that 2016 was a moment to take a deep breath and ask what went wrong, and then move forward again. The megalomaniacs, the greedy, those lacking in empathy and many corporate interests will always try to take over, but, just as meerkats and bonobos run on cooperation, so the best of humanity has been when we collaborate and cooperate. We must work for a feminized future not an avaricious masculine past. The future is liberal, collective and progressive, but it requires us not to walk past on the other side or hide in a dark room listening to Beethoven with our headphones on until the world blows over. Art may be the best way forward, for it is through artistic expression in different dimensions that we can see the world afresh.

Remember. Remember. Remember.

A Song for Hope

Malcolm McIntosh

The day was warm and I drove with the wind in
    my hair.
I stopped at Skylark Point to see the sea
And stare upward to the heavens
For the tiniest of birds to sing the sweetest of
    songs.
The corn does not yet lie in the fields
But waves golden in the breeze
For this is how we shall feed the millions
And sate our hunger for contentment.
I slept with the window wide open at South
    Allington
And in the morning light rain filled the air.
I awoke to the sound of cows lowing,
Pigeons cooing and blackbirds singing.
It wasn't cold, and the rain was soft.
We have many elysiums
And today South Allington is my Jerusalem
(o that that place was so peaceful today).
I could lay down my body in this place
And for that delivery.
Peace on Earth and goodwill to all people
(o that my life had delivered this).
But this is no lament
For as the body lies down in the soil alongside the
    warm cow
I return from whence I came
Dust to dust, ashes to ashes
Stardust to big bang
Love to love
And I looked down on Jerusalem
(o that dreams could come true).
I drove with the wind in my hair . . .

241

∼

Disrespect breeds disrespect, and violence breeds violence.

Meryl Streep

∼

First, we must start with the rhetoric.

Appendix
How to live healthily
(For everyone, anywhere)

I'm both a journalist and an academic. Six years ago when I was told I had terminal cancer, like Gould I set off on the long journey into the desperation of the internet cancer fluff and the enlightenment of lengthier, more informed articles on cancer, diet, lifestyle and well-being. I emerged quite quickly with a set of principles that are consistently being reinforced by new science, and by my experience, and by talking to other survivors. They are principles that, if adopted on a *societal* basis, would lead to a dramatic drop in chronic illness rates around the world. We all have to die, but the research presented here shows that there are many, many examples around the world which we can learn from where people die of old age – degeneration – rather than chronic illnesses. Can we learn? Can we remember? So, as with examples of the good society, an essential component of the good society is good health and social care in a civilized, intelligent society.

It is well known that at least one-third of cancers and heart disease could be prevented by changes in lifestyle. But, looking at the established research, and from experience, it is possible that many, many people could live longer, healthier lives if they were to heed the following. This is not just for those already suffering chronic disease, but also those who are now apparently healthy.

1. Think positive. Many people are cancer and chronic disease survivors. Whereas a positive cancer diagnosis used to be a death sentence, nowadays about 50% of cancer victims live more than a further 10 years. If the experts give you one month to live, you can make it two months, and, if they give you a year to live, you can make it two years – by following these rules. Two equals four.

2. Be strict 90% of the time, but allow yourself 10% for mistakes, indulgences and comforts. Enjoy life. Laugh a lot. But be consistent in the 90% – and be honest. Every day.

3. Give your immune system as much help as you can by lowering burdens on it.

4. Don't eat any ready meals and try to avoid all processed food, apart from obviously less harmful stuff like spaghetti and bread: but eat low-gluten and always organic. Eat complex, and eat high-fibre.

5. Lower your gluten intake: it's hard work for the (any) body to digest.

6. Drink lots of water: 2–3 litres a day. You need to flush out any toxins, especially on and after chemo. And never get dehydrated.

7. Stop eating red meat and all processed meat including bacon, ham and sausages.

8. Eat good-quality protein: eggs, chicken, fish – lots of it – and pulses; but make sure they're all organic. Add flax-seed oil to your diet for extra omega 3, 6 and 9.

9. Cut out almost all dairy, but you still need live, natural, organic yoghurt for your gut (make sure it has no added sugar). Milk contains a natural growth hormone that encourages cancers to grow. A modest amount of cheese is good as a source of protein, variety and calcium.

10. Eat high-fibre food, because you need to keep stuff moving though your gut and expel any cancer cells before they can take hold. Also, high-fibre food allows your gut to build the complex multiflora that is necessary to prevent cancer and other diseases.

11. Eat 5–8 portions of vegetables and fruit every day.

12. Sleep whenever you feel tired, wherever you are. Keep the body flexible and aerated by doing yoga or walking briskly every day. When you meditate, practise yoga or rest, learn to visualize so you can float away and give your overactive body a rest.

13. Walk as briskly as possible every day for at least an hour, however hard it is, and, if you can get out of breath, do so: it keeps the cardiovascular system going and gets the life force kicking. Get your adrenal gland working every day and producing endorphins – feel happy. A challenge is good, but stress is bad and produces cortisol which aids cancers. Laughter oxygenizes

the brain as much as yogic deep breathing and stimulates the heart of your immune system: the thymus gland.

14. All the research says that the best diet is a Mediterranean diet[208] (or a Japanese diet), with all colours of fresh vegetables, only cold-pressed extra-virgin olive oil, small amounts of mixed proteins, and a very occasional glass of red wine. Otherwise, it's best to quit alcohol altogether, except for the 10%. Also, vitamin D is very good for cancer patients. Recent research shows that it's the 13 litres of virgin olive oil per annum that Mediterranean people consume that is the key to the Mediterranean diet (other Europeans generally consume around 1 litre). The recent evidence is that there is a link between our over-simple diet and cancer. In other words, complex gut multiflora is very important in keeping healthy and stopping cancer. Two or three milk-free cups of pure coffee a day are good; do not drink instant coffee or take milk. Eat turmeric in curries at least once a week for its anti-carcinogenic and antioxidant properties.

15. Start the day with your new juicer juice: mostly fresh vegetables with an apple and carrot: vitamins A, C and E.

16. Cut out as much artificial sugar as you can: cancers love sugar, and obesity is a pandemic across the world. Organic chocolate, like vegetables, is good, as it's full of antioxidants, but chocolate cake and biscuits are not. Don't get overweight at all. Don't smoke or go near people who smoke.

17. Have a project on the go every day that will give you a reason for getting . . . dressed, off the sofa, and going. This may be grandchildren, it may be a job, it may be a garden, it may be helping out in the community. It may be writing a book.

18. If you follow these guidelines you will feel better within three weeks, but it will take three months before you have fulfilled the maxim that "you are what you eat". So be consistent and don't give up. Soon you won't miss sugar, salt or processed food – or alcohol.

Having cancer is like having a baby: everyone else is an expert. Do your own research and ignore most of them. Also, having cancer is not a battle, war or any of the stuff in tabloid newspapers: it's a natural degeneration of the body and you can slow it down by following the points above. You can't beat it, but you can live longer.

Over six years I have been consistent in the following areas: (1) (the toughest) walking hard for at least an hour a day (even on chemo or after radiation), which means at some point getting out of breath – so we are not talking about strolling! (2) keeping hydrated; (3) sleeping as and when necessary (friends have had to tolerate me just having a nap whenever and wherever!); (4) eating a varied diet to keep my gut flora active (many people only eat half a dozen types of food a week); (5) not drinking alcohol, but having two or so cups of strong black coffee a day; (6) keeping up the mixed vitamins; (7) basking in the sun for vitamin D; (8) keeping thin!

The latest genetic research seems to show that my siblings and I are genetically predisposed to certain types of cancer. It's known as Lynch syndrome and raises the possibility of testing at birth, which is not allowed under UK law at the moment.

But, if I had known about it, I would never have smoked and would have been more moderate in my alcohol consumption, and would have started testing for suspicious polyps in my gut in my late twenties. This all raises enormous ethical and cost questions for the twenty-first century. If you knew you could be tested, would you proceed?

My research and lifestyle is supported by surveying those groups of people who live longest around the world. Rarely are they a whole nation, except in the case of the Japanese, and in all cases they have resisted American fast food. Where they have been unable to resist, there has been an increase in chronic disease. Sometimes the research is too scientific and not observational enough, and I have found that standing and staring (politely) has taught me as much as anything. For instance, there is very little obesity in Italy and Japan despite the consumption of vast amounts of pasta in the former and rice in the latter. Why not?[209]

I've lived in Italy and Japan, and asked friends in these two countries to help with the nuances that can't be deduced from the big data (which is digital, not analogue) about why people in those two countries are so comparatively healthy. Their replies are very similar for both countries:

- The famous Mediterranean and Japanese diets.

- No snacking: you very rarely see Italians or Japanese eating or drinking in the street.

- A low consumption of sugar- or fat-heavy foods such as crisps.

- In Italy, family meals are still cooked at home and the tradition is still strong among all classes.

- Convenience foods and ready meals are nowhere near as ubiquitous as in the UK and are looked down on as inferior in quality and indicative of laziness.

- There is far greater aesthetic awareness. In both Japan and Italy, they are more conscious of the appearance of food.

- Italians and Japanese drink fewer soda drinks.

- People drink, but drink less, and in Italy it is culturally unacceptable to get drunk.

- However, in both countries the monitory evidence about smoking does not seem to have had an effect, and they have some of the highest smoking rates in the world: many people and places smell like last night's ashtrays – or London and New York last century.

Two stories from Italy perhaps show the difference between their attitudes to food and social meals and those in fast-food, frenetic nations. Most Italians stop for lunch and conversation for at least an hour. In one town we discovered that the parking meters also stopped from noon until 2:30 in the afternoon! The Pope finishes his Sunday prayers in St Peter's Square by wishing everyone *buon pranzo!* – "have a good lunch!"

The Japanese who live longest also drink copious amounts of green tea, which is an antioxidant, and practise *hara hachi bu*: eat until you are 80% full – because it takes 20 minutes for the stomach to tell the brain that it is full. *Ikigai* is also very important in Japanese longevity. It means "the reason for getting up in the morning" – usefulness and being wanted.

Earlier I mentioned being unexpectedly surrounded by the Greek monks of Mount Athos at London's Heathrow Airport: they live forever and have very few chronic diseases, dementia or Alzheimer's. They all have active lives and feel useful throughout their lives, whether this be through gardening or meditating, they grow almost all their food and, while some of them appear rotund, they often fast and never eat more than they need at any meal. And there are no women or female animals allowed on their peninsula, lest they be distracted. This is extreme, but they live a long time!

All the cases of longevity show that being positive, socially active and knowing what you eat and why you eat it is crucial. Through our lifestyles we can alter our children's predisposition to chronic disease, including mental health problems. As Irene Rea says, "The epigenetic modification of our genes – and the life stories of healthy nonagenarians – offer explanations about how diet, physical activity, stress and exposure to toxins and infections can subtly alter our genes and our predisposition to disease."[210]

None of the groups who live longest take expensive supplements – they get what they need from what they eat – and none of them go on "diets"; many come from relatively poor communities. You do not have to be affluent to live well, but you do have to be intelligent and adaptive to make the change from a poor lifestyle to a life-sustaining one that nourishes both body and soul.

Randomly, the ocean quahog clam has a lifespan of some 500 years, which it is thought to achieve by protecting its proteins from damage. This may be useful in studying Alzheimer's. Elephants and whales live long lives, the bowhead whale living up to 200 years, and one type of jellyfish actually gets younger every year, returning to its original form and then starting again . . .

Notes

Preface

1 John Kenneth Galbraith taught at Harvard for 50 years, and was honoured by two US presidents. In 1977 he made a major series for PBS/BBC called *The Age of Uncertainty*. He is probably best known now for a line from his best-selling 1958 book *The Affluent Society*: "private wealth and public squalor". *The Good Society: The Humane Agenda*, published in 1996, was described by *The New Yorker* as "common sense raised to the level of genius". He died in 2006.

2 One hundred and fifty is Dunbar's number: this refers to work carried out by Oxford anthropologist Robin Dunbar which estimated that the average size of physical communities from the Neolithic age onwards has been about 150: a number with significance in terms of the cognitive limit of the human brain. We can only maintain a maximum of 150 stable relationships at any one time, and this is as true for workplace communities now as it was for Neolithic man and woman.

Introduction

3 "Mark Zuckerberg rejects 'crazy idea' Facebook influenced US election result". *The Telegraph*, 11 November 2016; http://www.telegraph.co.uk/technology/2016/11/11/mark-zuckerberg-rejects-crazy-idea-facebook-influenced-us-electi. (Mark Zuckerberg on being accused of Facebook's algorithm subverting the results of the US election in 2016. At that time. 80% of Americans got their news feeds through Facebook.)

4 Ruchir Sharma, *Breakout Nations: In Pursuit of the Next Economic Miracles*. London: Penguin, 2012. Ruchir Sharma, *The Rise and Fall of Nations: Ten Rules of Change in the Post-Crisis World*. New York: W.W. Norton, 2016.

5 Shawn Donnan, "Lunch with the FT. Angus Deaton: Global Warning". *Financial Times*, 24–25 December 2016: 3. See also Jim Edwards, "There is a correlation between 'deaths of despair' among white people and voters for Trump". *Business Insider*, 18 January 2017; http://uk.businessinsider.com/angus-deaton-white-deaths-trump-2017-1. See also Harrison Jacobs, "The revenge of the 'Oxy electorate' helped fuel Trump's election upset". *Business Insider*, 23 November 2016; http://uk.businessinsider.com/trump-vote-results-drug-overdose-deaths-2016-11

6 Malcolm McIntosh, *Thinking the Twenty-First Century: Ideas for the New Political Economy*. Sheffield, UK: Greenleaf Publishing, 2015.

7 Julian Barnes, *Changing My Mind*. BBC Radio 3, December 2016.

8 Adam Curle, *Radical Peacemaker*, ed. Tom Woodhouse and John Paul Lederach. Stroud, UK: Hawthorn Press, 2016.

9 Zygmunt Bauman, *Postmodern Ethics*. Hoboken, NJ: Wiley-Blackwell, 1993.

10 Nelson Mandela *Conversations with Myself*. Macmillan, 2010.

11 John Gray, "What scares the new atheists?" *The Guardian*, "Review", 3 March 2015: 29-31.

12 The much-repeated quote is paraphrased from Vol. 13 of Gandhi's 98 volumes of writings (Ch. 153, page 241, published in 1913), where the actual text is: "We but mirror the world. All the tendencies present in the outer world are to be found in the world of our body. If we could change ourselves, the tendencies in the world would also change. As a man changes his own nature, so does the attitude of the world change towards him. [. . .] We need not wait to see what others do."

13 The BBC film *Frozen Future* was part of the "Nature" series, introduced by Michael Buerk and produced by John Dearing, with commentary by Gordon Clough, who spoke Russian but did not visit the scene. It was broadcast on BBC2 in 1990 and again by the Discovery Channel over the following years.

14 Stephen Hawking, *A Brief History of Time*. London: Bantam, 2011: 223.

Chapter 1

15 Dag Hammarskjöld, UN Secretary-General, 20 May 1956, in an address discussing the League of Nations at the New York University Hall of Fame ceremony on the unveiling of the bust and tablet for Woodrow Wilson.

16 Barbara Hepworth, *A Pictorial Autobiography*. Tate, 1993. Some statements by Barbara Hepworth, Barbara Hepworth Museum, St Ives, Cornwall, 1977.

17 Quoted in Stuart Rees, *Passion for Peace: Exercising Power Creatively*. Kensington, Australia: UNSW Press, 2003: 92.

18 *Great Lives: Dag Hammarskjöld*, BBC Radio 4, 26 August 2016; http://www.bbc.co.uk/programmes/b07pgvjz.

19 Quoted in *The Observer*, "The New Review", 7 June 2015: 12-15.

20 In Foreword to Gilbert Probst and Andrea Bassi, *Tackling Complexity: A Systemic Approach for Decision Makers*. Sheffield, UK: Greenleaf Publishing, 2014.

21 Partha Dasgupta, *Economics: A Very Short Introduction*. Oxford, UK: Oxford University Press, 2007: Preface.

22 https://www.youtube.com/watch?v=mGTR__LiueM

23 Antony Gormley, "Antony Gormley on sculpture's new roles". *Financial Times*, 2 October 2015; https://www.ft.com/content/f2e2dbb4-675f-11e5-97d0-1456a776a4f5

24 Brian Cox interviewed in *The Observer*, "The New Review", 18 September 2016: 11.

25 Andrew Dickson, *Worlds Elsewhere: Journeys around Shakespeare's Globe*. London: Bodley Head, 2016.

26 "Well, Shakespeare he's in the alley / With his pointed shoes and his bells / Speaking to some French girl / Who says she knows me well / And I would send a message to find out if she's talked . . ." (Bob Dylan, "Stuck Inside of Mobile with the Memphis Blues Again" [1966]).

27 Or Bob Dylan again: "Come you masters of war . . . / I just want you to know / I can see through your masks / You that never done nothin' / But build to destroy ("Masters of War" [1963]).

28 *The Observer*, "The New Review", 22 May 2016: 20.

29 B.P. Abbott *et al.*, "Observation of gravitational waves from a binary black hole merger". *Physical Review Letters*, 12 February 2016; https://physics.aps.org/featured-article-pdf/10.1103/PhysRevLett.116.061102

30 Kip Thorne of the California Institute of Technology, reported in *International Herald Tribune*, 12 June 2016: 5; and *New Scientist*, 13 February 2016: 5.

31 Lawrence M. Krauss, *A Universe from Nothing: Why There Is Something Rather Than Nothing*. New York: Simon & Schuster, 2012: 21.

32 Krauss, *A Universe from Nothing*: Epilogue.

33 In a letter to Shinaro Yamashuita, Giverny, 19 February 1920.

34 House of Commons, 11 November 1947.

35 Henry Mance, "Britain has had enough of experts says Gove". *Financial Times*, 3 June 2016; https://www.ft.com/content/3be49734-29cb-11e6-83e4-abc22d5d108c

36 Hawking, *A Brief History of Time*: 203.

37 Carlo Rovelli, *Seven Brief Lessons of Physics*. London: Penguin, 2014: 3.

38 Tim Adams, "Carlo Rovelli: 'Science is where revolutions happen'". *The Guardian*, 16 October 2016; https://www.theguardian.com/books/2016/oct/16/carlo-rovelli-interview-quantum-gravity-physics-science-is-where-revolutions-happen

39 Nora Barlow (ed.), *The Autobiography of Charles Darwin, 1809–1882*. New York: W.W. Norton, 1993: 139.

40 Gormley, "Antony Gormley on sculpture's new roles".

41 Baron C.P. Snow, *The Two Cultures: The Rede Lecture* (1959): 14-15.

42 Terry Eagleton, *After Theory*, London: Penguin, 2003.

43 David Morley and Bill Schwarz, "Stuart Hall obituary". *The Guardian*, 10 February 2014; https://www.theguardian.com/politics/2014/feb/10/stuart-hall

44 Quotes from James Baldwin, "The creative process". In *Creative America*. Ridge Press, 1962: 87; http://thenewschoolhistory.org/wp-content/uploads/2014/08/Baldwin-Creative-Process.pdf

45 John Berger, *Ways of Seeing*. London: Penguin Modern Classics, 1972: 64, 154.

46 Herbert Read, *The Meaning of Art*. London: Pelican, 1931: 190.

47 William Shakespeare, *Macbeth* Act V, Scene 5, lines 24-26.

48 Hester Lacey, "The Inventory: Colm Tóibín". *Financial Times*, 6 November 2015; https://www.ft.com/content/4be27716-826c-11e5-a01c-8650859a4767

49 Colin Firth, *Financial Times* advert for Chopard watches.

50 1,000,000,000; https://en.wikipedia.org/wiki/Billion

51 Thomas Pakenham, *Meetings with Remarkable Trees*. London: Weidenfeld & Nicolson, 1996. Thomas Pakenham, *Remarkable Trees of the World*. London: Weidenfeld & Nicolson, 2002.

52 Helen Macdonald, *H is for Hawk*. London: Jonathan Cape, 2014.

53 Helen Macdonald, "Identification please". *New York Times*, 21 June 2015.

54 Matthew Wilson, "Care for another tree?", *Financial Times*, "House and Home", 14–15 March 2015: 7-8.

55 Henry David Thoreau, *Walden, or Life in the Woods* (1854). London: Penguin Illustrated Classics, 1938: 80.

56 Gilbert White, *The Natural History of Selborne* (1789). London: Thames & Hudson, 1993: 162.

57 Quoted in *The Observer*, "The New Review", 7 May 2015: 15.

58 Barbara Hepworth quoted in Read, *The Meaning of Art*: 184.

59 http://www.hepworthwakefield.org

60 *The Philosophy of Andy Warhol (From A to B and Back Again)* New York: Harcourt Brace Jovanovich, 1975.

61 Reproduced on the museum wall of the Barbara Hepworth Museum and Sculpture Garden, St Ives.

62 Reverend Martin Luther King, "The three dimensions of a complete life". Sermon, St Paul's Cathedral, London, 6 December 1964. Given on his way to receive the Nobel Peace Prize in Oslo, Norway.

63 E.M. Forster, "Tolerance" (1941). In *Two Cheers for Democracy*. London: Penguin, 1951: 53-57.

64 On the occasion of the unveiling of her sculpture "Single Form" in memory of Hammarskjöld in front of the UN headquarters.

65 Brian Uruquhart, "Learning from Hammarskjöld". *New York Times*, 16 September 2011.

66 Preamble to the Charter of the United Nations.

67 John Carey, *The Faber Book of Utopias*. London: Faber & Faber, 1999.

68 Oscar Wilde, *The Soul of Man under Socialism* (1891).

69 Charlotte Brontë, *Shirley* (1849).

Chapter 2

70 *The Theory of Moral Sentiments*. Part IV, I, 17, 20.

71 Daniel Snowman, "An Interview with Eric Hobsbawm". *History Today*, 29(1) (January 1979).

72 William Skidelsky, "Niall Ferguson: 'Westerners don't understand how vulnerable freedom is'". *The Guardian*, 20 February

2011; https://www.theguardian.com/books/2011/feb/20/
niall-ferguson-interview-civilization

73 Eric Hobsbawm, *Age of Extremes: The Short Twentieth Century, 1914–1991*. London: Michael Joseph, 1994: 15.

74 Karl Marx and Friedrich Engels, *The Communist Manifesto* (1888). London: Penguin Little Black Classics, 20, 2015.

75 George Orwell, *Nineteen Eighty-Four* (1949).

76 Eagleton, *After Theory*.

77 Amartya Sen, *Development as Freedom*. Oxford, UK: Oxford University Press, 1999.

78 Tim Etchells, "A New Form of Exchange" (2016), Tate Modern, London, September 2016.

79 The Gini coefficient is a measure of inequality of a distribution. It is defined as a ratio with values between 0 and 1: the numerator is the area between the Lorenz curve of the distribution and the uniform distribution line.

80 Ian Morris, *Why the West Rules – For Now: The Patterns of History, and What They Reveal about the Future*. London: Profile Books, 2010. Ian Morris, "To each age its inequality". *New York Times*, 9 July 2015.

81 See Amartya Sen, "Adam Smith's market never stood alone". *Financial Times*, "Future of Capitalism", 12 May 2009; and John Plender, *Capitalism: Money, Morals and Markets*. London: Biteback, 2016.

82 John Kay, "The good market". *Prospect*, May 1996.

83 https://geert-hofstede.com

84 Charles Hampden-Turner and Fons Trompenaars, *The Seven Cultures of Capitalism: Value Systems for Creating Wealth in the United States, Japan, Germany, France, Britain, Sweden, and the Netherlands*. New York: Doubleday, 1993.

85 R.H. Tawney, *Religion and the Rise of Capitalism*. London: Penguin, 1922.

86 *The Seven Cultures of Capitalism*: 19.

87 Richard Whitley, *Divergent Capitalisms: The Social Structuring and Change of Business Systems*. Oxford, UK: Oxford University Press, 1999: 3.

88 Michael Porter, *Competitive Strategy*. New York: Free Press, 1980). M.E. Porter, "The five competitive forces that shape strategy". *Harvard Business Review*, January 2008.

89 W.Q. Judge, S. Fainshmidt and J.L. Brown, "Which model of capitalism best delivers both wealth and equality?". *Journal of International Business Studies*, 45 (2014): 363-386; http://www.jibs.net

90 Daron Acemoglu and James Robinson, *Why Nations Fail: The Origins of Power, Prosperity and Poverty*. London: Profile Books, 2012.

91 Sen, "Adam Smith's market never stood alone".

92 https://www.weforum.org/agenda/2017/01/these-are-the-most-inclusive-advanced-economies-in-the-world

93 http://www.kdfhs.org.uk

94 Robert Skidelsky and Edward Skidelsky, *How Much Is Enough? Money and the Good Life*. London: Allen Lane, 2012.

95 Wolfgang Münchau, "European values are more important than economics". *Financial Times*, 19 June 2016; https://www.ft.com/content/8278467a-34a5-11e6-bda0-04585c31b153

96 Walter Kempowski, *Swansong 1945: A Collective Diary from Hitler's Last Birthday to VE Day*, translated by Shaun White-side London: Granta, 2014. Reproduced in "VE Day: What the end of the war was like for those who were there". *The Guardian*, "Review", 8 May 2015: 20; https://www.theguardian.com/books/2015/may/08/ve-day-what-the-end-of-the-war-was-like-for-those-who-were-there

97 Ibid.

98 Christiane Amanpour, *Desert Island Discs*, BBC Radio 4, 30 September 2016. Slobodan Milosevic was put on trial by the International Criminal Tribunal for the former Yugoslavia (ICTY) in the Hague on charges of genocide but died in his cell during the trial in 2007. In 2008 the International Court of Justice found him guilty of knowingly allowing genocide to take place while in power and for not cooperating with the ICTY.

99 Isaiah Berlin, philosopher, born in Latvia and lived in the UK, speaking in 1992. Quoted in Hobsbawm, *Age of Extremes*: 1.

100 Yehudi Menuhin, violinist, born in New York City and lived in the UK, speaking in 1992. Quoted in Hobsbawm, *Age of Extremes*: 2.

101 Mark Thompson, "The sound and the fury: Why political language has failed". *The Guardian*, "Review", 27 August 2016: 4.

102 See, for instance, Robert D. Putnam, *Our Kids: The American Dream in Crisis*. New York: Simon & Schuster, 2015.

103 Kazuo Ishiguro, "Kazuo Ishiguro on his fears for Britain after Brexit". *Financial Times*, "Life and Arts", 1 July 2016; https://www.ft.com/content/7877a0a6-3e11-11e6-9f2c-36b487ebd80a

104 Ian McEwan, "Our country is changed utterly. Unless this summer is just a bad dream". *The Guardian*, 9 July 2016: 37; https://www.theguardian.com/commentisfree/2016/jul/09/country-political-crisis-tories-prime-minister

105 *Desert Island Discs*, 30 September 2016.

106 Horatia Harrod, "Chiwetel Ejiofor on Shakespeare, race and the Marvel universe". *Financial Times Magazine*, 14 October 2016; https://www.ft.com/content/684a4810-90d6-11e6-8df8-d3778b55a923

107 Lisa Pryor, "Our precious urban lives". *New York Times*, 28 October 2016; https://www.nytimes.com/2016/10/29/opinion/our-precious-urban-lives.html?_r=0

108 "Blair 'sorrow' over slave trade". BBC News, 27 November 2006; http://news.bbc.co.uk/2/hi/6185176.stm

109 Timothy Garton Ash, "Rhodes hasn't fallen, but the protesters are making me rethink Britain's past". *The Guardian*, 4 March 2016; https://www.theguardian.com/commentisfree/2016/mar/04/rhodes-oxford-students-rethink-british-empire-past-pain

110 *Today*, BBC Radio 4, 14 January 2016.

111 British sociologist and politician Michael Young coined the term "meritocracy" for his satirical novel *The Rise of the Meritocracy* (London: Pelican, 1958).

112 See, for instance, University College London, "Enabling social mobility through education: Working together to maximise HE progression"; http://www.ucl.ac.uk/

prospective-students/widening-participation/activities/
enabling-social-mobility-through-education

113 Simon Hattenstone, "Ken Loach: 'If you're not angry, what kind
of person are you?'". *The Guardian*, 15 October 2016; https://
www.theguardian.com/film/2016/oct/15/ken-laoch-film-i-daniel-
blake-kes-cathy-come-home-interview-simon-hattenstone

114 See Katherine Viner, "How technology disrupted the truth".
The Guardian, 12 July 2016; https://www.theguardian.com/
media/2016/jul/12/how-technology-disrupted-the-truth

115 Emily Bell, Director of the Tow Centre for Digital Journalism at
Columbia University, New York, USA, quoted in Helen Lewis,
"How Jeremy Corbyn won Facebook". *New Statesman*, 20
July 2016; http://www.newstatesman.com/politics/uk/2016/07/
how-jeremy-corbyn-won-facebook. Also quoted in Viner, "How
technology disrupted the truth".

116 See Malcolm McIntosh, *Managing Britain's Defence*. London:
Palgrave Macmillan, 1990.

117 "Legal and military failings of the Iraq war and its
aftermath". *The Guardian*, "Letters", 7 July 2016;
https://www.theguardian.com/uk-news/2016/jul/07/
legal-and-military-failings-of-the-iraq-war-and-its-aftermath

118 https://www.youtube.com/watch?v=4As0e4de-rI

119 Ruchir Sharma, *The Rise and Fall of Nations: Forces of Change
in the Post-Crisis World*. New York: W.W. Norton, 2016.

120 Economist Intelligence Unit (EIU), *Long-Term Macroeconomic Forecasts: Key Trends to 2050. A Special Report
from The Economist Intelligence Unit*; http://pages.eiu.com/
rs/783-XMC-194/images/Long-termMacroeconomicForecasts_
KeyTrends.pdf

121 Roland Ketts, "Out with the old". *New Statesman*, 16–22 Octo-
ber 2015: 28-29. Eamonn Fingleton, "After the FT's buyout let's
stop belittling Japan's success". *The Guardian*, 25 July 2015.
Harding Robin, "Landing of the rising building site". *Financial
Times*, "House and Home", 6–7 August 2016: 1. "Breeding
Bluefin". *The Economist*, 24 September 2016: 48.

122 For more on Japan's post-war foreign and defence policy, please see Malcolm McIntosh, *Japan Rearmed*. London: Pinter; New York: St Martins; London: Bloomsbury, 1968, 2012.

123 Justin Rowlatt, "Thomas Piketty: 'Indian inequality still hidden'". BBC News, 2 May 2016; http://www.bbc.com/news/world-asia-india-36186116. "Inequality in India: What's the real story?". World Economic Forum; https://www.weforum.org/agenda/2016/10/inequality-in-india-oxfam-explainer

124 Martin Fletcher, *Financial Times*, "Weekend Travel", 10–11 December 2016: 6.

125 See, for instance, Johan Norberg, *Progress*. London: Oneworld, 2016: 73.

126 Amartya Sen, "Quality of Life: India vs. China". *The New York Review of Books*, 12 May 2011; http://www.nybooks.com/articles/2011/05/12/quality-life-india-vs-china

127 McKinsey, "The power of parity: How advancing women's equality can add \$12 trillion to global growth" (September 2015); http://www.mckinsey.com/global-themes/employment-and-growth/how-advancing-womens-equality-can-add-12-trillion-to-global-growth

128 https://www.cia.gov/library/publications/the-world-factbook/geos/in.html

129 Li Wei, "Improving economic growth quality". *China Daily*, 2–8 January 2015.

130 "Chinese president addresses UK parliament". *The Guardian*, 20 October 2015.

131 "Pax Americana 'winding down', says US report". *Financial Times*, 10 December 2012; https://www.ft.com/content/4031c202-42f3-11e2-aa8f-00144feabdc0

132 "Cola conquest II: How Coca Cola took over the world"; https://www.youtube.com/watch?v=tpF_-BbaV1g; and http://i.imgur.com/59Zf2xw.jpg

133 "Blame Nixon for the obesity epidemic". *Los Angeles Times*, 27 June 2012. "Why our food is making us fat". *The Guardian*, 11 June 2012.

134 Deloitte, "2016 Global aerospace and defense sector poised to resume growth"; https://www2.deloitte.com/ly/en/pages/manufacturing/articles/global-a-and-d-outlook.html

135 Ibid.

136 Stockholm International Peace Research Institute (SIPRI), "Military expenditure"; https://www.sipri.org/research/armament-and-disarmament/arms-transfers-and-military-spending/military-expenditure

137 See Ramesh Thakur, "The eight deadly nuclear sins". *Japan Times*, 11 February 2016: 7; Edward Luce, "Obama's disappointing nuclear legacy". *Financial Times*, 25 May 2016: 5.

138 It was said that Thatcher kept a copy of Hayek's *The Road to Serfdom* in her handbag, but this is disputable: it is too big for a handbag. John Gray has also pointed out that she seemed to have missed the book's postscript, "Why I am not a Conservative". On the book's publication in 1944, Winston Churchill also brandished a copy in the House of Commons.

139 Martin Wolf, "Seeds of its own destruction". *Financial Times*, "The Future of Capitalism", 12 May 2009: 6-9.

140 Niall Ferguson, *Kissinger 1923–1968: The Idealist*. London: Penguin, 2015.

141 Press conference, April 2009.

142 "Six things Americans should know about mass shootings". The Conversation, 3 December 2015; https://theconversation.com/six-things-americans-should-know-about-mass-shootings-48934. Juliette Jowit *et al.*, "So, America, this is how other countries do gun control". *The Guardian*, 4 March 2016; https://www.theguardian.com/us-news/2016/mar/15/so-america-this-is-how-you-do-gun-control?CMP=share_btn_link

143 Lance Morrow, "The case for rage and retribution". *Time*, 12 September 2001; http://content.time.com/time/nation/article/0,8599,174641,00.html

144 Ibid.

145 "In buildings thought indestructible". *New Statesman*, 17 September 2001; http://www.newstatesman.com/node/154125

146 Quoted by Pankaj Mishra, "A generation of failed politicians has trapped the west in a tawdry nightmare". *The Guardian*, 1 January 2016. See also the Chilcot Report (http://www.iraqinquiry.org.uk) and my letter to the Guardian (see note 117).

147 Simon Heffer, "The American berserk". *New Statesman*, 11–17 March 2016: 25-27.

148 Richard North, "Arms and the man". *Financial Times*, "Life and Arts", 20 March 2016: 1.

149 Barney Henderson and Chris Graham, "Donald Trump: Torture 'absolutely works', says US President in interview with ABC News: Thursday morning briefing". *The Telegraph*, 26 January 2017; http://www.telegraph.co.uk/news/2017/01/26/waterboarding-absolutely-works-donald-trump-discusses-torture.

150 "Teju Cole talks to Taiye Selasi: 'Afropolitan, American, African. Whatever'". *The Guardian*, 5 August 2016; https://www.theguardian.com/books/2016/aug/05/teju-cole-taiye-selasi-interview-known-strange-things

151 Jennifer Schuessler, "Ta-Nehisi Coates asks: Who's French? Who's American?" *New York Times*, 27 October 2016; https://www.nytimes.com/2016/10/28/books/ta-nehisi-coates-asks-whos-french-whos-american.html

152 Sources: Dave Mosher and Skye Gould, "How likely are foreign terrorists to kill Americans? The odds may surprise you". *Business Insider*, 1 February 2017; http://uk.businessinsider.com/death-risk-statistics-terrorism-disease-accidents-2017-1. Alex Nowrasteh, "Terrorism and immigration: A risk analysis". Cato Institute, 13 September 2016; https://www.cato.org/publications/policy-analysis/terrorism-immigration-risk-analysis

153 Hari Kunzru, "Another Day in the Death of America by Gary Younge – review". *The Guardian*, 14 October 2016; https://www.theguardian.com/books/2016/oct/14/another-day-in-the-death-of-america-gary-younge-review-usa-gun-culture

154 See for example John Paul Lederach, "Beyond violence: Building sustainable peace". In Eugene Weiner (ed.), *The Handbook*

of Interethnic Coexistence. New York: Continuum Publishing, 1998: 236-45; http://www.colorado.edu/conflict/peace/example/lederach.htm

155 Charles Dickens, *A Tale of Two Cities* (1859).

156 Christiana Figueres, @CFigueres, 5 October 2016.

157 Gillian Tett, "Lunch with the FT: Ban Ki-moon, *Financial Times*, 18 September 2016; https://www.ft.com/content/6bb80314-5c72-11e5-a28b-50226830d644

158 *The Ammerdown Invitation. Security for the Future: In Search of a New Vision*; http://www.forceswatch.net/sites/default/files/Security_for_the_future.pdf.

159 Ibid. See also The Ammerdown Group, *Rethinking Security*; https://rethinkingsecurity.org.uk. See also Malcolm McIntosh and Alan Hunter (eds.), *New Perspectives on Human Security*. Sheffield, UK: Greenleaf Publishing, 2015.

160 Paul Rogers, *Irregular War: ISIS and the New Threat from the Margins*. London I.B.Tauris, 2016.

161 Stockholm Resilience Centre, "The nine planetary boundaries"; http://www.stockholmresilience.org/research/planetary-boundaries/planetary-boundaries/about-the-research/the-nine-planetary-boundaries.html

162 United Nations Global Compact, *Architects of a Better World: Building The Post-2015 Business Engagement Architecture* (2013): 4; https://www.unglobalcompact.org/docs/about_the_gc/Architecture.pdf

163 Michael Tomasky, "Q&A with Michael Sandel: From market economy to market society". *The Daily Beast*, 7 March 2012 [my emphasis]; http://www.thedailybeast.com/articles/2012/07/03/q-a-with-michael-sandel-from-market-economy-to-market-society. Michael J. Sandel, *What Money Can't Buy: The Moral Limits of Markets*. London: Allen Lane, 2012.

164 Sandel, *What Money Can't Buy*: 11.

165 Eagleton, *After Theory*: 123.

166 Pankaj Mishra, "Humiliated rage and furtive envy". *The Guardian*, "Review", 25 July 2015: 2-4. See also Norberg, *Progress*.

167 Dasgupta, *Economics: A Very Short Introduction*.

168 *The Ammerdown Invitation*.

169 Joseph Stiglitz, *Globalization and its Discontents*. New York: W.W. Norton, 2002: xiii.

170 "Lunch with the FT". *Financial Times*, "Life", 26–27 March 2016: 3; *Start the Week*, BBC Radio 4, 4 June 2016; interview with the *New Statesman*, 17–23 June 2015: 33-34.

171 Jonathan D Ostry, Prakash Loungani and Davide Furceri, "Neoliberalism: Oversold?". *Finance & Development*, 53(2) (June 2016).

172 For more on the case of Chile, see my previous book *Thinking The Twenty-First Century*.

Chapter 3

173 I am obviously enormously grateful to the many surgeons (three major operations totalling 12 hours), radiotherapists (one programme of 6 × 15 minutes), radiographers and radiologists (20 CT scans) chemotherapy nurses (37 weeks in four sessions plus one in total) and oncologists who have advised me in the last six years. In particular, I would like to acknowledge Dr Matt Burge at the Royal Brisbane and Women's Hospital in Australia and Dr Mark Beresford at the Royal United Hospital in Bath, England, for their care and patience with a very inquisitive patient. They are as confounded by my lack of mortality as I am, and can only ascribe it to my plan and being at the long tail at the far end of the bell curve. Having given me all the treatment the medical profession can think of, they say, "Keep doing whatever it is you're doing." Patient, heal thyself. This book is part of my good life: be useful to society and to yourself.

174 Ian Tucker, "Daniel Lieberman: 'Dieting is a disaster for everyone'". *The Observer*, 22 September 2013;

https://www.theguardian.com/science/2013/sep/22/
dieting-disaster-evolution-daniel-lieberman

175 See also "Public misinformed on obesity", *New York Times*, 2
November 2016; and Denis Campbell, "Three in four Britons
unclear on obesity link to cancer: Poll", *The Guardian*, 9 September 2016; https://www.theguardian.com/society/2016/sep/09/
three-in-four-britons-unclear-on-obesity-link-to-cancer-poll

176 Ben Martynoga, "Inside the home of Sally Davies, England's
chief medical officer". *Financial Times*, 29 May 2015; https://
www.ft.com/content/91fb7c0a-ff9c-11e4-bc30-00144feabdc0

177 Material for this section on the birth of the UK's National
Health Service is drawn from the following sources (in alpha-
betical order by author): Francis Beckett, *Clem Attlee: A Biog-
raphy*. London: RCB, 1997; Tony Benn, *Diaries: 1940–1990*.
London: Arrow Books, 1995; John Bew, "Welfare wrapped in
a patriotic flag". *New Statesman*, 4 December 2014; John Bew,
Citizen Clem. London: Riverrun, 2016; Barbara Castle, *Fight-
ing All the Way*. London: Pan Books, 1993; Frank Field, "From
cradle to grave". *New Statesman*, 30 November 2012; Michael
Foot, *Aneurin Bevan 1945–1960*. London: Davis-Poynter, 1973;
Roger Hermiston, *All Behind You, Winston*. London: Aurum
Press, 2016; John Jacobs, *Beveridge 1942–1992*. London: Whit-
ing & Birch, 1992; Dominic Sandbrook, "One giant of a man".
The Daily Mail, 19 June 2009; *Social Insurance and Allied
Services* ("The Beveridge Report", Cmnd 6404, HMSO, 1942).

178 The Beveridge Report, paragraph 7.

179 John Bew, *Clement Attlee: The Man Who Made Modern Britain*. New York: Oxford University Press, 2017: 539.

180 Friedrich von Hayek, *The Road to Serfdom*. London, Routledge, 1944.

181 Francis Beckett, *Clem Attlee: Labour's Great Reformer*, 2nd
edn. London: Haus Publishing, 2015; http://hauspublishing.
com/the-annex-blog/by-october-1907-attlee-was-a-socialist-an-
extract-from-our-attlee-biography

182 The Beveridge Report, paragraph 9.

183 Akin Oyedele and Skye Gould, "These are the 10 biggest employers in the world". *Business Insider*, 23 June 2015; http://uk.businessinsider.com/biggest-workforces-in-the-world-2015-6

184 David Blumenthal, "Fidel Castro's health care legacy". The Commonwealth Fund, 28 November 2016; http://www.commonwealthfund.org/publications/blog/2016/nov/fidel-castros-health-care-legacy

185 The data for this section on global healthcare is derived from a number of sources: http://www.commonwealthfund.org, based in the USA; http://www.who.int, a UN agency; http://www.worldobesity.org; http://www.cancerresearchuk.org; and Colin Pritchard, "Britain's NHS is chronically underfunded, but great value for money . . . for now". The Conversation, UK, 25 October 2016; https://theconversation.com/britains-nhs-is-chronically-underfunded-but-great-value-for-money-for-now-67579

186 William Sitwell, *Eggs or Anarchy: The Remarkable Story of the Man Tasked with the Impossible: To Feed a Nation at War.* London: Simon & Schuster, 2016: 272.

187 William Shakespeare, *Macbeth* Act V, Scene 5, lines 26-28

188 T.S. Eliot, *Four Quartets*. New York: Harcourt, 1943.

189 Atul Gawande, *Being Mortal: Medicine and What Matters in the End*. London: Profile Books, 2014: 9.

190 Dylan Thomas, "Do not go gentle into that good night" (1951).

191 Gawande, *Being Mortal*: 259.

Chapter 4

192 John Kenneth Galbraith, *The Good Society: The Humane Agenda*. New York: Houghton Mifflin, 1996.

193 Francis Fukuyama, *The End of History and The Last Man*. New York: Free Press, 1992.

194 *Bulletin of the Atomic Scientists*, 25 January 2017; http://thebulletin.org/press-release/it-now-two-and-half-minutes-midnight10432

195 "McGuinness confirms chuckle image". BBC News, 7 November 2007; http://news.bbc.co.uk/1/hi/northern_ireland/7083818.stm

196 https://www.youtube.com/watch?v=IN05jVNBs64

197 Mick Cleary, "Nelson Mandela: South Africa's 1995 Rugby World Cup winners pay tribute". *The Telegraph*, 6 December 2013; http://www.telegraph.co.uk/news/worldnews/nelson-mandela/10500559/Nelson-Mandela-South-Africas-1995-Rugby-World-Cup-winners-pay-tribute.html

198 Amartya Sen, "Why India trails China". *New York Times*, 19 June 2013; http://www.nytimes.com/2013/06/20/opinion/why-india-trails-china.html

199 "Six things Americans should know about mass shootings". *The Conversation*, 3 December 2015; https://theconversation.com/six-things-americans-should-know-about-mass-shootings-48934; Juliette Jowit *et al.*, "So, America, this is how other countries do gun control". *The Guardian*, 14 March 2016; https://www.theguardian.com/us-news/2016/mar/15/so-america-this-is-how-you-do-gun-control?CMP=share_btn_link

200 Bee Wilson, *First Bite: How We Learn to Eat*. New York: Basic Books, 2015.

201 Quarry Bank Mill, Cheshire, England, was built in 1794; https://www.nationaltrust.org.uk/quarry-bank#Overview

202 Yuval Noah Harari, "This much I know". *The Observer Magazine*, 28 October 2016.

203 Oxford Martin Programme on Natural Governance; http://www.oxfordmartin.ox.ac.uk/research/programmes/natural-governance

204 Otto Sharmer, *Theory U: Executive Summary* (2007); http://www.presencing.com/sites/default/files/page-files/Theory_U_2pageOverview.pdf

205 Pankaj Mishra, *Age of Anger: A History of the Present Parody*. London: Allen Lane, 2017.

206 *RSA Journal*, 4 (2015); https://medium.com/rsa-journal/reality-bytes-b4f7b046edfd

207 Shawn Donnan, "Nobel economist Angus Deaton on a
    year of political earthquakes". *Financial Times*, "Life and
    Arts", 22 December 2016; https://www.ft.com/content/
    bbf54b3e-c5f3-11e6-9043-7e34c07b46ef

Appendix

208 Note that not all who live around the Mediterranean eat well,
    or follow "the Mediterranean diet".

209 There is a lot of useless information on the internet, but, if you
    are patient and trawl through it all, after a while some themes
    emerge which are supported by the more rigourous research,
    and are outlined above in the 16-point plan. For this section
    I cannot quote all the hundreds of sources I have read over
    six years, but the following are useful, and easily accessible.
    The advice distributed to me in cancer wards in the UK and
    Australia, based on work by the Royal Marsden Hospital in
    London, is less than helpful as it is based on getting any calo-
    ries into you at the expense of quality or a changed diet, but
    you have more fortitude than that, so try harder. Dan Buettner,
    Thrive: Finding Happiness the Blue Zones Way. Washington,
    DC: National Geographic, 2010; Dan Buettner, *The Blue Zones:
    Nine Lessons for Living Longer.* Washington, DC: National
    Geographic, 2008. For health in the UK in World War II, see
    Sitwell, *Eggs or Anarchy*; and for dietary change at a national
    level, read Wilson, *First Bite*.

210 Irene Maeve Rea, Jennifer Rea and Ken Mills, "People in
    their nineties reveal the secrets to ageing well". *The Con-
    versation*, 25 February 2016; https://theconversation.com/
    people-in-their-nineties-reveal-the-secrets-to-ageing-well-52237